SPECTACULAR COMPUTER CRIMES

WHAT THEY ARE AND HOW THEY COST AMERICAN BUSINESS HALF A BILLION DOLLARS A YEAR!

Buck BloomBecker
Director, National Center for Computer Crime Data
Santa Cruz, CA

Dow Jones-Irwin
Homewood, Illinois 60430

To Linda, my connection to reality
To Mia, my connection to awe
And to all those whose trust made telling these stories possible.

Sponsoring editor: Susan Glinert Stevens, Ph.D.
Project editor: Joan Hopkins
Production manager: Diane Palmer
Compositor: Carlisle Communications, Ltd.
Typeface: 11/13 Century Schoolbook
Printer: Arcata Graphics/Kingsport

Library of Congress Cataloging-in-Publication Data

BloomBecker, Buck.
    Spectacular computer crimes : what they are and how they cost American
business half a billion dollars a year / by Buck BloomBecker.
      p.   cm.
    ISBN 1-55623-256-X
    1. Computer crimes—United States. I. Title.
HV6773.2.B55 1990
364.1'68'0973—dc20

                        89–25672
                        CIP

Printed in the United States of America
1 2 3 4 5 6 7 8 9 0 K 7 6 5 4 3 2 1 0

CONTENTS

INTRODUCTION

Spectacles help us focus . . . if we can see through them.

This book is an attempt to bring focus to my 10 years work at the National Center for Computer Crime Data, collecting information about computer crime—both the spectacular and the relatively ordinary. Since the Center is a clearinghouse for such information, I have been able to draw on case studies as well as conversations with criminals, victims, and security professionals. I have also drawn on more than a few frustrations experienced in taking this organization from its birth to its current stage of adolescent struggle for identity.

Computer crime is changing. To protect our computers—and ourselves—we need to replace yesterday's myths with today's realities. The worst myth, the basis of most others, is that computer crime is a technologists' problem. In reality, computer crime victimizes us all. The first five chapters of this book offer the National Center's perspective on the realities of computer crime, as well as offering some insights into the history of the leading myths and the mischief associated with them.

If you, the reader, are not currently involved in the field of computer security, the goal of this book is to make you curious about the current realities of computer crime. Thus, the second and third sections of the book describe computer security, both in theory and in practice. Computer crime costs you money and threatens your security in a number of ways. In these pages I will offer just a few of the more interesting illustrations of its importance to your life. There are concrete things you can do to help battle computer crime, once you agree that the topic is too important to be left in the hands of the technologists alone.

Looking to the future, the final section of the book considers the growing use of computers in crimes related to politics, and the struggle over software rights. Chapter 18 focuses on the "Internet Worm," which interfered with thousands of computers. This chapter argues the need for a community of computer users who take responsibility for making their use secure.

If you are a computer professional, computer crime is probably not a novel concept to you. If you have heard of some of the cases in this book, I hope you will be interested in reading concise and detailed descriptions that go beyond the headlines.

This book is also supporting material to help computer security professionals better communicate the importance of their work. Computer crime *fighting* should be the career of the future. Upper management and government policymakers will play a large role in determining whether it is. The National Center has provided facts and figures in several statistical reports on computer crime to try to urge more respect for the role of computer security. But stories often move people when numbers can't.

I have tried to appeal to both technologists and others who care about our technological society by balancing the technical and the nontechnical aspects of the problems involved in computer security. That effort started with the decision to name the book the way I did.

There is a degree of danger in naming a book *Spectacular Computer Crimes*. As one who has often railed against the hype that accompanies media treatment of some computer crimes, I am perhaps the last person who might be expected to use a title that engages in the same sort of sensationalism. My purpose in choosing this provocative title is to acknowledge the irony I face, as well as to exploit it.

Computer crimes are often spectacular. They are "unusual, notable, or entertaining," as my dictionary defines *spectacular*. But these crimes can be boring and mundane as well. Thus, one challenge I set for myself is to enlarge your understanding of the definition of computer crime to encompass the many crimes which are not spectacular, but which are costing us millions—if not billions—and putting both our personal and national security at risk.

The greater challenge, the one which most profoundly motivates my attempt to further publicize computer crime, is to convince you that spectacular events need more than spectators. I often fear that the information bath our communications and computer revolutions have created leaves us too "data shocked" to respond to the problems we read about in the papers, hear on the radio, and see on the television every day. We are all victims of computer crime in a variety of ways, ways I will spell out in a number of the chapters of this book. We need not tolerate computer crime as the price of progress. We can fight it. We need to.

Computer and communication technologies are central to our cultural survival. They are key components of military systems. They are increasingly the basis of new business systems, new scientific research strategies, new forms of literary expression, and new ways of thought.

But unless computer systems can be trusted, the value of these applications is uncertain. Computer crime challenges the very premise of trustworthiness. Computer criminals are members of a disorganized army of volunteer systems analysts who inadvertently demonstrate the vulnerabilities of our computer systems. They tell us that computer systems cannot always be relied on. How will we, as citizens of the computer age, respond?

The obstacles to response are formidable. Already we have grown accustomed to see the limitations as well as the promise of this technological breakthrough. Computer error has become the cop-out of the 80s. People who can barely spell the word *computer* blithely explain problems they do not begin to understand by declaring "The computer must have done it." So quickly and so pervasively has the computer entered our lives that few people pause very long when told that some bureaucratic foul-up is computer error.

We may be able, as a society, to tolerate irresponsible employees blaming computers for their own mistakes, or those of system designers and policymakers. I doubt it. I believe we underestimate the costs of inefficiency and poor design hidden behind the excuse of computer error. But the costs of computer crime are clear—and significant.

In our shock over the changes resulting from computing, we have had little time to react. Some of those who reacted most quickly have become phenomenally wealthy. (I am not talking about computer criminals here, since none that I know of have made the computer-crime killing that abounds in fiction.) I refer to the entrepreneurs who have become millionaires, a few even billionaires, by producing a better product and selling millions of them before the competition caught up. Invent a better mouse (we might update the Emerson apothegm), and the world will beat a path to your door.

Many of us are "appliance operators," reacting much more tentatively to technological change than the entrepreneurs. We have adopted enough computer and communication technology to make our lives work a bit better. But we have not devoted the time to computing necessary to feel totally comfortable with the changes it has brought.

I write this book using a word processing program whose capabilities I understand fairly well. Yet I know that I'll be able to do things with it in a year that I can't do now. And there are all sorts of software packages at my "workstation" (which I got when it was only a desk) that I haven't had a chance to master because I've been trying to finish my book without spending all my evenings learning their intricacies.

Chatter with friends and acquaintances convinces me that I'm not alone. Most of the computer users I know are busy, motivated, ambitious people. They had full lives before they bought their first computer, and they didn't go through their schedules and get rid of a number of time-drains to make it possible to devote a day a week to mastering computing. We make do, sometimes learning only what we really have to, sometimes taking advantage of a lull in other commitments to learn something new because it is fun.

In the midst of this chaos, it is hard to pause and contemplate the significance of the computer revolution. (In the midst of this chaos, it is even hard to pause and find time to read a book like this. For having done this you have earned my respect and gratitude. I'm committed to making your investment of time worthwhile.) Yet computer crimes, both the spectacular and the mundane, offer us just such a perch amidst the rush of technological change. See how the system has broken down and you can appreciate how it works, how it doesn't work, and why it is important to us that it continue to work. Computer crime, like all crimes, forces us to focus on what we value most and what we're willing to do to protect it.

We are heroes and heroines all, trying to stay sane while the computer and communication revolutions threaten many of the verities we grew up with. Join me as I tell the story of a number of heroic efforts to achieve, to restore, or to augment the security of our computer-dependent society.

Buck BloomBecker

PART 1

COMPUTER CRIME: FROM MYTHICAL TO MUTUAL COMMUNICATION

Myths aren't lies. They are far more powerful. They are the stories we tell to explain realities we are having trouble grasping.

In simpler times, the mystery of the changing seasons, the wonder of birth, the anguish of death were all explained by myths. Now we need myths to come to some comfortable view of the mysteries of computing.

The power of myth is in its pervasive persuasiveness, the danger in its simplicity.

Everyone knows about computer crime. You can probably recall the movie *WarGames*, the hundreds of articles about the "Internet worm," and maybe some of the more widely publicized cases listed in the table of contents. The media coverage tends to support a very simple view of computer crime, one that encourages superficial interest and discourages serious involvement. This attitude, I fear, is central to the media's thrust, which is communicating myths rather than encouraging communication.

Jerry Schneider's story, in chapter 1, demonstrates the genesis of the computer crime myth and underlines its inadequacy to protect us from greater danger. Stan Rifkin's story, in chapter 2, shows how a belief in the myths of computer crime can lead to a very unhappy, brief career as a computer criminal. The myths exposed, the remainder of this section focuses on three basic questions about computer crime: Who really does it? To whom? What is computer crime anyway?

The agenda of computer crime fighting must start from answers to these questions. If we are going to rely increasingly on computers, as all seem to agree we should, how to protect ourselves from their misuse will be a matter of growing concern.

A key step in this process is defining *responsible computing*. Once we have disabused ourselves of the limitations resulting from the old myths, we can begin to discuss the requirements for creating the kind of computer security our society really needs. A tension must be attended to: We want both security and growth in the use of computers. To respond to these seemingly conflicting goals requires realistic definitions of both the problems and the solutions. Parts Two and Three discuss preventive and reactive strategies. Implicitly—and occasionally explicitly—they raise the issue of defining which social responsibilities our thoughts about computer crime should respond to. In Part Four this question becomes more dominant. We need to discuss not only how we secure our computers, but why, and on whose behalf. This is the most significant challenge this book presents. The research I have done and the people whom I've spoken with in preparing this book convince me that you are up to the task.

CHAPTER 1

THE MYTH OF
COMPUTER CRIME

JERRY SCHNEIDER: THE IMPOSTOR

Jerry Schneider wasn't like the other hackers at Hamilton High. "Phone phreaking," he told a *Los Angeles Times* reporter, "didn't prove to be any great challenge to me . . . . I was more into setting up large-scale computer systems." On October 10, 1976 Schneider attacked one of those larger systems. He had found a spectacular challenge, electronically robbing money for *60 Minutes* while the nation watched.

"The way a banker makes money is to move money around as fast as he can," said Dan Rather, as he began that night's *60 Minutes* segment entitled "Dial E for Embezzlement."

"Bankers are hell-bent to speed up their systems with instant communications and electronic wizardry. Trouble is, the bank thieves are as up-to-date as the bankers, and sometimes a step ahead . . . . Faster banking can lead to faster stealing, as some sadder and wiser banks are beginning to learn."

The problem captured in brief, Rather introduced Schneider as a solution: "Sometimes it takes a thief to catch a thief. In the hills back of Hollywood there's a man who operates just that way. He's Jerry Schneider, a convicted computer thief."

Schneider was cool. Four years of intense media attention had given him the experience necessary to look calmly and securely into the camera while explaining himself somewhat elliptically.

"If somebody's after money, okay—which is the goal here—from banks, they're going to do it any way they know how to do it."

In hushed tones, Rather explained how Schneider was about to prove his point. Telephone touch tones chimed in the background as he spoke:

"Collusion with an insider at my own bank got Jerry the phone number of the Credit Department. He already had my own bank account number from a bank card that lets me overdraw my checking account by $500, no questions asked. Jerry is talking to a clerk in New York, trying to get him to jack up my credit limit from $500 to $10,000."

Over the phone, the voice of a bank clerk was heard. "Can I help you?" he asked.

Schneider, telephone in hand, responded, "Yes. Account 1–3–5–0–0–0–1–2."

Rather explained: "If the clerk says yes, the clerk will enter that into the bank's computer."

CLERK:

Credit limit?

SCHNEIDER:

$10,000.

Rather's response was incredulous: "It isn't that easy! You can't simply call on the telephone and get one's credit extended from $500 to $10,000!"

Schneider disagreed: "Yeah, you can."

If any career could have been built on public relations, certainly it was that of Jerry Schneider, digital detective. Behind his telephone he had reached the public affairs equivalent of the cover of *Rolling Stone*. In 1976, as now, *60 Minutes*, one of America's leading television shows, was seen by millions. And any one of them worried about the growing danger of computer crime had only to contact Jerry Schneider in Los Angeles. Yet, more than a decade later, Schneider is more associated with offshore banking (an industry under close government scrutiny due to the criminal exploitation of offshore tax havens) than with detecting computer crime. Understand why Jerry Schneider is not, and probably never was, a real computer security consultant and you begin to distinguish the reality of computer crime from myth.

As an avowed computer security consultant, Schneider was that perfect mythical mixture of good and evil, the confessed sinner. Offering his services to those fearing computer crime, he seemed acceptable, even establishment, while still offering the titillation that comes with having pulled it over on the telephone company. (Not too many people in the pre-deregulation days distinguished between Pacific Telephone and Telegraph in Santa Monica and "Ma Bell.")

What Schneider could do, thousands of others might also do, Donn Parker warned Rather's *60 Minutes* audience. Parker, the gaunt "American Gothic" computer-crime consultant, estimated that there were some 400,000 computer programmers in the United States. Of these, he guessed, "there might be a hundred thousand who would have the skills, knowledge, and access and be in a position of trust where they could so something [like Schneider did on the air] in some undetected fashion successfully."

As early as 1976, it was clear that computer crime was growing, and the news show had facts and figures to show how much. "In John Reed's own Citibank," Rather reported, "million-dollar, hundred-million dollar transactions fly across the wires, part of hundreds of billions of dollars moving across the world every day . . . It's all being fed directly into computers, which talk to other computers, and soon even visible records will disappear as the whole system moves to no-paper transactions."

Moving the focus from wire transfers to embezzlement, Parker commented: "The average computer-related bank fraud in embezzlement, based on my file of cases, is just a little under $500,000 per incident . . . It's automated crime."

As I watched Jerry Schneider back in 1976, I had no idea that he was going to change my life. I sat in my communal living room, having become fully committed to an alternative life-style just months before, and having grown somewhat jaded about computer crime. I had done a few book reviews on the topic, read about Schneider already, and didn't know Donn Parker from a hole in the wall. I had no idea that I would soon embark on a career that would involve telling the story of Jerry Schneider hundreds of times a year as I attempted first to spread and then to update the computer-crime myth.

In the mythology of computer crime, the story always ends with the criminal achieving fame and fortune. A spectacular computer crime is committed. The criminal is caught, his exploits sensationalized in the media, and his computer wizardry made to seem awesome. He is punished lightly and becomes a computer security consultant capitalizing on his media fame.

(Any feminists taking offense at the last paragraph should rest assured that it is intended to be descriptive and not sexist. The myth has no room for women, though a few would easily fit. This is just one of the ways in which the myth diverges from reality.)

It is not accidental that Jerry Schneider's story bears such a striking resemblance to the central myth of computer crime. *60 Minutes* was the most influential of Schneider's many appearances in the press. The late 70s were good times for stories about computer crime, as the public began to react with awe—and fear—to the growing use of computers.

An odd ecology resulted. Criminals, normally too embarrassed to seek publicity, became a hot commodity if they committed a computer crime. The media, always looking for a new and spectacular trend, happily credited the criminals with skills often far beyond their grasp. To bring the two together, computer security consultants offered legitimacy and perspective to both the media efforts and the claims of the criminals. No one did this more than Donn Parker, then—and perhaps now—the world's most quoted expert on computer crime.

Schneider was one of the 26 criminals interviewed by Parker in a study sponsored by the National Science Foundation. This was the first, and for quite some time only, national study on who commits computer crime. Parker's profile of the computer criminal was given even wider publicity through his book, *Crime by Computer,* and his innumerable media interviews since.

Parker thus set the stage for the discussion of computer crime through the 70s. In *Crime by Computer,* he wrote: "Perpetrators are usually bright, eager, highly motivated, courageous, adventuresome, and qualified people willing to accept a technical challenge. They have exactly the characteristics that make them highly desirable employees in data processing." Though, as will be seen, Parker has since added considerable sophistication to his views, most of the media and the public have not.

I was one of the participants in this sensationalism about computer crime. "Computer Crime, Career of the Future?" was the title of a speech I started giving in 1978, trying to alert my listeners to the dangers of ignoring this new technological threat. As director of the newly formed National Center for Computer Crime Data, I was eager to spread the word, and stories like Schneider's made the job much easier.

"If you commit a computer crime," I told computer professionals, security consultants, and anyone else who would listen, "the odds are that you will not be detected, reported, or punished very heavily if you should come to the attention of the law." In *Computer Careers Magazine* I continued the theme, writing:

> Jerry Neal Schneider, one of the more famous computer criminals, is, I think, a real inspiration for anyone seeking employment in the field . . . After detection, his career took off . . . Trading on his fame as a computer criminal he went into business as a consultant to people who did not want to be ripped off by computer criminals.

With the perspective of several years work since that article discussed Schneider, I can see how dangerously oversimplified my discussion was.

Jerry Schneider's story doesn't have the ending that the media, my colleagues, and I reported. It is a far more alarming story, one which suggests that the computer-crime myth is dated, and that far greater dangers face us than the myth would have us fear. If we can't predict the appearance of a lot more Jerry Schneiders, our myths aren't going to be sufficient to protect us from various types of future social mischief far more troubling than computer crime.

WFI: HACKING THE INTERNATIONAL BANKING SYSTEM?

It looks like Jerry Schneider's got it made. His brief computer-crook-turned-consultant career ended, he has managed to evoke the ire of bankers, Congressional representatives, regulators, and internal revenue agents in his latest role. According to *The Wall Street Journal* and his own promotional literature, WFI is now the world's largest sales organization for offshore banks. And Jerry Schneider, the kid who ripped off Pacific Telephone's computers in 1971, is its sole owner.

Charges of fraudulent uses for offshore banks reverberate throughout the country. Schneider and WFI, however, have never been charged with using offshore banks fraudulently, nor ever sued for anything more sinister than falsifying testimony for offshore banking services.

Wood, plants, and a skylight dominate the Beverly Hills office of WFI, Schneider's corporation. Aside from the intercom I spoke through to gain entry, it all seemed quite normal, tucked between a classical music shop and a health food store. A pleasant receptionist handed me sample copies of some of the publications currently available from WFI. Men in suits with briefcases came and went, and the receptionist checked off boxes on a form indicating whether those who contacted the office bought any books, subscribed to Schneider's *Private International Money Letter,* or signed up for any seminars. Behind her, a bronze plaque indicated that WFI belonged to the Los Angeles Better Business Bureau. As luck would have it, I got there the same day as WFI's latest brochure, offering two-day seminars in Los Angeles, Boston, and Cancun. For $385, the brochure announced, I could learn about "Using Offshore Banking for Profit, Privacy & Tax Protection."

Who would have thought that the ham radio fan of the early 60s, the phone phreak's phone phreak in the 70s, would become the international banker of the 80s?

Not Los Angeles District Attorney Investigators Ron Maus and Frank Kovacevich. It was almost Christmas 1971 when they interviewed John Nicholas. They sat in the office of the Chief Special Agent of Pacific Telephone, Vic Esposito, along with Special Agents Lees and Kinsel of the phone company. Nicholas had come to PT&T to talk about Jerry Schneider, and the security officers were eager to listen. Lees had been on Schneider's track for about three months previously, ever since a customer had tipped him off about equipment Schneider was selling. But Lees needed evidence of what Schneider was up to. Now there was solid proof, and alarming proof at that.

Nicholas had worked for Arcata Electronics, one of Jerry Schneider's customers. Schneider, Nicholas said, had offered him a job as warehouse manager that September. After about a week, Nicholas began to wonder what was going on in his new job. He would arrive at 8 in the morning and find his boss unloading telephone equipment from a truck that looked like it belonged to the Pacific Telephone and Telegraph Company. It was the same style, the same color, and even had the authentic PT&T logos. Schneider said he had purchased the items he was unloading through a Pacific Telephone salvage outlet, but a lot of them looked new to Nicholas.

By the end of the month, things were more curious. On September 30th, Schneider asked him to pick up equipment from a Pacific Telephone office in Century City, Los Angeles. The next morning, at about 6:30, Nicholas took the key he'd been given and opened the gate at 2010 Avenue of the Stars. He parked the phoney phone company truck and identified himself to a security guard named Adams.

Adams would later tell Maus about his visit from Nicholas (who was no saint himself). He remembered a young man, about 22, looking kind of sleepy, coming into the garage one morning in what appeared to be a telephone company van. Adams asked Nicholas who his supervisor was, "Mr. Schneider," Nicholas replied. "And the location of the job?" Adams went on. "LAT&T on West Washington Boulevard," answered Nicholas. "I was satisfied he was there on legitimate business," Adams told Maus, "so I assisted him in loading his order."

The order consisted of telephone equipment listed on a genuine pink PT&T purchase order form. Schneider was emphatic that Nicholas should only pick up the items shown on the list. Each item, Schneider said, would have a clearly marked number corresponding to the numbers on his list.

The truck packed to half-capacity, Nicholas left, waving to Adams, but signing and leaving no receipts.

Two weeks later, Nicholas made another pickup for Schneider. This time he had no help in loading the van. No security guards were at the location when he arrived.

Earl Eugene Watson went to work for LAT&T a bit later than John Nicholas. He, too, soon was asked to make a pickup for Schneider. He told Ron Maus that Schneider had described a recent acquisition, a telephone "that was impossible to get," one with which Schneider could gain access to the telephone company computer and order equipment directly from PT&T. It had 16 buttons, Watson recalled, 4 of them red buttons on the right side.

After a month or two in Schneider's employ, Nicholas and Watson had had enough. They concluded, as Watson told Maus, "Schneider's business with PT&T just wasn't what he represented it to be." Run the business legitimately, they told him, or we'll go to the authorities. Schneider would later dispute their version of these facts, accusing them of blackmail.

According to Watson, Schneider replied, "I can't carry on a completely legitimate business. There isn't enough profit for the overhead. I would have to close down." Schneider said he would close the business down, telling Nicholas and Watson they were no longer needed. By the next Monday, Maus noted, "LAT&T was back in business, minus the services of this witness [Watson] and John Nicholas."

When Maus went to the deputy district attorney in charge of the case, they realized they had a bundle on their hands. A burglary was no challenge. Prosecuting Schneider for illegal entry of Pacific Telephone buildings and theft of their phone components amounted to little more. But how were they going to explain to a jury the fact that Schneider *ordered* those items he was stealing?

Maus found that Schneider had considerable access to the PT&T ordering system. He would check the PT&T catalog for a specific item and learn its seven-digit code number. Then, he would use the 16-button key card dialer he'd so happily shown to Watson and place his orders directly into the phone company's computerized inventory system. Schneider valued his phone highly, keeping it in what Alan Watson, his bookkeeper, described as his "secret room," located next to the bathroom and his office.

Ultimately, Schneider himself would be widely interviewed, describing his criminal achievements to those whom he hoped might hire him as a consultant.

The key to Schneider's crime was his knowledge that a person who impersonated a PT&T employee could gain remote electronic entry to the company's inventory system. Once admitted to the use of the system, he merely had to learn the proper ordering codes.

"To get into the network took a bit more detective work on my own," he told Robert Sherwood of Control Data Corporation. "I got the ordering number by calling a supply room which was attended. I found this [room's] number on an equipment guide list in . . . a [trash] can. I then posed as another supply attendant. I said, 'Do you know what the new number is for the computer?' He said he didn't know they changed the number. Then I said, 'Oh yeah, I got a bulletin with the new number. Isn't it 6−2−7 etc.?' and he threw back what the number was to me. So through a candidly imposed question, I retrieved the telephone number and the switch network number of the ordering system and thus I got into the system."

Schneider pleaded guilty to receiving stolen property, eliminating the need for the district attorney's office to use the computer knowledge the case had brought it. Despite initial estimates putting the losses suffered by the phone company at hundreds of thousands of dollars, the case was settled based on the inventory Schneider had on hand the day Maus, Kovacevich, and quite a few others came to serve a search warrant at his office. Schneider was sentenced to 40 days in a minimum security facility in southern California.

Afterwards, holding court for *Datamation's* Edith Myers as he recuperated in Los Angeles's Cedars-Sinai Hospital, Schneider would display a blowup of a four-color photograph of himself and his father taken while Schneider was in custody. In dressy clothes and posed on a hillside, Schneider looked not like an inmate, but a vacationer at a resort. "He seemed quite proud of what we had done," Myers recalled.

Crime was not to be Schneider's last resort, however. Out of jail by July of 1972, Schneider was vigorously pursuing a career in computer-security consulting by October 16, 1972, when he met with Donn Parker and Shig Tobuka of Project RISOS at Lawrence Livermore Laboratory. Project RISOS was an attempt to understand the personality characteristics of assorted security threats, including computer criminals. The value of contributing to the nation's fund of knowledge about computer crime was not lost on the now 21-year-old Schneider. When he met with Parker and Tobuka, Schneider brought "Bill Myland, an investor" along with him. Myland videotaped part of the conversation. (The videotape was for "promotional purposes," Schneider explained as they spoke in the Airport Marina Hotel in Los Angeles.)

Schneider told Parker of his plans to sell a report on what he had done to AT&T in New York. "He is also willing to sell his report to others and claims he is making plans to write a book," noted Parker afterwards. "He is also negotiating with . . . an English writer who is writing a book on computer security . . ."

Publicity had accompanied Schneider from the day of his arrest. The headline spanning all the columns of the Wednesday, February 9, 1972 *Los Angeles Times* read "Massive Phone Thefts Uncovered." *People* picked the story up, including Schneider's picture as a chubby youngster as well as a contemporary pose with a taller, svelter Schneider smiling from his "house-cum-sauna." Smaller publications around the country told the tale of Schneider's fall from and return to grace. Described in articles like "How to Steal a Million from a Computer," and "A Computer-Age Sherlock Holmes," Schneider was hot copy, a one-man distillation of the key roles in computer crime.

In the *Los Angeles Times*, Michael Seiler captured the spirit of Schneider's press efforts in an article entitled "How He Folded, Spindled, and Mutilated the System." "There is something in many of us that is fascinated by the skillful thief," Seiler wrote, "the person who uses nerve and cunning to rip off a corporate empire." Seiler reported on an interview at Schneider's office, describing the outer office as "empty except for some dirty cafeteria dishes on the floor and a framed poster leaning facedown against one wall. The poster is a blowup of the front page of the *Times* for February 9, 1972 . . . . the headline says 'Massive Phone Thefts Uncovered.' "

Flanked by two advisers, Schneider told Seiler, "We provide technical services, lectures, and advice to people who use computers." Gerald Mollner, Schneider's marketing adviser, put it more bluntly: "The details of what he did, are what he sells now. He's converted his illegal activities into legal activities and he's selling his knowledge to other businesses."

At the same time, Schneider was enjoying more than a little interest from within the computer community. He kept in touch with Donn Parker, asking for a letter of introduction to support his submission of a paper to the National Computer Conference, then the major computer event of the year. Parker wrote to Carl Hammer, the program chair for the conference. Parker's letter appears carefully crafted:

> We spoke of a unique situation at the FJCC [Fall Joint Computer Conference] concerning a young man convicted for perpetrating a computer-related crime who is submitting a paper to the NCC [National Computer Conference]. His name is Mr. Jerry Schneider. He has paid for his crime and is now intent upon using his knowledge and skills he has acquired to advise computer systems users how to protect their organizations from losses, injuries, and damage. In no way do I support, endorse, condone, or encourage the use of Jerry's methods to acquire these skills and knowledge, but I suggest that the publication of a paper by him could be of particular value to the computer field as long as it doesn't glorify or encourage repetition of his acts. Therefore, I suggest you give particular attention and consideration to his submission.

The next day, Schneider submitted "A Quantitative Examination of Computer-Related Theft of Property and Protective Analysis" to Dr. Hammer, Chair of the Science and Technology Program for the National Computer Conference.

Yet somehow, Jerry Schneider doesn't seem to have made it in the world of computer-security consulting. In fact, he no longer offers those services. In 1975, he told the *Examiner's* Larry Kramer that his clients included Xerox, McDonnell-Douglas, the U.S. Government, IBM, Honeywell, and Control Data. No computer-security professionals I've spoken to can confirm or deny this list. Parker reports confronting Schneider over his claims. "Jerry maintained that he'd done consulting," Parker recalled. "He gave me some double-talk but he admitted that no one ever paid him for his services." Parker concluded that Schneider "used the term *consulting* rather loosely."

By 1977, Schneider told Parker that he was out of the computer security business. "I sincerely appreciate all the favors you passed to me in the past," he wrote. "I have one more easy one. At this time, I have nothing to be gained by talking to the press, I am not trying to promote anything. I have a fixed income at what I am doing now and do not want to change things. I would appreciate that you do not pass my name on to reporters as a source of information on computer security."

To find out what Jerry Schneider was up to these days, I called the number for WFI. I must admit I felt a bit nervous as I gave my real name and asked for an introductory package of information about offshore banking.

Not much later I received a reply. With the excitement of a teen, I opened the package I'd been sent. The cover letter was inviting. "Private international banking has never been simpler," it promised. My own offshore bank seemed to be almost within reach. "You need no banking or money management experience whatsoever," my letter continued. "The management firm does the work. You get the benefits."

My ardor cooled somewhat as I looked through the rest of the package. I noticed the Century City high-rise, and the sticker indicating an address change to a slightly lower-pressure part of Beverly Hills. I looked at the finance form, noticed I would need a minimum net worth of $300,000 and decided that I should ignore the offer of expeditious service at the letter's end.

"If you are seriously interested, I can expedite your offering immediately by phone by calling me at (213) 855–1000," wrote Richard Dobbs, a "financial consultant." "Otherwise I look forward to receiving your written request." (I couldn't help wondering why he would look forward to my written request if I wasn't seriously interested.)

Two weeks passed. I resisted all temptations and delighted to find yet another piece of correspondence from WFI, this time from Jerome Schneider himself. (One of Schneider's high school classmates told me that Schneider had his name legally changed to Jerome a few years ago.)

"I recently sent you an invitation to receive our all-new International Bank Offering Memorandum without cost or obligation," Schneider wrote. "To be sure you will receive your copy, simply sign, complete, and return the enclosed Memorandum request form and a Memorandum will be sent within 24 hours."

Schneider threw in a great teaser. "I am pleased to report that we have uncovered a new international financial center in the Caribbean that offers benefits far exceeding those offered by today's traditional centers," his form letter continued. But Jerry was no fool. Only those who wanted his Memorandum could get his latest tip. "I prefer to keep the name of this country confidential until I speak with you by phone or send you the Memorandum. You can reach me toll-free."

The flyer beneath his letter was a bit more detailed than the first, listing the benefits that could be mine with my own bank.

> Guaranteed Privacy: Strict offshore banking secrecy laws legally shield your financial records from aggressive competitors and overzealous government investigators.
>
> Asset Protection: Your assets placed in an offshore bank are immune against judgment, seizure, or writs of execution, none of which is recognized by certain offshore jurisdictions.

WFI's qualifications were listed as well:

> Headquartered in Century City, Los Angeles, WFI has counseled, advised, and helped establish offshore banks for large corporations, small companies, and individuals . . . . WFI has established over 100 separate offshore banks—more than any other organization in America.

"I am frustrated and angered when I think about Jerry Schneider and WFI," says John Shockey, Special Assistant in the Enforcement and Compliance Division of the U.S. Controller of the Currency's Office. Shockey nearly shouts, decrying the effects of offshore banks on the banking community.

Schneider has been able to avoid the reach of many angry opponents. Since at least 1982, Jerry Schneider has been under Congressional investigation, with the IRS, the Controller of the Currency, and other agencies looking into his affairs from time to time. However, Schneider has consistently asserted the legality of WFI's operation and has even offered to work with the office of the Controller of the Currency "to put an end to offshore bank fraud."

Schneider, having demonstrated the vulnerability of a computer system, is now demonstrating a much more striking vulnerability, that of the international banking system. Unfortunately for those to whom he offers his service, this system is far less vulnerable than it may sometimes appear. Thus Schneider must sometimes soft-pedal the risks that his banks present to customers. At other times he must soft-pedal the benefits they offer to crooks.

Insulation from regulation is always a big selling point for offshore banks. The Senate Permanent Subcommittee on Investigations (PSI) reported in 1982 that WFI offered its prospective clients buying banks in the Northern Marianas "circumvention of banking and securities laws of the United States." In an "Offshore Bank Offering Memorandum" distributed in 1982 and in a September 16, 1982 "Status Report," WFI claimed that neither the banking nor the securities laws of the United States apply to the Northern Mariana Islands. "These claims have been adamantly refuted by both the United States and Northern Mariana Islands government officials with whom PSI spoke," a Congressional investigator reported.

The potential illegal uses of offshore banks are more serious. Charles Morley, the PSI's chief investigator, said in a staff report that WFI has chartered and sold 150 banks to American clients in such jurisdictions as St. Vincent, Montserrat, Anguilla, and the Northern Marianas. About the function of these banks, Morley said, "We have determined that illegal uses abound, and legitimate uses are extremely limited."

The nature and uses of these banks were a prominent issue in a libel suit brought by Schneider against *Los Angeles Times* reporter Doug Frantz. In the lawsuit, Schneider takes issue with Frantz's statements that "offshore banks can be the ticket to money laundering, tax evasion, and frauds" and Frantz's allegations that "All sorts of con artists use offshore entities to issue reams of impressive-looking letters of credit, certificates of deposit, and cashier's checks that are not worth the paper that they are written on."

A Senate Governmental Affairs Committee permanent investigations subcommittee charged that WFI had contributed to "the proliferation of offshore private banks of the type used to hide illicit stock deals." Republican William Roth has subpoenaed Schneider's records for hearings on a growing trend in the sale and use of offshore banks for tax evasion and other unlawful purposes.

Robert Serino is deputy chief counsel at the Office of Controller of Currency in Washington D.C. He says of offshore banks, "They give people credibility, they give people what looks like money that they can do deals with. They turn out to be worthless."

One ex-federal investigator said he saw undercover observers from three other government departments in the audience at a recent Schneider seminar.

To understand how Jerry Schneider continues to successfully operate his offshore banking business, despite recurrent claims of illegal uses of such banks by their owners, is to understand the importance of the "virtual reality" that computers encourage, and our consequent vulnerability to "reality crimes."

Schneider, like many overweight kids, used to create imaginary worlds to escape the scorn that he suffered. Shy and obese by age four, he spent his early years in his own overly large shadow. He had no friends; he was picked on and called Fatso, his mother would later report.

"The telephone was his whole life," his mother told Michael Seiler. Schneider felt inferior and tried to act big.

"I built a tremendous telecommunications system in my home at age 10," said Schneider in 1974. "I had developed a tremendous search for knowledge in electronics, electronic systems, systems bugging, systems testing, and things like that."

By age 12 or 13 Schneider's love affair with telephones had grown. He got a telephone repair worker's cap and belt so he could pretend to be a telephone repair man. In high school he asked PT&T for equipment to train his high school electronics class. He applied for a job as a technician with Pacific Telephone after high school. Both requests were turned down.

JERRY SCHNEIDER AND THE MYTH OF COMPUTER CRIME: VICE AND VIRTUE IN THE VIRTUAL WORLD

The significance of Jerry Schneider and his various careers, begins with the implications of the computer crime myth. Why do we want to read about the computer criminal turned detective? Why do we want to read about sensational computer crimes?

I suggest that the computer criminal is the new Prometheus. In mythic form, this type of criminal is our symbolic ally in the fight against computers and the bureaucracies they often serve. A classic martyr, Prometheus was killed, according to the ancient Greek stories, for stealing fire from the gods and bringing it to humankind. His death was a slow torture, as Zeus tried to force him to foretell who would overthrow the reigning gods.

We turn to the mythic computer criminal to help us counter the deification of computers that we see all around us. If I cannot get my modem to work, or I've just crashed my disk, rather than feel stupid, I can identify—at least for the moment—with someone who wins that battle that I all too often lose.

But cognitive dissonance requires more. The psychological theory says we try to make our ideas and our emotions consistent. We may resent the demands computers place on us, but we are not ready to revolt against them. Since we want to be at peace with the growing use of computers, we must have a mythic figure to assure us that the machines can be trusted, particularly after we've learned that their users can be tricked. The hero must replace the antihero. Thus the myth of the criminal-turned-consultant. We will be protected, our stories tell us, by those whom we most admire. They will tame the monster and then make sure that none other directs that monster against us.

On a more practical level, the computer crime myth seems to serve all those concerned with the issue of computer crime. For the criminals, it suggests that a market exists for their ultimate enrichment. If nothing else, they can exploit the market to sell books or seminars.

For the media, myth touches the deepest reaches of the questing soul; and as Joseph Campbell has recently demonstrated, it may even sell TV space or books.

For the computer security professional, the myth serves to sensitize potential customers to the fact of vulnerability, even if its focus is dramatically skewed.

Jerry Schneider was able to distort reality. He created a false phone company, a questionable computer security company, and hundreds of banks existing in virtual but not much other reality. Currently exploiting the limitations of the international banking system, Jerry Schneider is a master of illusion on a global scale.

What does he know that others don't?

It has only the slightest to do with computers. It has much more to do with the fact that much of life is spent dealing with virtual realities. We accept computer representations of reality because they work and make life easier for us. Why, for instance, send piles of gold around the world when marks in merchants' accounts will accomplish the same purpose? And why keep bulky paper accounts when computers can store the same information much more cheaply and efficiently?

Like many children, Jerry Schneider created alternate realities to allow himself to escape from the harsh rejection he felt. But unlike others, Schneider had the unfortunate combination of gifts and flaws that kept him from escaping from his escape. His expertise in science was sufficient to allow him to stand out, winning science fairs, being president of the high school radio club. But it wasn't a solution to his temper tantrums or the embarrassment of needing a nose job.

Schneider wound up a master of illusion in a world where the illusions he mastered have enormous value.

Why did he succeed? Because few of us want to create adequate policing for the new realities. This is the challenge of computer security. This is the reason that those who would protect our computers need to update the myths that endanger them. The myth that computer crime is about computers, and not computer systems, proves dangerous when looking at a history like Jerry Schneider's. It is his interest in systems, whether or not computers play a significant part, that is crucial to our understanding. Wherever there is a system with loopholes, people who understand systems will be there to exploit it. Many of those systems surround us in everyday life. To protect them, we can start by understanding the systems awareness shown by computer criminals.

CHAPTER 2

A VICTIM OF THE MYTH OF COMPUTER CRIME

STANLEY MARK RIFKIN:
THE COMICAL CRIMINAL

Dan Wolfson was watching the 1976 *60 Minutes* segment featuring Jerry Schneider. The sometime photographer, sometime media broker was a friend of Stan Rifkin's from childhood. His friend was soon to make a slight alteration in Wolfson's life. A year before Wolfson hit the papers for harboring Rifkin, he told CBS radio correspondent Steve Palma that "Stan . . . could do computer theft as it was stated in the [*60 Minutes*] program. . . ."

Wolfson called Palma the day after Rifkin was arrested for the theft of $10.2 million. Several newspeople had spoken to Wolfson about a story, and he had turned down one or more offers. Wolfson asked if Palma had any advice on how to deal with the reporters.

The myth of the computer criminal was worth a few bucks to Wolfson. But it cost Stanley Mark Rifkin a lot. Wolfson was ultimately able to sell a few photographs. The picture UPI bought was captioned: "Stanley Mark Rifkin, 32, smiles in this picture taken, minutes after his arrest, by Dan Wolfson, who rented the apartment where Rifkin was arrested. Rifkin, a computer wizard, is charged with defrauding a Los Angeles bank of $10.2 million. Wolfson was also arrested . . . during the telephone interview with UPI."

Though considered a very able computer programmer, Rifkin demonstrated that he was a poor excuse for a computer criminal. If Jerry Schneider's "career" can be characterized as a triumph of systems analysis, the computer crime career of Stanley Rifkin can only be seen as a systems analysis failure. Schneider shows that computer criminals may pose threats that have little to do with computers. Rifkin, in contrast, shows that skill in computing may not correspond to skill in committing crime.

"Diamonds," Gary Goodgame said. Diamonds would be the best solution to Stanley Mark Rifkin's problem.

It was the middle of the summer in 1978, and Rifkin sought attorney Goodgame's legal advice. Claiming to represent a Fortune 500 corporation, Rifkin told Goodgame that his principal wanted an "untraceable commodity" so that it could deal with another corporation. There were "political reasons" for his concern, Rifkin explained. Rifkin knew nothing about diamonds, so he would need assistance. Goodgame suggested that Lon Stein, a diamond broker, could help.

At the time, Rifkin was creating a back-up system for the wire room of the Security Pacific National Bank in Los Angeles. The wire room was the hub of a communications system which handled between two and four billion dollars in fund transfers for the bank every day. The back-up system would allow the bank to continue to make fund transfers if its primary system crashed. To create this back-up system, Rifkin had to learn how the current system worked and to be sure that all of the key elements were carried over into the system he was helping design. There were no specifications available to explain how the money-transfer system worked, so Rifkin interviewed a number of bank employees who worked in the wire room to find out. This research provided Rifkin with an excellent opportunity to educate himself as well.

As his education continued, Rifkin's interest in diamonds continued to grow. He met with Lon Stein for the first time in June of 1978 and asked if Stein could buy 10 million dollars worth of diamonds for him. "Impossible," Stein replied. He said that the quantity was too large, it could not be done in a single transaction, or even a small number of large transactions.

Rifkin persisted. He and Stein spoke many times between June and October, discussing different methods of payment and different ways in which the diamonds might be purchased. Finally, they agreed that Stein would go to Geneva to see if he could arrange the transaction with Russalmaz, a Soviet government agency that sold diamonds.

Shortly before October 25, 1978, Rifkin left his work at National Semi-Conductor for "personal reasons." On that day, he went to the Security Pacific wire room. Rosemary Hanses, who worked in the wire room, met Rifkin at the door and asked him what he was doing there. He replied he was "doing a study." Indeed he was. Rifkin timed the operators and took counts of transactions to see if the wire-transfer system was working any better than it had previously. Apparently it was not. Rifkin decided to continue with his plan to rob the bank.

To transfer money through the wire system, it was necessary for an authorized employee to use a code symbol. Looking at a slip of paper on the wall inside the wire room, Rifkin was able to copy the code. Then he left. He went to a pay phone located nearby and called the wire room. He identified himself as Mike Hansen of the International Department of Security Pacific Bank. He requested that $10.2 million be transferred to an account at the Irving Trust Company in New York. From there the amount was to be transferred for credit through the Wozchod Handels Bank in Zurich, Switzerland.

The pieces of Rifkin's plan were beginning to come together. Russalmaz maintained an account in the Wozchod Handels Bank. Alex Malinin, the Russalmaz director, had previously received a telegram from a Mr. Nelson, ostensibly of the Security Pacific Bank. It identified Lon Stein as a representative of the bank who was going to purchase diamonds for the bank from Russalmaz. Mr. Nelson, the head of the wire room at Security Pacific, had not sent the telegram. It was Rifkin who sent it, two weeks before he transferred the $10.2 million.

Stein flew to Geneva on the 25th of October and soon went to work. Between noon on October 26 and the evening of October 27, he purchased $8.145 million worth of Soviet diamonds.

After he transferred the funds, Stan Rifkin went home and, in his words, "thought a lot about taking the next step." He decided to proceed. The next morning he boarded a plane for

Switzerland. On arrival he called Russalmaz. The money had not yet been credited to their account. He waited. Finally the Zurich bank received telegraphic confirmation that the money had been transferred to its New York account with Irving Trust. They called Russalmaz in Geneva to tell him the money was there, and the transaction was virtually complete.

The next day, Rifkin picked up a baggage ticket from the managing director of Russalmaz. He boarded a plane for Luxembourg, assured that the diamonds would accompany him. En route, he turned to Jacques Spalter, the man sitting next to him, and confided, "I am a very wealthy man now."

But it was not until he arrived at his hotel in Luxembourg that Rifkin finally looked at the diamonds. Only then was he sure that the scheme had really worked. "I was aghast," he would later recall. "I didn't have the slightest idea what to do." He decided to return to the United States.

Rifkin took the diamonds and removed several of them from small packages, putting them into a smaller number of larger packages. By doing so he also reduced their value, since graded diamonds are worth more than those mixed up with others. The small packages had each contained only diamonds of the same grade. Rifkin put the bunch of diamonds into a transparent container made to store folded dress shirts.

By October 29, Rifkin was back in Los Angeles. He called attorney Goodgame and told him that he desperately needed to speak with him. He said he had not taken Goodgame's advice, but had absconded with the diamonds he had purchased.

On October 30, Rifkin met Goodgame in L'Ermitage Hotel in Beverly Hills. He had checked into the hotel as Mr. Garnet. Rifkin filled an ashtray to overflowing with diamonds and gave Goodgame three of the stones. He told Goodgame that he had made an unauthorized wire transfer from Security Pacific National Bank. Rifkin added that he had acquired a new identity and was going to "places unknown." He also gave Goodgame documents to dissolve the company through which he had purported to purchase the diamonds. The next day, Goodgame and his attorney appeared at the Los Angeles office of the FBI and told all.

Rifkin was on the move. On November 1 he was in Rochester, New York, at a hearing concerning rate increases for the Rochester telephone company. He was there to see Paul O'Brien, whom he had last seen during the summer of 1976. Once they were alone, Rifkin told O'Brien that he had received payments in the form of cash and diamonds as a result of a West German land deal, and he wanted to convert the diamonds to cash. For this purpose Rifkin wanted O'Brien to set up a New York City-based diamond brokerage. Rifkin told him that he could not be contacted while O'Brien was thinking the proposition over since "Stanley Rifkin" was not in Rochester. Rifkin explained that he had done something several months ago that he had always wanted to do—he had disappeared. The discussions continued, with Rifkin giving O'Brien $6,000 to initiate their relationship.

O'Brien agreed to approach his superiors at the telephone company to arrange a leave of absence to handle Rifkin's business affairs. He was to discuss the leave on Friday afternoon, and Rifkin was to call him Saturday morning.

For a while, things looked good for Rifkin. On Friday, the president of the phone company agreed to O'Brien's request for leave. But a few hours later, the news hit Rochester.

O'Brien was watching television Friday night, November 3, when he saw a news item concerning a multimillion dollar bank theft in Los Angeles. The story identified the thief as Stanley Rifkin and identified the victim as Security Pacific National Bank. The prospect of working for Rifkin instantly diminished markedly in value. Immediately, O'Brien attempted to reach the FBI in Los Angeles, Unable to do so, he called the Buffalo, New York office of the FBI. After considerable delay and confusion, the agents there were able to take O'Brien's information and act on it.

After he confessed to Goodgame, Rifkin's days were numbered. FBI agents spoke with officials at Security Pacific National Bank and confirmed that the unauthorized wire transfer had taken place. They interviewed Lon Stein. He admitted going to Switzerland and purchasing diamonds at Rifkin's request. The bank ordinarily tape recorded all telephonic fund transfers, and it had recorded Rifkin's call as Mike Hansen as well. Stein listened to the recording and identified Rifkin's voice. Goodgame had turned the diamonds Rifkin gave him over to the FBI. Stein identified them as similar to the ones he had purchased.

In an effort to find Rifkin, FBI agents checked his last known address, an apartment in Sepulveda, California. They gathered background on Rifkin from his driver's and vehicle license information and interviewed former employees of Rifkin's company. The agents got an arrest warrant charging Rifkin with interstate transportation of stolen property.

The investigation continued. Rifkin's girlfriend, Mary Bruskotter, was located, along with relatives, former associates, former employees, and others believed connected to Rifkin. No one knew where he was.

At this point, O'Brien contacted the FBI. The FBI obtained his consent to record any calls Rifkin might make to him. When Rifkin called O'Brien on November 5, Rifkin knew he was in trouble. O'Brien advised him to turn himself in. "One against the FBI is real bad odds," Rifkin admitted. But he rejected O'Brien's offer of help should he surrender. Instead, he asked O'Brien to send back the $6,000 "in a plain brown wrapper" to a post office box in the name of Daniel Wolfson. Wolfson was living in Carlsbad, California, near San Diego.

Postal authorities gave the FBI the address that Wolfson used when he obtained the Post Office box that Rifkin was using. They also reported a change of residence card that Wolfson had filled out.

Late in the evening on November 5, 1978, FBI Agents Robin Brown and Norman Wight knocked on Daniel Wolfson's door. Wolfson denied them entry at first, saying he would talk, but only at his doorway. The agents showed him Rifkin's picture. "Is he here?" they asked. Wolfson said that he wanted to talk to his attorney to determine his rights. "Do you have anything to hide?" Brown asked. "I haven't trusted the government since Watergate," Wolfson replied.

Brown said that Rifkin was a wanted federal fugitive. He said he wanted to come in and talk. Holding his arms on each side of the door frame, Wolfson refused. Brown warned him that failure to cooperate might be considered harboring a federal fugitive.

Brown asked Wolfson how long it had been since he had seen Rifkin. "I want to talk to my attorney," Wolfson replied. Brown persisted. "Is Rifkin here now?" he asked. "I don't know," Wolfson replied.

Finally Brown told Wolfson that they were going to enter, using force if necessary. Wolfson moved aside.

As the agents began to search, Rifkin appeared in the doorway of a vacant bedroom, saying, "Here I am." The agents identified themselves and arrested Rifkin. Rifkin asked to be allowed to put on underclothes before leaving for jail, and the agents accompanied him to a bedroom.

As they frisked him, Rifkin told the agents he and Wolfson had practiced this the previous day. The agents advised Rifkin of his rights, but before they asked any questions, Rifkin said, "I guess you want the diamonds." He pointed to a black and brown canvas suitcase and removed a plastic shirt case from it. Inside it were thirty packets of diamonds.

After his arrest, Rifkin offered to teach computer crime to the FBI. His offer was refused. Out on bail, Rifkin soon came to the FBI's attention again.

On February 9, 1979, Patricia Ferguson met with Joseph Sheehan. She told him that she represented a principal who wanted to move funds and who needed access to a bank. "You must have larceny in your heart," she told Sheehan. She went on to explain the principal was "Stanley Rifkin—Security Pacific Electronic Fund Transfers."

Shortly afterwards, Rifkin himself met with Sheehan and told him he wanted to make a wire transfer of between $1 million and $50 million from the Union Bank in Los Angeles to the Bank of America in San Francisco. Once the money was there, Rifkin would arrange for the purchase of bearer bonds and flee to Mexico City. This time, Rifkin told Sheehan, he would "do it right."

Unlike Goodgame and O'Brien, Sheehan did not turn Rifkin in to the FBI. He did not have to—he was an FBI agent working in an undercover capacity. Rifkin was arrested once again.

Within two weeks, Rifkin pleaded guilty to two of the charges against him and the government dropped the rest.

On March 26, 1979, Rifkin was sentenced. His attorney, Robert Talcott, argued that he was a "unique individual" and urged a unique and imaginative sentence. "What is so unique about the offense?" asked Judge Matt Byrne. The Judge noted that Rifkin had numerous opportunities to abandon his plan, and that there were many stops along the way that required rethinking and remotivating his decision to commit the crime. Defense attorney Talcott argued that Rifkin was motivated by an unconscious desire for self-annihilation. Everything Rifkin did, his attorney argued, was designed to result in capture and punishment.

The Court seemed more interested in deterrence than in finding a unique sentence for Rifkin. Judge Byrne dismissed the defense's suggestion that Rifkin assist financial institutions in studying their wire transfer systems to prevent crimes such as his own. "If he can't deter himself, how is he going to deter others?" the Court asked.

Assistant U.S. Attorney Katherine Stolz urged the Court to consider that society needed protection from the likes of Rifkin. Stolz called Rifkin a con artist, a manipulator, and a habitual liar. She scorned the idea that Rifkin could be of value to financial institutions concerned about computer crime. "I doubt that the Security Pacific Bank would want him on their premises for any purpose," she said.

Rifkin spoke on his own behalf. "I feel there are two me's," he explained. "One is rational, one not." The irrational Rifkin would rise up from time to time, he continued, and his conscience would not always rise up to meet it. When that happened, he would take a step forward toward committing his crime.

Rifkin was sentenced to eight years in federal prison. The Court stated that it hoped this would serve as a warning that a crime such as Rifkin's is serious, not just because of the money involved, but also because of Rifkin's continuing pursuit of criminal activity.

Meanwhile, the diamonds were much in the news. The Security Pacific Bank brought a civil suit against Rifkin and ultimately got them. The diamonds were not of the best quality, however, and were hard to sell. Ultimately the bank took a considerable loss, and some of the gems appeared as part of a Mother's Day "hot rocks" promotion by May Company in Los Angeles.

What made Stanley Rifkin do it?

The most obvious explanation for a theft is the thief's desire for money. This explanation, however, is not the only one. The sum of $10.2 million is enough to motivate most people, it is true. But wouldn't anyone who was thinking about spending the money have taken a bit more time planning how he would convert the diamonds into cash, and how he would keep his fortune from being traced? Rifkin seems to have been too caught up in the technology of his crime to do the rudimentary systems analysis that would have forced him to address these basic questions.

Another explanation that would seem to fit some of the facts of this case is the "mountain climber" analogy. Maybe Rifkin committed his crime because of the challenge. The statement he made to agent Sheehan, that this time he wanted to "do it right," makes this explanation plausible. Many people who deal with computing have noted the existence of a game-playing mentality which takes delight in rising to the challenge of beating a computer system. I discuss this mentality in the next chapter, calling it the "playpen" attitude towards computing.

But how do we explain the indecision that Rifkin claims followed him from beginning to end? Although the statements he made at the time he pleaded guilty are obviously self-serving, they suggest that he never totally committed himself to the venture. Referring to the diamonds, Rifkin said, "I never thought I'd get them." The statement is one plausible explanation for Rifkin's apparent failure to develop a logical plan to deal with the jewels should his scheme succeed.

Rifkin certainly had an abundance of experience with electronic fund transfer systems. He wrote a memorandum in 1976, while he was working for Payment Systems, outlining several frauds involving automated teller machines. This expertise certainly helped him understand the Security Pacific system. It did not, however prepare him to fence stolen diamonds.

Though some of his friends called him charming, others who knew Stan Rifkin called him a loner. His lack of ability to carry out the crimes he attempted certainly reflected an absence of people in his life whom he could trust in undertaking illegal activities.

Rifkin's attorney suggested he was suicidal. At one point Talcott argued that his client had done everything he could to get himself arrested short of hiring a skywriter and writing a confession over the beach at Malibu. His offer to teach a course in computer fraud for the FBI after his arrest and his rapid admission that he'd committed the crime once he was arrested both suggest he was out of contact with the realities most criminals focus on. Perhaps these questions did not challenge him, and thus were ignored. Maybe he just focused on computer crime and not its consequences.

Sitting in court at Rifkin's sentencing, I was struck by what an unimpressive figure this world-famous computer criminal cut. Short, pudgy, balding, he was the kind of guy one could easily pass on the street without noticing. He had about as much adventure to him as a ream of tractor-feed paper. I couldn't help but feel that Stanley Rifkin had bought a perverted version of the American dream and bargained away his computer skills for a brief fling as a publicized and infamous celebrity. He was, I believe, a victim of the computer crime myth. Filling an ashtray with diamonds, talking about a new identity, and going to "places unknown" is the kind of derring-do that may give a TV criminal a quick shot of macho enthusiasm. But it is also the type of behavior, both on television and in real life, that seldom does a criminal much good. Like much macho behavior Rifkin's posturings were much like the pretenses of Jerry Schneider. As Schneider pretended to be a telephone man and then to run a telephone company, Rifkin pretended to be a romantic criminal. Unfortunately for him, at least in the short-run, he lacked Schneider's talent for pulling such impostures off.

After a couple of years, the fun went out of giving my "Computer Crime: Career of the Future?" speech. Or maybe the "wannabe's" got to me. It would start with the introduction. Whoever introduced me would always get a big laugh just by telling the audience the title of my speech. Some added, giddily or slyly, "It's a how-to lecture." Then after the speech ended, the "wannabe's" would come to me with larceny in their eyes and a computer crime scheme almost evident on their furrowed brows. "You'd never guess the holes in my company's system," an otherwise calm computer programmer would exult. My stab at irony hadn't worked. My attempt to rouse the citizenry to action was too subtle. I needed to say what I had to say.

Now I speak on "Why I'm Not a Computer Criminal," focusing on Stanley Mark Rifkin's tragicomic flirtation with crime. Think of the humor of it—a diamond thief who knows nothing about selling diamonds! This international money transfer expert came to Los Angeles without funds! He had to sell a few diamonds and instantly got himself reported to the Beverly Hills Police. Nothing is as good a remedy to the pretensions of computer wizardry as a good laugh at a supposed wizard's expense.

Logic, I like to remind folks, is against the computer criminal. Rifkin tried to succeed as an amateur where many professionals have failed. And logically, unless he was willing to become a professional criminal, the odds against his success were about as high as those that would face a professional criminal trying to do a programmer's job without any experience or training.

Many people might be attracted to computer crime because they, perhaps like Rifkin, like the thrill of achievement. First, unlike Rifkin, they would have to succeed.

But even success has its price. What is achievement without the opportunity to brag about it? Success at crime requires secrecy. That means the criminal must be ready to suffer the agony of unrequited self-love. When I lecture about this point, my audiences often tell me jokes like the one about the rabbi who played golf on the highest holy day of the Jewish calendar,

Yom Kippur. God punished him, the joke explains, by allowing him to shoot a hole in one.

Perhaps Rifkin saw his escapade as a great adventure, and perhaps in his world it was. But how much more adventure would he have had were he acting with courage and significance like Jan Hanasz, the Polish TV Pirate in Chapter 14, instead of just risking arrest for the high-value diversion of wire transfer information?

Most of all, there is every evidence that computer crime did not improve Stan Rifkin's life. It has dogged him ever since his arrest.

THE ANCIENT COMPUTER CRIMINAL

If Jerry Schneider is computing's Great Impostor, Stan Rifkin is its Ancient Mariner. Almost from the beginning of his "celebrity," Stanley Mark Rifkin asserted his right to be left alone, to prevent his crime from being commented on. He sued *Esquire* in 1982 for libel and invasion of privacy because they had run an eight-page dramatization of Rifkin's theft. While in the SPC Treatment Center in Los Angeles, he argued (as his own attorney) that he had "steadfastly guarded against the commercial or public use of his name and likeness." Rifkin went on to list 127 statements from the article that he claimed were all false.

Rifkin's suit was ultimately dismissed, but that did not keep him from threatening to sue me when I published an earlier version of the above account. I believe my suggestion that he was like an idiot savant was the most vexatious to him, though he also made some references to my trips around the country talking about him in computer crime speeches.

Rifkin's desire to put the past behind him ran into other difficulties as well. His conviction was the first opportunity for the Association for Computing Machinery to discipline someone for violating its code of ethics. The wheels were turning, and a trial was being planned when Rifkin quit the Association rather than risk being thrown out.

After his release from federal prison, Rifkin went to the Washington, D.C. area and became active in the Washington Chapter of the IEEE (Institute of Electrical and Electronics Engineers), joining the board of directors, as well as holding office in the local chapter. Rifkin chose not to disclose his criminal conviction when he ran for chair of the chapter. When the media got wind of it, Rifkin's tenure soon ended.

But it did not end without bitterness or controversy. A member of IEEE who was in the thick of the debate noted: "A lot of us were upset with the way the media exposed this. They made it seem that Rifkin was in a position of responsibility. The chair doesn't involve funding, it's just training for more senior positions in the organization."

FORGIVENESS AND DENIAL

While writing the first chapter of this book, I became aware that Jerry Schneider had sued *Los Angeles Times* reporter Doug Frantz for libel and invasion of privacy. He argued that his conviction in 1972 had been sealed and thus could not be commented on. The fact that he commented on it freely for several years after the record was sealed seems not to have deterred Schneider in the least.

Rifkin, too, argued in lawsuits that stories about his computer criminality invaded his privacy. As a rule, criminals lose this argument unless a very long stretch of good behavior separates their crime from the reports on it. Implicitly, society has a right to continue to protect itself from a criminal by publishing information about the crime. But saying that Schneider and Rifkin have no remedy at law does not end the discussion.

We don't know what to do about computer criminals once they've done their time. After the media has lionized them, real competitive life returns these criminals to problems which may well have preceded their computer crime. A recent conclave on computer ethics addressed a hypothetical question based on the Rifkin experience at the IEEE. The results suggest how far the members of our profession and those who know it well are from agreement about acceptable sanctions for computer crime.

Of 24 participants, 10 thought it unethical to run for office in a computer professional society without mentioning a felony conviction for computer-related crime. The majority saw no ethical problem. When the question turned to sanctions, seven thought the professional society unethical if it did not remove the individual from office once his or her failure to disclose was known. An even greater majority found no ethical failure on the part of the society. These troubling results suggest that much more discussion on ethics is needed amongst computer professionals.

It looks like the current concern over computer viruses will lead to many more questions about appropriate sanctions for computer crime. In 1989, two major legislatures, those in New York and California, considered bills which would bar computer criminals from computer-related work. California proposed to bar those arrested for computer crime from computer courses in college or graduate school.

While we do not yet have rational responses to questions surrounding computer crime, it seems precipitous for either legislature to adopt so radical a sanction. The problems in defining the terms alone are nightmarish, the consequent difficulties in implementing such law laughable, and the economic significance perhaps not very desirable. Better to have democracy in action—a cooperative effort between the professional societies and the legislatures to develop relationships and sanctions supported by those most knowledgeable about the problem.

I would suggest, as my modest contribution to the discussion, that it is important to distinguish between forgiveness and denial. Psychologists and theologians say that forgiveness is very good for someone who has been the victim of any harm or crime. They also say it is unhealthy to deny that something bad happened to you. So the difficult question posed by the controversy over limited sanctions is the extent to which we can forgive a criminal without denying what he or she has done. One way, it would appear, is to allow information about the crime to be freely available.

Stanley Mark Rifkin may have finally achieved the goal he sought years earlier, to depart to parts unknown. There are many people I spoke with in the IEEE who miss him. It isn't that easy to get chapter presidents, one told me. The last anyone had heard, Rifkin was living somewhere around Pittsburgh.

CHAPTER 3

WHO ARE THE COMPUTER CRIMINALS?

MARVIN MAKI: THE ORDINARY COMPUTER CRIMINAL

The first computer criminal I encountered and the first the Los Angeles District Attorney's Office prosecuted was Marvin Maki. This man was a mythbuster from the word go.

I met Maki at a Hyatt Rickey's in Palo Alto, California, in 1981, somewhere between the three-bean salad and the ambrosia on the bounteous lunchtime buffet. He and I were two of the participants in a panel discussion on computer crime sponsored by *Computer Decisions* magazine. Maki wasn't young and didn't seem to be at all like the stereotype I'd read about except for the fact that he was white and male. He was pissed. It had been three years, but he still couldn't get over the fact that he'd been forced to give up a large number of stock options when he pled guilty to stealing computer services from his former employer, Manufacturing Data Systems, Inc. (MDSI) in Ann Arbor, Michigan.

Maki still didn't see what the big deal was. He used the MDSI computer, it was charged, to produce a punched tape to run W and R Tool's manufacturing machines and to process the company's accounts receivables. Maki, from his point of view, simply did what people in industry do in this situation. He saw nothing wrong with it, or so he said.

Maki argued that if W and R had requested that MDSI work with them to fix the programs they were using, MDSI would have agreed. He had simply cut out the request phase of the process. He had also learned the access codes used by MDSI's

French and English offices and had used them to get access to the MDSI system. MDSI had changed its domestic codes after Maki left (complaining of low pay) but had not taken the additional step of changing the foreign codes.

Ten years of studying computer crimes convinces me that there is much truth and more than a bit of exaggeration in Maki's claim that he was doing what many others did. Donn Parker noted that a news article about Maki's case was posted at a defense facility in Newport Beach, California after Maki's arrest. "Their people do this, too," Parker noted.

In our discussion for *Computer Decisions,* Maki (given the alias Ben Johnson) offered his defense: "I've known a lot of people who have taken unauthorized computer time," he said. "They're working on a project and they start running over budget, so they get in and take a little extra time. The computer is just sitting there anyway." (Maki did not laugh when I responded to his comment by noting that Gary Trudeau had mocked this attitude when he titled one of his collections of cartoons *But the Trust Fund Was Just Sitting There.*)

Part of the problem in computer crime is the difficulty of changing common practices which disregard others' rights. Though still grieving his lost stock options, Maki was able to see and express the other point of view. "I have come to the conclusion," he told us on the panel, "that this type of thing is wrong—because you're still using an unauthorized resource. The company is there to make money and you're taking profits out of the company."

Many white-collar criminals, criminologists tell us, lack Maki's insight and still rationalize their crimes by saying that they were doing what others they work with do. This is the heart of the theory of "differential association." This criminological theory suggests that white-collar crime is best understood as what occurs when a group of people push the limits of corporate dishonesty beyond the acceptable. In general, this theory warns those who run organizations that their employees will be no more honest than they are, and some will be much less so. Whether because of causation or rationalization, employees who perceive their bosses or their co-workers as unethical will act less ethically. This, it appears, was the case with Marvin Maki.

The point that struck me was how ordinary Maki was. He was a working stiff from the San Fernando Valley, quite close to the Los Angeles District Attorney's office where I worked. He was involved in computer crime because he had failed to observe some rather novel property rights that were not as clearly protected as other such rights. I would be most surprised if Maki left MDSI with a computer, an electric typewriter, or a copy machine. The rights to these items were well established in his mind, I'll bet. But the right to use a computer is not yet viewed as a valuable property right that cannot be interfered with. Not yet.

The worst thing about the computer crime myths is all the real criminals they neglect to warn us about. There are far more Marvin Makis than Jerry Schneiders or Stanley Mark Rifkins. Most computer criminals get on-the-job training. In the National Center for Computer Crime Data's most recent survey, employees committed 75 percent of the computer crimes prosecuted throughout the United States. Many of the crimes these people commit are just like the crimes employees used to commit before computers were installed. Sales clerks used to take cash from the register. Now they might falsify a transaction at a point-of-sale computer terminal and *then* take some cash from the register. Computer security professionals planning strategy must be aware that *these* are the people taking the money. Security against a teenage genius who appears in one of every thousand cases is very different from security against an employee who resembles every other employee in background and skills.

There are a number of types of computer criminals, however, and they can be categorized according to their perceptions of the computer environments around them. Perhaps some day a serious criminologist will study those who commit computer crimes and offer us the benefit of the discipline that such social scientists lay claim to. Thus far, the field of computer criminology has escaped extensive academic attention, allowing journalists and security consultants to opine in the absence of contradiction. In the words of sociologist Jack Katz, "The social sciences leave the serious academic investigation of elite deviance to . . . the ethical philosophers, who exploit qualitative case materials in the innocuous forms of delightful illustrations from literature, lively hypotheticals, and colorful histories documented by others." Katz is the author of the recent book, *Seductions of Crime.*

At least since Jerry Schneider appeared on *60 Minutes* in 1976, the differences between journalists' and security consultants' definitions of computer crime have been insignificant. Both groups tend to arrive at their definitions from quite limited observation of a few criminals, and both seem more inclined to sensationalize the issue than to encourage intelligent action.

Astonishingly, the descriptions remain similar even though the crimes they are applied to may vary considerably. In the past few years, computer viruses have been the hot topic in the media's discussion of computer crime. (Several cases of viruses, worms, and other malicious programs will be discussed in the following pages.) Consider the thumbnail wisdom offered by *Time* magazine on the topic of viral criminology: "The virus writers tend to be men in their late teens or early 20s who have spent an inordinate portion of their youth bathed in the glow of a computer screen." The magazine, whose cover story about viruses (in the September 26, 1988 issue) was probably seen by more people than any other prose treatment of the topic, goes on to quote a columnist for *Scientific American* describing the perpetrators of viruses as "nerds." "They live in a very protected world," says A. K. Dewdney, "both socially and emotionally. They leave school and carry with them their prankish bent."

This view of virus spreaders is virtually identical to the view of computer criminals Donn Parker offered to the public in the mid-1970s in his first book, *Crime by Computer.* Based on a survey of a small number of computer criminals who allowed him to interview them, Parker wrote: "Perpetrators are usually bright, eager, highly motivated, courageous, adventuresome, and qualified people willing to accept a technical challenge. They have exactly the characteristics that make them highly desirable employees in data processing."

Parker's view soon became the norm. F. W. Dennis, a security professional, echoed it in an article in *Security World,* a publication written for the security profession. "The common denominator," Dennis observed, "in nearly all cases of computer fraud has been that the individual is very much like the mountain climber—he or she must beat the system because it is there." Dennis spoke without the benefit of even the few interviews Parker had conducted.

If all the computer criminals fit within the stereotype created by Donn Parker and eagerly spread by the media, there would be no need to worry. We could simply assume that people who spread viruses are like all other computer criminals, and that computer criminals are like all other computer nerds, and move on to more challenging topics.

Such a point of view, however, is at best a historical relic and at worst an invitation to ignore the realities that confront us in the war against computer crime. The computer criminal of the 1990s may know absolutely nothing about computers—or know just enough to be dangerous. We must go beyond the stereotypes in talking about who commits the wide range of computer crimes.

Unless we are content to distrust all people who are interested in computers, the stereotypical view is of little use anyway. What can a personnel director do if he or she is told not to employ any computer "nerds"? This description not only covers few of the most dangerous computer criminals we might encounter, but many of the most valuable employees a computer user or manufacturer would want to employ.

Indeed, if we were to devise a personality test designed to spot the computer criminal, the first and most difficult task would be to create a test that did not also eliminate most of the best minds who have made computing what it is.

Such a test, as valuable as it might be, has yet to be created. In the meantime, it seems that the best we can do is to look at the computer crimes people have committed and try to reason from the crimes to the apparent motivations of the criminals. Starting from this perspective, we can at least develop some sense of how to predict and prevent computer crime.

The computer crimes that the National Center for Computer Crime Data has analyzed over the last decade or more suggest that there are a number of different types of environments in which computer crimes have occurred. These environments are the computer systems *as seen by the computer criminals themselves* when they decide to commit computer crimes. For the criminal, this perception of the computer system in question makes it easier to decide to commit the crime. For this reason, we at the Center call the environments "criminogenic environments."

If you want to know who would want to pry into your personal history, rob your bank, or destroy the program that controls the traffic lights in your city, the best answer we can provide is to look at the computer environment as a criminal might see it and try to understand why this environment might become an invitation to computer crime.

For example, one type of computer criminal might see the computer environment as a playpen, a place to try the computer games that seem most fascinating. Another might see it as a battle zone, a place where life is miserable and anything done against the enemy is justified.

When we at the Center first studied the motivations of computer criminals, we listed seven environments which seemed to correspond to the motivations of the computer criminals we'd spoken with and studied. Now, having looked at the crimes discussed in this book and many others, and having spoken with several of the people who committed those crimes, we've found that the original seven environments stand up reasonably well. We have added one additional category to describe the new data that has emerged.

The purpose of the rest of this chapter, then, is to summarize eight computer crime environments, and to describe the criminals we've seen according to the types of environments they seem to be responding to. Since computer viruses are so much in the news, we will focus on them to some degree, demonstrating that the criminals likely to commit this sort of computer crime are much the same as those likely to commit other computer crimes.

THE PLAYPEN

Ours is a society torn by its unacknowledged ambivalence towards addiction. Most public opinion polls taken during the closing months of the 1988 U. S. presidential elections indicated that our population believes illegal drugs are a major problem. Yet we have seen little movement toward governmental involvement in the fight against alcoholism, and even less toward eliminating the price supports on tobacco, despite the Surgeon General's warnings about the health dangers of nicotine for the last twenty or more years. If anything, the prevailing attitude seems to be that any addiction is okay as long as it boosts the aboveground economy.

This background is necessary if we are to understand the playpen attitude towards computer crime. Getting students, workers, and hobbyists "hooked" on computing is a major goal of a major sector of the American economy and of the economies of most of the economic powers in the free world. (If computer devotees reading this think our use of the word *hooked* is inappropriate, consider also the literacy campaign urging young people to become "hooked" on books.)

Outside of a few parents who have voiced fears that their children are overdoing their concentration on computers, and the seldom-heeded complaints of "computer widows" and "widowers" whose mates have turned to computer bulletin boards as their major recreation, most of us are delighted when our children or co-workers get bitten by the computer bug.

Well we should be. The prospects for growth in the computer industry are agreed upon by virtually all, and the extent to which learning computer skills assures a better economic future cannot be gainsaid. But as often happens when an enthusiasm sweeps our culture, there is seldom much attention paid to the negative side of excessive interest in computing. The first criminogenic environment exists when people have forgotten that sometimes they must leave the playpen and accept the notion that computing is more than just a game.

The seeds of the playpen attitude are planted early. By 1989, students in 99 percent of all the school districts in the

United States had at least one computer available to them. Increasingly elementary schools are encouraging their students to learn the rudiments of computing. Sometimes it is hard to convince the students to temper their newfound love of computing. Think of the dilemma expressed unknowingly by the mathematics teacher who spoke of the enthusiasm her 9- and 10-year-old students exhibited when she allowed them to use the school's computers. "They are so excited," she said, "that they fight to get on the system. Some of them even erase others' names from the sign-up lists to use the computer or destroy the sign-up lists altogether." The idea that this was not good preparation for the students' moral lives seemed never to have occurred to her.

College students often show little moral development beyond that of the 9- and 10-year-olds. In visiting numerous campuses as a lecturer on computer ethics, I'm constantly amazed at how serious a problem cheating is. It is not just sign-up lists that are stolen, but programming assignments, or even other students' passwords.

These examples demonstrate the fact, obvious to anyone who has played computer games or watched others play them, that using a computer can be intrinsically satisfying. They also suggest that the yearning for the satisfaction that comes from using a computer can lead to a violation of others' rights. When computer crime results from the attempt to gain satisfaction from working with a computer, I categorize it as an example of the playpen perception getting out of hand.

Unfortunately, both for society and for those who need the guidance, there is no standard within the computer community to define precisely when the playing has gotten out of hand. If a student uses an hour of computer time without permission, one university computer department may consider it criminal theft of service, while another views it as an exercise of commendable ingenuity. As the popularity of computing grows, it becomes even harder to define precisely what the computer community is. With most children exposed to computers in schools and increasing numbers of adults using computers at work or at home, computing has broadened from a scientific activity to a popular one. It is hard enough to get scientists to agree to standards of a technological nature; harder still to get them to agree to standards of behavior or ethics. But now scientists are a minority of those who use computers. Unless we involve parents, employers, and the computer industry, developing standards for our computer-using society is going to be increasingly difficult—and increasingly more important if we are to combat the playpen attitude toward computer crime.

Virus creators may be motivated by the playpen point of view. An article in a 1988 issue of 2600 (the self-proclaimed "Hacker Quarterly") expressed this perspective poignantly. "The Dark Side of Viruses" written under the pseudonym "The Plague" explained the author's moral views about creating viruses:

> I was asked whether I had any moral feelings about viruses, or whether I thought that they were wrong, or evil, or whatever. My feelings are the following: I don't care one way or the other. If people's data is destroyed, then so be it. If people are stupid enough to accept pirated software then they deserve to be punished.

The author's stated reason for creating viruses was not to punish pirates. Speaking with the reverence for technology that marks those in the playpen, he said, "The beauty of the computer virus is that it perfectly mimics a real virus or small organism, thus having the potential of being a great tool in artificial intelligence."

The IBM Christmas Tree virus is an example of the dangers the playpen attitude presents when yoked with the power of the virus technology. In this case, a German student created a program to send a couple of his friends holiday greetings in the form of a graphic representation of a Christmas tree. He included an electronic version of the old chain-letter concept, instructing the program to contact all the people listed on each recipient's distribution list. Whenever someone executed the Christmas program the student had created, it not only displayed a Christmas tree on their screen, but sent copies of the program to all those on the distribution list. This little program evaded a serious attempt to restrict its distribution in Germany and wound up spreading to such an extent within the IBM corporation that IBM had to shut down its electronic mail system for two days until they could control it. Estimates have put the number of countries visited by this virus at 130!

In our discussion of Robert Morris in Chapter 18, "The Sorcerer's Apprentice," we will see that authorities at Cornell found Morris to have been singularly irresponsible in failing to contemplate the potential consequences of letting a computer worm loose that ultimately affected as many as 6,000 computers. Morris was so caught up in the specifics of the task he had set himself that he paid no attention to anything else.

Kevin Mitnick is the only "certified" computer addict I have heard of. The subject of Chapter 12, "The Willie Horton of Computer Crime?" he has been sentenced to a one-year jail term followed by six months in a therapy program designed to deal with addictive behaviors. Harriet Rosetto, the administrator of the program, has never dealt with computer addicts before. However, she finds the focus of addiction far less important than its cause. "People who are addicted are hiding from feelings, usually feelings of shame and low self-esteem," Rosetto explains. Consequently, it is her plan to treat Mitnick with a combination of the 12-step philosophy and Judaic ethics. The 12-step program is based on the insights and experiences of Alcoholics Anonymous. The Judaic ethic stresses concepts like responsibility, priorities, and justice.

If the therapy that works for substance abusers with a variety of motivations can work for computer abusers, we may find the new field of computer criminology coming of age.

The increased illegal use of telephone connections by hackers and others seeking to use computer systems without paying the data communication fees charged by the long-distance carriers is another problem often associated with the playpen attitude. Often it appears necessary to a young computer enthusiast to steal "connect time" to communicate on all the bulletin boards he or she is interested in. The easiest way to solve this problem, many seem to feel, is to use an access code that has not yet been discovered by the victimized telephone company as no longer valid.

Playpen crimes are usually justified in the minds of the players as involving small losses to the victims. When the victim is a large organization like a telephone company or an unsuspecting corporation whose computer has been turned into a hacker's playground, the hacker's rationalization usually includes the idea that such a large corporation won't miss the amount.

But it is a mistake to assume that the computer criminal committing a playpen-type crime is unlikely to do any damage. Before computer viruses gave all computer criminals a way to extend the harm they could do exponentially, ordinary computer criminals showed that their computer games could be very troublesome.

The playpen motivation may even help explain major bank robberies involving computers. When Stanley Mark Rifkin pleaded guilty to charges arising from his theft of $10.2 million from the Security Pacific National Bank, he described his reaction when he first took possession of the diamonds he had purchased with money stolen from the bank: "I was aghast," he said. Rifkin further explained his failure to hide the diamonds by saying that he hadn't made any plans for this contingency. Implausible as this story may seem to those of us used to thinking of thieves as simply motivated to have or to sell whatever they steal, it is consistent with the general ineptitude at crime that Rifkin demonstrated throughout his sorry history as a computer criminal.

The security implications of the playpen attitude are fairly clear: norms are needed to define allowable and excessive computer use. These norms will certainly require more specificity about the kind of work that can be done on office computers and the kind of software that can be used on office systems. An employer may not care about whether a systems analyst uses her home computer to contact bulletin boards long into the night, but may well tell her to leave any software she downloads from those bulletin boards at home, lest they contain contaminated programs.

THE LAND OF OPPORTUNITY

Unlike the game players in their playpen, those who see the computer environment as a land of opportunity seem to be motivated not so much by challenge as by lack of challenge. Where the game-playing hacker might try hundreds of codes to find one which gives entry to a new computer system, the employee motivated by the land of opportunity delights in discovering that on-the-job training has provided excellent preparation for computer crime. The best preparation for this kind of computer crime is simply doing one's job and noticing the loopholes every system has.

For example, a German who operated a computer printer that printed paychecks got the idea of pressing the REPEAT button when his paycheck was being printed. When nothing happened after the first repetition, he printed many more. Hardly the genius the media would have us think all computer criminals are, this computer criminal took several checks and tried to cash them all at the same time!

"Data diddlers" are the most common type of computer criminals. These are people who commit crimes by changing data about to be processed by a computer. As detailed in Chapter 9, "The Street Computer Criminal," word got out in Oakland that the Bay Area Rapid Transit ticketing machines were quite generous. They not only produced tickets, but would return your money if you put in a $5 bill that was folded just right. Several traditional criminals added computer crime to their rapsheets when they were caught attempting to capitalize on this bug in the ticketing machines. (Even tired commuters became suspicious when they saw people spending half an hour buying tickets.) Sammie Marshall, Harold Rossfields Smith's accomplice in chapter 6, exploited a loophole he seemed to have learned of at an earlier time. Wells Fargo Bank was $21.3 million poorer before the loophole was plugged.

Perhaps the best example of the land-of-opportunity attitude on the part of virus criminals appears in those cases where viruses were planted as an attempt to help one's business. In Chapter 12 we discuss one such criminal.

One needn't be a professional criminologist to note that, for many people, motivation is directly proportional to opportunity. Obviously, the better the security, the less opportunity for crime. Thus, whether we are talking about security against virus spreaders or any other kind of computer criminal who sees systems as lands of opportunity, the key is good, systematic, and extensive security. Simple measures—such as taking particular care that employees do not process their own accounts, rotating employee's assignments, and looking for signs of any irregular work habits—help companies reduce their vulnerability to insiders who see the company computer as a land of opportunity. To guard against outsiders, the obvious first step is to reduce the access they have to the company's computer.

To reduce the danger of infected software, employees in organizations using computers must exercise great care before using software from public bulletin boards or from unknown sources.

THE COOKIE JAR

Not all criminals are rational. A gambling debt, a drug habit, or sudden losses in a market dive may all lead an employee to see funds or other valuables in a computer system as the best solution to that employee's most pressing problem. As though the computer system were a cookie jar, the "hungry" criminal dips into the computer to take what he or she needs. In such circumstances, the criminal's motivation is much more pressing than a chance observation of a loophole in the system's security.

Criminologists have identified situational pressures as frequent accompaniments, if not causes, of white-collar crime in general, and the experience of the National Center for Computer Crime Data bears out the assumption that these pressures have led to computer crime as well.

One head teller at a bank in New York City stole $375,000 from dormant accounts there. His crime was discovered when a bookie raid disclosed evidence that he was betting up to $7,500 a day and making only $10,000 a year at his job.

A Denver, Colorado brokerage clerk financed numerous gambling trips to Las Vegas with the funds he derived by falsifying the records of an accomplice's stock holdings with that brokerage company.

A Los Angeles bank teller explained his theft of funds from a test account to which he had transferred them by claiming that his wife needed the money to pay off someone blackmailing her after some cocaine transactions. Though the probation officer dismissed the explanation as farfetched, he noted that the man had serious debts, whatever their cause, and needed more money than he had to pay them.

Since the cookie jar is usually viewed as the source of money or some other easily cashed item, it could be a while before virus spreaders who demonstrate this motivation come to light. Perhaps, in a rather perverse way, the only addiction virus spreaders allow themselves is compulsive computing. (More likely, however, we simply haven't a large enough data base to find examples of the unshareable needs leading people to create viruses.)

To avoid exposing themselves to people whose needs drive them to cookie-jar crimes, companies must thoroughly investigate employees before they are hired. But situations change, and security must be responsive to these changes. Maintaining good relationships between employees, their supervisors, and management in general may mean that the employee will seek help before a problem grows to the point where it is unshareable.

THE WAR ZONE

More than computer crime in general, virus crimes involve hostility and malice, since few virus crimes offer tangible rewards. Thus it is not surprising to find categories of computer crime that are particularly well suited to describing these types of attacks. The "war zone," and the "soapbox," which is discussed in the next section, reflect angry views of the computer environment. In the case of the war zone, the criminal sees the computer not as a solution to life's problems but as a symbol of their cause. Disgruntled employees, feeling that management is out to get them or that they have already been hurt unfairly, may express their resentment in attacks on the company computer.

The case of Donald Burleson in Chapter 7, "The Computer Insecurity Director," demonstrates the effects of battle-zone thinking. Burleson, according to a fellow employee, was the kind of guy who was mad about everything. A tax protester, he sued his employers for withholding taxes from his pay. Three days after he was fired from USDPA & IRA, an insurance company, he planted a "worm" program in the company system.

Unlike a virus, which can propogate into other systems, a worm can move around one system, but nowhere else. Burleson's worm was capable of destroying 168,000 records of employee commissions.

The implications of the Burleson case are staggering. If one angry employee can destroy that many records, what could others do? What if the enemy was a multinational with hundreds of interconnected computer systems?

In Sacramento, California, three employees of the State Department of Justice, apparently annoyed by their paltry pay increases, deleted certain arrest records from the state's criminal record system. Tales of computer library tapes erased, misfiled, or mislabeled are legion.

In one of the most extreme cases we've seen at the Center, an employee of a large produce company, feeling cheated out of a substantial pay raise, created a shadow corporation for revenge. The computer representation of the corporation was slightly less efficient than the real corporation. On the books it looked like there was a bit more spoilage of vegetables, a bit more theft off the docks, and so forth. All of the difference between the real corporation and the shadow corporation went into the pocket of the vengeful employee, whom the corporation had put in a position of unchecked trust.

Increasingly, the Center is finding that ex-employees make up a significant portion of those prosecuted for computer crime. In many cases their crimes are either motivated by a desire for revenge or are simply a matter of continuing to use the services of their former employers. Marvin Maki appears to be best described as this latter sort of criminal.

As in the case of the cookie jar, good management is the best prevention against battle-zone computer crime. When employees have no acceptable avenues to express resentment toward their employer, management should not be surprised when they use unacceptable avenues instead. Employee resentments may be well founded. Corrective action will not only reduce the threat of the resentful employee, but will also demonstrate to all employees the folly of perceiving the computer as a war zone.

THE SOAPBOX

More than any of the other categories of computer crime motivation, the soapbox seems to have been made for the virus crime. In the war zone, the criminal got back at an employer through the employer's computer. Those with a soapbox point of view are attempting to make a broader statement or to inflict more extensive suffering. Some see this type of computer crime as a way to strike out against computers: others see it as a way to strike out against computer users. Some see little difference between the two.

Technological terrorism is one of the threats that viruses make much more real. For two decades, bombing computer installations has been a symbol used to protest against capitalism. In Italy, the Red Brigades produced a telling document, Resolutions of the Strategic Directorate, which articulated the rationale for such violence. It called increasing computerization of the West part of a sinister plot to "maximize social controls." The Resolutions go on to argue that because computers are instruments for the "repression of the class struggle . . . it is important to attack, unravel, and dismember these networks of control."

Katya Komisaruk, the "Princess of Computing" discussed in Chapter 13, clearly falls into the area of symbolic technological terrorism. Likewise, Jan Hanasz, the Polish TV Pirate of Chapter 14, was viewed in this manner by the Polish authorities who prosecuted him, even though most Poles thought him a hero.

Previously, when we at the Center commented on the bombing of computer centers, we noted happily that as long as the "enemy" used physical bombs and not logic bombs, we were in good shape. Unfortunately, there are signs in the recent cases involving viruses that terrorists are gaining technological savvy they previously lacked. The Israeli virus seems to have been planted by someone who supports the Palestinians, since it was set to go off on the fortieth anniversary of the State of Israel. The Chaos Computer Club in Germany has engaged in several acts of computer crime which seem designed as much to make political statements as to achieve any technological goals.

Yale sociology professor Scott Boorman has argued that viruses can become the weapons of the future. "Software attacks," he wrote, "often best carried out with the aid of well-placed insiders, are emerging as a coherent new type of systematic offensive warfare." Boorman's comments appeared in *Signal,* a military electronics journal.

Even the relatively benign motives of the World Peace virus demonstrate the importance of the soapbox motivation in computer crime. The fact that hundreds of thousands of Macintosh users all over the world received the message from one source is a mighty inducement to anyone who would like to be heard. This bodes ill for the future.

When physical bombings were the biggest problem posed by technological terrorists, physical security was the most obvious solution. Now that program warfare has been demonstrated to be much more feasible, security must include careful protection of strategic computer systems from unknown programs and certain types of data files. Traditional security for strategic systems is based on different models, and needs to be revised.

THE FAIRYLAND

The least obvious and thus most dangerous environment leading to computer crime is the "fairyland." This category of computer criminality runs completely counter to the widely held view of computer criminals. In the fairyland environment, criminal acts are committed by people who are not even aware that they are doing anything wrong. Because computers are still new to many people and because of the complexity of their operations, computer users may easily lose sight of the consequences of their behavior.

In the days before viruses, fairyland cases often involved wire transfer crimes in which innocent clerks actually transferred large amounts of money for criminals who duped them. In one case described in Thomas Whiteside's *Computer Capers,* a scheming operator convinced his girlfriend to transfer $2 million to his bank in New York. He told the girlfriend that he simply wanted to play a joke on a friend at the New York bank.

The man and the money disappeared before the girlfriend realized that she had been conned as well as jilted.

As with communicable biological diseases, computer viruses are a particular threat because they are spread unknowingly. The thousands of copies of software that contained the World Peace virus were created almost entirely by people who had no idea that they were doing so.

The analogy to communicable diseases is also applicable in discussing security against this type of computer criminal activity. Without educating potential virus spreaders about their responsibilities and the dangers viruses present, we will not be able to establish good security against computer viruses.

Even if a computer user's ignorance of computing does not facilitate a crime, it may stand in the way of effective security. One of the best traditional security protections in business is nosy employees. If a large number of people see a business document with unusual entries on it, one of them may bring it to the attention of the company's auditors or security staff. We lose some of the advantage of this kind of security as we computerize our businesses and make it harder for human nosiness to help us. If the people who love computing (those who have a playpen attitude) could teach those who live in a fairyland, security might be dramatically increased.

THE TOOLBOX

As Freud said, sometimes a cigar is just a cigar. So for some of those who commit crimes, a computer is just a computer. In these cases the computer is not the target, but simply an implement in a crime that in no other way involves computing.

Increasingly, purveyors of vice are recognizing the potential uses of computers to conduct illegal business. Criminals involved in gambling, prostitution, and drug distribution have all taken advantage of the data processing capabilities of the computer. A data base program keeps track of illegal activities as well as legal ones, and a spreadsheet shows profit and loss regardless of what one is selling.

Clearly all computer viruses involve computing. But in some cases, the only purpose of a virus is to allow the creator to accomplish another goal. Several years ago Vault Corporation, a California computer company selling copy protection software, threatened to introduce a "killer worm" program into its software. The effect of this program, the manufacturer claimed, would be to cause disk crashes whenever someone tried to copy software without authorization. User resistance was predictably strong, and the company decided against using the program. This is the sort of application that could be even more dangerous if a virus instead of just a worm were used.

In "The Computerized Con" in Chapter 4, computers were merely the bait used to part a number of personal computer users from their funds in business opportunity and boiler room frauds. The operator of these frauds had certainly managed to operate without computers as bait in the past, but the opportunity to use a new technology seemed to be attractive.

CYBERPUNK SPACE

In the last few years, a new genre of science fiction has arisen under the evocative name of "cyberpunk." Introduced in the work of William Gibson, particularly in his prize-winning novel *Neuromancer,* cyberpunk takes an apocalyptic view of the technological future. In *Neuromancer,* the protagonist is a futuristic hacker who must use the most sophisticated computer strategies to commit crimes for people who offer him enough money to buy the biological creations he needs to survive. His life is one of cynical despair, fueled by the desire to avoid death. Though none of the virus cases actually seen so far have been so devastating, this book certainly represents an attitude that should be watched for when we find new cases of computer virus and try to understand the motivations behind them.

The New York Times's John Markoff, one of the more perceptive and accomplished writers in the field, has written that a number of computer criminals demonstrate new levels of meanness. He characterizes them, as do I, as cyberpunks. Early (and not always accurate) accounts of Kevin Mitnick's case, suggested that his malice was on a par with other cyberpunk computer criminals. As Chapter 12 demonstrates, the accounts reflect media myth-making more than Mitnick's malice.

THE FUTURE OF COMPUTER CRIMINOLOGY

The categories I have listed are not mutually exclusive, exhaustive, or chiseled in stone. I encourage readers' responses, particularly if it appears I have missed a significant attitude. The categories may not be of much use when we try to predict behavior, unless we can develop tests to determine how potential suspects perceive computer environments. These categories do suggest a way to look at the computer crimes that have already occurred and to inspect the computer environments we're responsible for to see how they might be viewed. The future will see more people learning enough about computers to commit more sophisticated variants of crime, with their motivations ranging through all I've listed and doubtless others as well. The time to start cataloging the known motivations is right now, since computer criminals are not going to wait before taking action.

CHAPTER 4

WHO ARE THE VICTIMS OF COMPUTER CRIME?

ROY HOUSTON: THE COMPUTERIZED CON

A PARANOID'S GUIDE TO COMPUTING

Dennis Macleod was not a mere spectator to the drama of computer crime. He was a victim. As unlike the mythical victim as anyone could be, he was no large corporation with money to spare. In fact, he was sharp, more than merely computer literate, and experienced in the world of advertising after a 15-year career in broadcasting.

When Macleod saw an ad in the *Seattle Times* offering $300 a week in "rentals" for the use of his computer, it seemed too good to pass up. The requirements were within his technical grasp. Only owners of IBM PCs available from 9 A.M. to 9 P.M. could apply. That fit him, and he needed the money. His wife had lost her job. "She was flat on her back," Macleod said, "taking heavy doses of medication." Running a business involving their computer was just his wife's speed, since she couldn't spend too much time on her feet.

Macleod called a number for Mutual Telecommunications Network (MTN), and found himself talking to a mechanical voice. The voice told him that he could make money while his computer did the work. Dutifully, he answered the mechanical voice's questions, providing the necessary information for his credit to be checked. The voice said that if he wanted to be considered as a "syop" (or system operator) for MTN, he would have to send a $660 deposit by October

10, 1987. (He ignored MTN's use of non-standard terminology. System operators are usually called "sysops.")

Macleod sent the money. He understood, based on the prerecorded messages, that he would be using a Watson board to collect information for MTN. The board was a special piece of hardware which could be used for computer-generated phone calls. He would have to type in names and phone numbers from the phone book, but once he did, the Watson board and his computer would do the rest. And every hour his computer spent collecting information would make Macleod $3 richer.

I asked Macleod if he was at all suspicious, listening to the recorded messages offering him much-needed cash. On the contrary, he replied, "I had no human contact for several months." Seemingly he trusted the machines more. (In light of his subsequent dealings with the humans behind MTN, this was a reasonably logical response.)

Finally, Macleod was able to speak to a real person when "Bill Sims" called him. Macleod believes, based on several face-to-face conversations, that "Sims" was really Roy Houston. "He [Houston] told me the rentals were for information collection, and said the Attorney General's office had given it the OK," Macleod later recalled. "He just didn't mention anything about a trivia game or a television show."

Macleod received the Watson board and the software to run it. There were problems with the software. By November 20, 1987 he was started. He and his wife plunged into the business, running up over 1,300 hours worth of rentals before the year's end. "We were depending on MTN," he says.

ELECTRONIC ENVELOPE STUFFING

Jim Petrakis doesn't find Macleod's story all that surprising. "If I read the ad," he said, "and it offered a Macintosh user like me the way to putter with my hobby and still pay some costs, it could be just the right thing to come along." Petrakis, a postal inspector, is one of many law enforcement officials who have looked closely at MTN. According to Macleod, at least 1,600 PC owners sent in deposits for Watson boards and programs to do MTN's bidding.

"We have gotten complaints," Petrakis says. "Some people have remitted funds and gotten nothing. Others have not been paid for the time they spent. Most have a net loss."

In addition to the *Seattle Times,* MTN advertised in the *Hartford Courant, Los Angeles Times, Sacramento Bee,* and other mainstream newspapers in Louisiana, Georgia, Iowa, and Florida. Pierce Jensen was another of MTN's victims. The data processing manager used to be in sales. He saw an ad in the *Los Angeles Times* and responded. "It's cheaper now to let computers do your pitching for you," Jensen said. He was told that the Watson board and software he ordered were worth $2,400. Natural Microsystems, the Natick, Massachusetts manufacturer of the Watson circuit boards, listed their price at $399 at the time MTN was asking for the $660 deposits. (This price, however, does not take into account the cost of the software MTN also provided.)

Jensen was angry when he did not receive anything for four months. Eventually, he succeeded in getting the board and software after feeding false information about threats by disgruntled owners to Houston's successor as president of MTN. Once he received the board, Jensen said to himself, "Now that I've got my board, to hell with them."

Norm Cabana was less fortunate. The Fairfield, California resident was calling other residents of Fairfield at the rate of 400 per day. "I'd like to take their hide and nail it to the barn door," he told reporter Katherine Kam, complaining about the wages he claimed MTN owed him.

Macleod, Jensen, and Cabana were but three of the 1,600 syops MTN acquired in the last few months of 1987. In October of that year, Houston claimed in an interview with *PC Week* that MTN was hoping to build a nationwide system of 500 syops, covering every major area of the country. These syops, he explained, would be used to conduct nationwide telemarketing campaigns for clients while taking advantage of local telephone rates.

Pull out a throw-away paper and look in the classifieds. You are likely to find a listing of "business opportunities," some of which are frauds. One classic is the envelope-stuffing fraud.

Generally, Postal Inspector Petrakis says, the victim of this type of fraud sends money for a starter set of envelopes to stuff but receives nothing in return. MTN did not send equipment to all who paid for it. Its record was even worse for sending the "rental" fees to computer owners who had put down deposits on Watson boards.

THE BINARY BOILER ROOM

By the time the earliest syops received their equipment, the only "client" for MTN's services was Trivia Masters Productions. Headquartered in Atlanta's CNN Center, Trivia Masters purported to be putting together a TV game show. The calls syops like Jensen, Cabana, and Macleod were making invited people to compete in the Trivia Masters game.

Imagine it, perhaps 1,600 people making computerized calls—some, like Norm Cabana, making as many as 400 calls a day. And those who received the calls found themselves listening to a computerized voice asking questions such as: "John the Baptist was known for his diet of (a) locusts and honey or (b) peanut butter and crabgrass."

In the music category, the listener would hear a synthesized version of the Beach Boy's song chanting "Ba ba ba, ba ba bra ann." The mechanized voice would then ask, "Is this the opening to a song called 'Barbara Ann'?"

In the general information category, the voice asked: "How many days of the week begin with *T?*"

"The questions they are asking are ridiculous," said Henry Huerta, coordinator of the Florida Department of Consumer Affairs. Yet, according to Macleod, Trivia Masters was signing up as many as 80 players a day. Perhaps it tells us something about the current relationship in our society between people and the machines we use that so many people could be convinced to participate in the Trivia Masters game by a computer simulation of a voice.

To answer the questions, participants touched different tones on their telephone. Every correct answer was greeted with prerecorded cheers, applause, and whistles. (Pavlov lives!)

Not too surprisingly, many of the participants in this contest got the initial questions right. "While other contestants are dropping like flies," the prerecorded message informed them, "you're still in there." To continue to compete, and perchance to win a $500 prize, participants were told to call another long-distance number.

Completing three rounds at this long-distance number gave the participants a chance to win even more money—this time $5,000. (Either no one stopped and asked for the $500 prize, or no records were kept of such an event.) Now it was getting serious, and those who were still playing were asked to send a $20 "entry fee" to participate in the special game that offered not only the $5,000 prize but a chance to appear on the game show. "Are you willing to take time from work for a free trip to Atlanta?" the computer asked, neglecting to specify when, where, or by whom the taping would be done.

Ed Smith, president of the Better Business Bureau office in Atlanta, wrote to Trivia Masters at the address it gave consumers, asking for proof that it was planning a game show. As of May 1989 he had not received an answer.

The existence of the game show is only one of the unanswered questions vexing investigators and frustrating the many victims. Rhonda Brambley, one of those who received a call from Norm Cabana's computer, managed to get Trivia Masters to accept $10 instead of the $20 entry fee they had requested. But in return she was given a number to call which had been disconnected. "I'm an honest person," she told reporter Katherine Kam, "and I can't believe someone would do this. I can't figure out how they can manipulate my phone and someone's computer to do this."

Don Steinberg, a reporter for *PC Week,* commented: "Principals believed to be running the trivia game operation have eluded investigators' inquiries by hiding behind a sophisticated web of computerized voice-messaging systems and forwarded telephone numbers that have effectively prevented callers trying to reach them from speaking with anything but a computer."

The technology is baffling, but when joined with the complexities of our legal system, it provides the kind of environment con artists can thrive in. Trivia Masters was more than MTN's first (and possibly only) client. Prior to January 1988, James Ray Houston was listed as president of both MTN and Trivia Masters. In February 1988, Ray Poje, currently listed as president of MTN, told the Fairfield *Daily Republic* that Houston had stepped down as MTN president. But Dennis Macleod doubts that this is true.

"Houston and Poje have been buddies the last 10 to 15 years," Macleod claims. "Houston, Poje, and Lance O'Brien were like three stooges, collecting $1,500 a week," when Macleod met them in Atlanta in January of 1988. Poje disagrees. "Trivia Masters is not paying me," he said in February 1988. "I've been stiffed for $250,000." Poje blamed the Trivia Masters bad fortune on bad press. "It seems like any time we get any newspaper coverage it's bullshit" he told the *Republic*'s Kam.

I wonder how Ray Houston's mind works. It's hard to imagine the kind of thinking, values, and training that leads one to set people up to lose money while he tries to avoid landing in jail.

Did he wake up one night from a troubled sleep and run into the streets of some sunbelt suburb yelling, "Eureka, Eureka, I've perfected the two-level, computer-assisted, combination business-opportunity and boiler-room fraud"?

Or did he emerge from a pop psychology seminar convinced that he had a gift to give the world? Was he moved by nothing more than the desire to make the computer operators of the world richer and happier by providing them with new ways to make money with their machines?

Did Houston work out the details, considering the advantages of two-level versus three- or four-level versions of his con game, or did the structure come to him in an intuitive flash?

I'd like to ask Ray Houston these questions, but he's nowhere to be found. When he was running his two companies he was hard enough to get to, a maze of voice mail messages insulating him from the telephonic world. It was quite an irony—the man who was selling automated communication devices to hundreds of computer owners was using the same equipment to fend off their calls when he didn't keep his word.

Ray Houston is a historic figure in the world of computer crime because he seems to live out some current fantasies with an abandon that most of us would never dare to emulate. Who, I suggest, wouldn't like to turn their computer into a machine that produced income? The people on the "sucker lists" that folks like Houston buy and sell certainly thought it was a great idea.

And who, after being shuttled through six voice menus and pressing six buttons before being told they've called the wrong number, doesn't wish that they, and not the voice mail system, were calling the shots? What greater revenge than to create a voice mail system more restrictive than the rest—one sufficient to avoid telephonic contact for months?

Of the many syops whose money MTN collected, none had a closer view of the operation than Dennis Macleod. In January 1988, around the time that Houston was to step down from the presidency of MTN, Houston invited Macleod to Atlanta. The national management had split, Houston wrote, and he was offering Macleod the president's job. "I said I had no experience, but Houston said it was no problem, they could train me."

Macleod was skeptical. "I've been fed some pretty serious bullshit," he thought. Still, in the hole from his investment in the Watson board, he accepted the free trip to Atlanta that went with the invitation. "I wanted to see how much I could get from them," Macleod explained.

"I started getting scared when I met these people," Macleod said. Noting Houston and his associates' lack of computer expertise, Macleod concluded, "They're real stupid, thieves, or both." Conversations with Houston increased Macleod's concern. "Houston talked about how the government was always two years behind in investigations of fraud. He talked about how the people involved in Trivia Masters were like pet cows ready to be milked," Macleod noted bitterly.

He couldn't understand Houston's cynicism. "After having screwed these people over, he thought they were going to sit still again," Macleod said. Houston told Macleod of a mailing list of 5 million participants in other game shows whom he considered prime targets for the revised Trivia Masters "competition."

While in Atlanta, Macleod was given a contract. "They were looking for a fall guy," he says. "They put all their criminal bullshit down on paper and asked me to take charge of it." Instead, Macleod contacted radio station WOR in New York and the Atlanta Postal Inspector's office. He returned to Seattle and set up a bulletin board to serve as a clearinghouse for others who had been victimized by MTN's operation. "For my $660 I'll scream as long as I can," he told me. "The son of a bitch will pay." At last accounting, he claimed, "I'm about $5,000 in arrears from these clowns."

THE MUSCLE-BOUND ARMS OF THE LAW

In February 1988, the Fairfield *Daily Republic* reported that "officials in Georgia, Washington state, Louisiana, Wisconsin, Iowa, Ohio, Maine, and Florida are investigating Trivia Masters after receiving hundreds of inquiries." As of August 1989, none of those investigations had eventuated in any action against Trivia Masters or MTN, save one.

Washington state Deputy Attorney General Kathy Muir reported that "we wrote them [Trivia Masters and MTN] a letter saying that they were in violation of Washington law, and they assured us they would not do business in Washington." Washington's law prohibits the use of automatic dialing machines like those provided by MTN.

Though Florida is the home of MTN, Consumer Affairs department coordinator Henry Huerta reports, "We're not investigating. We got no bona fide complaints, only inquiries." In response to "lots of inquiries about whether the company is legitimate," Huerta said, "we told them to follow their own conscience. We don't tell people what businesses to invest in."

Ed Smith of the Better Business Bureau of Atlanta expressed similar deliberation. "Our experience with them is limited right now," he said. "We're asking people to exercise normal economic precautions."

Jim Petrakis was promoted from the Los Angeles Postal Inspector's Office to the Washington, D.C. office. His replacement, Tom Dugan, reports that his office's investigation is "still open. It's a good, prosecutable case," he says. "The guy ripped a lot of people off."

While in LA, Petrakis was quick to add that none of the complaints against MTN, even if proven, would necessarily be sufficient to establish that MTN had violated the law. "Investigation of this sort of case usually requires letting the suspected fraud play itself out," he explained. "While something like this is going on it is hard to determine whether what we have is a bad business or actual fraud. If all the victims were paid tomorrow, there would be no fraud." The key is intent. To prove a case of fraud, it is necessary to show that those charged intended to cheat their victims.

Ray Houston knows well the meaning of fraudulent intent. In 1982 he was sentenced to 16 months in jail after being convicted of operating a talent agency without a proper license and of 29 counts of false and misleading advertising. He was acquitted on an earlier charge of wire and mail fraud.

Petrakis also explained why it is unclear whether the computer owners who made calls for Trivia Masters would be prosecuted for operating computerized "boiler rooms." He defined a boiler room as a scheme in which telephones are used "to contact potential victims throughout the country, and to convince them to send money in order to receive a promised benefit. People are lulled into sending money and then do not receive the benefit promised." By the time the consumer realizes he or she has been taken, Petrakis added, the boiler room operators have changed names, locations, or phone numbers.

"It is possible that some of the people involved in these kinds of contracts are not aware of the law and are violating it. Or they may not be aware of what the computers are telling people. It is not clear if they are independent contractors or employees." It is hard to imagine a juror or a prosecutor who would not sympathize with a computer owner who has himself or herself been fleeced of $600 and not paid any of the promised rental fees. But what about the people who received the phone calls and believed they were playing a trivia game? Is there no protection for them? This is a question our legal system has not yet addressed.

WE ARE ALL "USEES"

This has been a very political chapter in a very political book. I hope that you, the reader, recognize that people like Pierce Jensen, Dennis Macleod, Norm Cabana, and Rhonda Brambley deserve your sympathy and support. In truth, each was playing against heavy odds. Each confronted a technology they did not understand, one combining telephones, computers, and the law. Each made a mistake, but one you and I might be equally likely to make if we are not forewarned.

Computer security, properly understood, should protect these people, not just the corporate and governmental owners of large mainframe systems. In short, the definition of computer crime should include consumer protection for those who own computers and those who rely on them. With the ever-decreasing cost of personal computers, and their increasing use in schools and work, the number of computer owners (and buyers) will continue to grow. Unfortunately, the crest of consumer protection occurred before the personal computer became a social institution. Mark Silvergeld, director of the Consumer's Union, put his finger on the problem. "Consumer groups are grinding out the old basics," he said. "Intellectual property issues are too abstract for most consumer groups."

The area of consumer protection is much broader than just warnings about nondelivery of Watson boards or failure to pay computer users rent for the use of their computers. If a company like MTN can send out a thousand boards that will be used to enlist unsuspecting computer owners in a fraudulent enterprise, one that cheats equally unsuspecting recipients of computerized game show come-ons, we have a much more serious problem to address. Computer-age consumer protection requires some effort to protect people from deceptive computer applications. Even more, it requires attention to the mechanics of various applications, and some sort of warning so that consumers do not inadvertently use illegal or unethical applications on their computers.

We are all "usees." Unlike a computer user, a usee is someone who relies on computers whether he or she uses one or not. We are all usees of the IRS's computers; we are all usees of the computers that keep track of our social security benefits, that calculate the rates we pay for insurance, and that keep track of credit reports about us. Eventually, the law will progress to the point that it protects usees against unfair or harmful computer applications, in addition to protecting the more immediately obvious rights of computer users.

But eventually can be a long time, particularly if Silbergeld is right about the amount of help we can expect to get from traditional consumer protection groups. And this is where the politics of this chapter—and this book—come in. As long as computer crime is seen as a spectacle, we will view it as a struggle that doesn't involve or endanger us. Once we see that every one of us can be the victim of computer crime, we begin to realize that it is no longer possible to ignore the challenges of computer security.

And as long as we're at it, who do you think pays when a major corporation suffers from computer crime? I'm willing to bet that far more of the cost is recovered through increased charges to consumers than reduced salaries of corporation executives. There's no escaping it. Directly or indirectly, we are all victims of computer crime. (If you have any doubt about that, take a look at our chapters on computer viruses.)

CALLING DENNY MACLEOD

When last I spoke with Denny Macleod, he was full of fire, moving and shaking his Rebel bulletin board and trying to find ways for the victims of MTN's operations to make some money with their Watson boards. He had contacted a user group of Watson board owners, and noted that he knew of a dozen business plans that its members were circulating. He spoke of other centers for the bulletin board at Travis Air Force Base, in Boston, in South Carolina, and in Texas. He had mailed a letter to 1,033 victims encouraging them to work together and was getting replies from 6 to 8 of them on his bulletin board every day.

Macleod had spoken, when interviewed in February 1988, of filing a class action suit. It never materialized. "People kicked it around on the bulletin board, but it died," he said. "Not many of the people have any money, and $660 isn't enough to fight about. Anyway," he continued, "people feel so stupid when they realize they'd been had."

But Macleod was still willing to fight. "If I let them get away with it, they'll come back and do it again," he argued.

Dennis Macleod is no longer in Seattle. None of the victims, investigators, or reporters who wrote about him know where he is. David Bresnahan says Macleod took a job with a radio station "somewhere in the boonies" and promptly lost interest in fighting MTN and Trivia Masters. Bresnahan runs Emerald Communications, a computerized telemarketing business which employs a number of the victims of the two-level fraud. There is no more Rebel bulletin board, no more effort to help the victims of MTN. No prosecution has eventuated in any jurisdiction, and no more money has been distributed to the victims since February 1988. There has been no TV trivia contest. I wish I didn't have to end this chapter so somberly, but as Walter Cronkite would say, "And that's the way it is."

CHAPTER 5

HOW—AND WHY—DO WE DEFINE COMPUTER CRIME?

JOHN TABER: THE LONE STRANGER

Sit down at a table with several computer security experts and claim "In the history of computer crime, no one has had greater impact than John Taber," and none will argue. Of course, few will know who you're talking about, though most of them are likely to care.

Computer security is the Rodney Dangerfield of computing. It often gets no respect, particularly from senior managers who are inclined to invest the resources they control into production or marketing. These areas more obviously produce profits. The security professional must either prove the case for a bigger budget with facts and figures, or scare the dickens out of management with stories of computer crime. By 1980, the basic points of the argument were well known. Combine scary numbers with scary stories, the thinking went, and you've got your best shot at making computer security seem important. The myths of computer crime, bolstered by numbers of questionable reliability and dubious applicability, provided the tools for security professionals' efforts

Taber came out of nowhere and challenged this reigning computer security orthodoxy. He demonstrated how much of the statistical and anecdotal evidence of computer crime was myth and not scholarship. Having left the statistics' validity sadly shattered, Taber returned to the obscurity in which he had previously lurked. In two very influential law review articles, and in testimony before Congress, this IBM programmer, (speaking in a nonrepresentative capacity) threw down the gauntlet to all those people who argued that computer crime was a serious problem requiring legislative attention. His challenges to the field can be summarized in four questions:

1. Can computer crime be defined?
2. Can it be measured?
3. Can we tell how serious of a problem computer crime is?
4. Is there a basis for laws against computer crime?

These questions still challenge anyone who argues the case for increased attention to computer security, as I do in this book. Consequently, the rest of this chapter will be spent attempting to offer reasonable responses to Taber's tests.

CAN COMPUTER CRIME BE DEFINED?

One of the biggest problems facing computer security is the lack of agreement in the field as to the definition of a computer crime. Different definitions proliferate, ranging from the very narrow definition John Taber offered back in 1980 to the expansive definitions now in favor.

Taber defined computer crime saying: "There are genuine computer crimes. By genuine computer crime is meant a crime that, in fact, occurred and in which a computer was directly and significantly instrumental." In 1980, Taber reviewed the 375 files in the data base maintained by Donn Parker at SRI in Menlo Park, California. Taber found only two he accepted as falling within this definition.

Parker has since offered a more expansive definition of computer crime in his most recent book, *Fighting Computer Crime*. Describing why he considered the Rifkin case discussed in Chapter 2 a computer crime, Parker offered two reasons:

> Many people claim that this was not a computer crime . . . The perpetrator did not use a computer directly; neither did any person in collusion with him. He merely telephoned a computer terminal operator who innocently caused computer activity by entering data through a

terminal. The crime could also have been perpetrated if telex communications had been used, as in other funds transfer systems. Therefore, computers were not essential to the crime . . .

I have identified the case as both a computer abuse and a computer crime because it easily satisfied my definitions of both categories . . . The perpetrator made unauthorized access to a computer terminal area and used his special computer skills, knowledge, and access to gain the necessary information by observing terminal displays and operations. In addition it is an important case from which to learn how to make computer applications terminal areas, and management procedures more secure. It also demonstrates the high position of trust occupied by computer security consultants and the need for controlling their activities.

Parker used abuse as a general term, defining it in *Fighting Computer Crime* as "any intentional act associated in any way with computers where a victim suffered, or could have suffered, a loss, and a perpetrator made, or could have made, a gain." He also appears to accept a legal definition such as "a computer crime will be any act as specified in a computer crime statute in the applicable jurisdiction of the statute."

At the National Center for Computer Crime Data we agree with Parker in part, defining computer crime as that which the law in a specific jurisdiction defines as computer crime in its computer crime law. This is a relatively narrow, relatively precise definition. Using it, we can compile statistics concerning computer crime prosecutions from year to year and know that we are making a contribution to the fund of knowledge available to computer security professionals interested in reducing the incidence of computer crime. At the same time, we view the task of computer security as much broader. Here we part from conventional wisdom.

The current battle in the field of computer crime centers on whether computer crime is designed to protect information or computer systems. Advocates of the former point of view include the Data Processing Management Association (DPMA) and Donn Parker. The National Center for Computer Crime Data is the advocate of the latter.

The prelude to the DPMA's "Model Computer Crime Bill" expresses the rationale of the information perspective, basing it on Parker's analysis, as communicated to Congress and the DPMA.

In contrast, it is the position of the National Center for Computer Crime Data that the purpose of computer crime laws is the protection of computer and communication systems, not just information.

There are two main differences between the two positions: what theirs leaves out, and what ours leaves in. They would have difficulty prosecuting the theft of media with no information on it, such as blank diskettes, denial of services, or the spreading of a virus. We would include the theft of components, fraudulent representations concerning a computer's capabilities, and the physical destruction of a machine as computer crimes. More significantly, I believe, the definition we favor would communicate to the various publics involved that the goal of computer crime law is to safeguard computer systems so that they can be used effectively and safely for all the purposes for which a computer might be found useful.

COKE AND CHIPS TO GO

As an example of the difference between protecting information and protecting computer systems, consider this case:

The Compaq Corporation was experiencing drug problems in 1987, according to Detective Ray Daniel of the Houston Police Department. The company hired a private investigative firm to work undercover investigating both drug sales and the theft of components for the Compaq computers being produced in Houston. A buy program was set up, not unlike the myriad sting operations which have been used in the last two decades. Working together, a private investigator and Detective Daniel arrested several dozen people for sales of stolen computer chips or of drugs. To Daniel, who couldn't tell me the type of chips involved, the difference between chips and other stolen merchandise was negligible. "It's just stuff people steal in order to buy drugs," the narcotics officer calmly told me. "On the street, they say 'steal or deal,' " he explained.

As this book went to press, James Kaatz was one of the few people arrested in this operation who had not pleaded guilty. Those arrested by Houston Police Department who had pleaded guilty received sentences up to 18 years.

Should this case be considered computer crime? The answer, I suggest, lies in a consideration of the goals we want computer crime law to serve. Though not spectacular, this sort of case demonstrates a real problem faced by computer manufacturers. Trafficking in stolen computer components is big business. It involves competition between major computer manufacturers here and abroad. It also has significant implications for our military security, since so much of our military posture depends on state-of-the-art computer systems which rely on the latest chips.

Kaatz and the others arrested with him have been charged with theft, receiving stolen property, or trafficking in illegal drugs. As long as these charges are adequate to put them away, there is no need for additional laws. If, however, investigators find it difficult to prosecute the theft of chips under existing law, then it is time for computer crime law to step in. In California's Silicon Valley, law enforcement officials and private security directors are working together to fight the theft of high-technology components. Lack of money, not changes in the law, seems to be their biggest problem. Under a pilot project, the District Attorney's Technology Theft Association was able to compile an admirable record of successful prosecutions. The project was not renewed, however. It was a victim of the state's budgetary constraints.

These kinds of considerations, not abstract arguments from definition, are the key to defining computer crime. To define computer crime we must first ask why we are defining it. New computer and communication technologies are being put to use in almost every home, office, and school. We need to protect those who use them, own them, or rely on them. When defining computer crime, this is the question we must ask: are we adequately protecting those who need our help? This pragmatic social concern, not some academic search for ideal definitions, should guide the emerging definition of computer crime.

John Taber asked why we need computer crime laws when we don't having filing cabinet crime laws. My response, as might be guessed, is that filing cabinets do not play as significant a role in our lives as computers. We passed laws concerning motor vehicle crimes when automobile use became widespread in society. Proponents of laws punishing drunk driving were not required to explain why no laws concerning drunk horse-riding had not been passed. (In fact unless the laws and ethics promoted in this book are effective, some day we will probably have an organization analogous to the Department of Motor Vehicles enforcing responsible use of computers).

CAN WE MEASURE COMPUTER CRIME?

There is a talmudic type of earnestness surrounding those who argue whether our society can or cannot measure the amount of computer crime. The argument has raged since John Taber attacked the validity of the SRI data base of computer crime information compiled by Donn Parker. In 1980, Taber submitted his most thorough and sweeping critique to a journal that I was editing. I had to publish Taber's critique, despite my fears that it would be damaging to my work. The National Center for Computer Crime Data had been given the opportunity to make a copy of Parker's data base. An attack on Parker was an attack on us. So I asked Donn Parker to reply to Taber. His response was surprising and frank: "The Computer Abuse Research Project is not a rigorous sociological statistically based computer crime study. . . . Its mandate was to collect and report on incidents of reported abuses involving computers to explore the technological implications of such abuses, and to conduct legal research on the technical adequacy of the law."

In defense of his data base, Parker explained that "specific research results are based on subsets of applicable cases. For example, computer abuse perpetrators were characterized on the basis of information in 26 interviews with such persons, and the average reported gross loss per case in a subset of 42 cases of banking-related abuse was found to be $430,000."

He explained the failure of reports to specify the subsets on which his research was based, noting "we have loosely called the computer abuse file of reported cases a computer crime file when to take the time to explain and define our precise meanings for a general audience would be secondary to another theme."

Since then, Parker, having seen his own research misinterpreted too often for his liking, has become the leading advocate of the "you can't measure it" position in computer security thinking. He acknowledges the role Taber played in changing his opinion. Taber's article was "probably a turning point," Parker recently told me. "It made me delve further and understand the dangers of putting out quantitative information on a subject that can't be quantified." Parker now claims that all computer crime statistics are invalid. Harold Highland, former editor of the influential publication *Computers and Security,* endorses the same position. A recent article summarized the views of Parker, Highland, and Canadian computer security consultant James Finch, saying: "All three agree that since only a small proportion of computer crimes are reported to the police, it is impossible to come up with a reliable statistic."

On the other side of the discussion, increasing numbers of researchers and computer security consultants are producing figures about computer crime. The interested reader will find reference to this research in the concluding chapter. The National Center for Computer Crime Data is in the nonagnostic camp, having produced *Computer Crime, Computer Security, Computer Ethics,* and *Commitment to Security,* two statistical reports on computer crime and security.

To give the agnostics their due, criminology has long noted the difficulties in measuring any type of crime. In an excellent summary of the problems with crime statistics, two student editors of the *American Criminal Law Review* quote a former public information director of the Baltimore City Police Department: "No one knows how much crime there really is because the number of crimes known to the police is only a small percentage of all the crimes actually committed. The hypocrisy is that those that interpret them pretend they show everything."[1]

Where the National Center for Computer Crime Data parts company with the agnostics is on the question of how to react to an imperfect world. We agree with Morrissey that the nub of the problem with crime statistics is their responsible use. We agree with Parker who has noted sadly that the statistics about

---

[1] L. Center and T. Smith, "Crime Statistics - Can They Be Trusted?" Vol. 11 *American Criminal Law Review* 1973, p. 1047.

computer crime that he has published in the past have been abused. We at the Center have had the same experience.

But there is a need to report on computer crime as accurately as possible. The Center does this by studying prosecution statistics and by being clear that this is what we are doing. We are convinced that this information is valuable, particularly in commenting on the effects of the nation's 49 state computer crime laws and the 2 federal computer crime laws. In *Commitment to Security,* our latest report, Stan Stahl, our director of research, summarizes our position thus:

> The National Center for Computer Crime Data believes that, without ongoing statistical and other mathematical analysis, we will never adequately solve the numerous legal, ethical, moral, and technological problems surrounding the areas of computer crime and information security. We agree with Galileo, who wrote "The book of nature lies open before our eyes . . . it is written in the language of mathematics." The nature of scientific inquiry is to use statistics and other forms of mathematics as the way to explicate the truth. It is this fundamental scientific principle that the Center applies to its own research.

CAN WE TELL HOW SERIOUS A PROBLEM COMPUTER CRIME IS?

Taber argued that "there is no evidence that computer-based fraud and embezzlement are increasing." Parker now agrees. We at the National Center for Computer Crime Data do not have enough information to agree or disagree, but we do have some relevant information. From our two "computer crime censuses," we can say that prosecuted computer crime is growing dramatically. We estimated only several hundred prosecuted computer crime cases per year in 1986. In our 1989 report we estimated several thousand cases prosecuted per year. These are only extrapolations from our prosecutor surveys, but they do suggest a clear growth to us.

The advantage of the information about prosecuted cases is the light it sheds on our use of the existing computer crime laws. Our surveys of computer security professionals suggest that the average annual loss from computer crime is about one-half billion dollars. Yet our census results indicate that 60 percent of the prosecuted cases involved a loss of less than $10,000 and 87 percent involved losses of less than $100,000. Our surveys of computer security professionals also indicate that only about 6 percent of the serious computer security incidents were reported for prosecution. Thus we can look at the prosecution data, compare it to the data garnered from computer security professionals, and conclude that our laws are not being used to prosecute the most important cases. This data is useful to a computer security professional, a prosecutor, or a legislator considering computer crime laws.

SHOULD WE PASS LAWS AGAINST COMPUTER CRIME?

John Taber wrote in his 1980 article:

> Computer crime is a media creature, largely fed by the computer security industry press releases, that has superseded the earlier creature, the "computer error." In 1970, the California state legislature, exasperated by media reports of "computer errors," contemplated enacting licensing requirements for data processing professionals. It was an unwise plan to end "computer errors . . . ."
>
> "Computer crime" has gone farther in legislation than "computer error." Computer crime laws, hastily and carelessly drawn, have already been enacted in about a dozen states, and are being considered in many more. A federal bill is pending as well. None of them is necessary, and it is appalling that they are justified by such inadequate research.

I wonder what he was thinking in 1989, as Vermont was the only state left without a computer crime law. Of those laws, several have proposed barring computer criminals from "computer-related professions."

If his goal was to prevent the passage of computer crime laws, Taber was not at all successful. But if his goal was to change the way the security profession views computer crime, he has been dramatically effective. His few articles and one appearance before Congress played a major role in bringing about the agnosticism that currently holds sway amongst some very influential computer security consultants. Has he won the battle but lost the war?

I believe so. The issue today is not whether there should be computer crime laws, not whether computer crime is a meaningful concept, but how to combat the problem. Ever since computer viruses demonstrated that computer crime is a problem for every computer user, Taber's critique has been a historical artifact. It remains important, however, as a challenge to all of us in the field to improve our analytic skills.

PART 2

THE THREE KEYS TO SECURITY

Arguments about computer security strategies sometimes seem to be about as sophisticated as the beer commercials in which advocates challenge each other menacingly snarling "less filling" and "more taste." Champions of computer crime laws, computer security awareness, and computer technology tend to push their passions, leaving the possibility of a synergy between the three strategies unexplored. Just as a geometric figure needs at least three sides to enclose a space, so a computer security strategy needs all of these elements working well together to protect a computer space.

That sanity shared, I must confess that security awareness is my passion. Get the best technology, pass the stiffest laws, and it won't amount to diddley unless there are people committed to making them work.

Getting people to care about security enough to become committed to it is not an easy task, especially if those people are not part of the security department. The Wells Fargo case described in Chapter 6 illustrates both a weakness in technological controls and a weakness in motivating Wells Fargo's supervisory staff to use the security policies that the bank had already established.

Caring isn't enough. Employee awareness programs may turn around the attitude of an occasional malcontent who would otherwise become the security vulnerability that Chapter 7's Donald Burleson represented as USPA & IRA's computer security director. But such programs are much more effective motivating the vast majority of employees that will cooperate for the good of the organization once they have been told clearly and emphatically exactly how they can cooperate.

Security strategy should make success in computer crime technically difficult to achieve and even more difficult to disguise. The security technology in USPA & IRA's system made detecting Burleson and proving his guilt relatively easy, suggesting one of the many sorts of security that responsible computer users will adopt when appropriate. Another key strategy is the disaster recovery planning that the company used, including the creation of the back-up copies which kept Burleson's acts from being a disaster instead of a relatively minor annoyance.

We need computer crime laws to focus public and employee awareness on the importance of keeping our computer systems secure. The laws should be a loud statement of commitment to protect our citizens from abuse of the computer systems that are increasingly part of our lives. If a law doesn't fit the facts, as in the Olson case, it is not the worst catastrophe. If no change, occurs after a court points out the problem, it's worse. But even this is less of a problem than the fact that few computer crimes are prosecuted. Laws only deter people who believe the laws will be enforced.

We have barely begun to fashion social strategies for computer security that recognize the importance of carefully balancing the three components discussed in this section. Perhaps its combination of messages of hope and horror will provide the motivation to develop effective computer security strategies that honor the responsibility of computer users to those who rely on the computers.

CHAPTER 6

AWARENESS

HAROLD ROSSFIELDS SMITH:
THE DIGITAL DEVIL

I never expected that studying computer crime would bring me close to Mohammed Ali. But I stood next to him one day in 1982, delighted at my luck. I hadn't paid much attention to boxing since I stopped watching the Friday Night Fights with my father in my teens. But like many of my generation, I was entertained by Ali's antics, impressed by his antiwar stance, and encouraged by his ability to keep landing on his feet. To be in his presence was a treat, even in the men's room of the Los Angeles federal courthouse.

Like me, Ali had come to see the sentencing of Harold Rossfields Smith that June day. The case meant a bit more to the Champ than it did to me, since Smith had stolen $21.3 million on behalf of two organizations that bore Ali's name. "Ali's totally innocent," prosecutor Dean Allison had told me. "He's a teddy bear—shrewd, but not sophisticated. His attorney told him not to get involved with Smith, but he's a sucker for a pitch."

Ali was not the only one taken in by Harold Rossfields Smith. Smith was drawn to celebrities. He had gained support from Sammy Davis, Jr. and Shirley Bassey, and didn't seem to hesitate to ask anyone he could get close to to help him in his latest scheme.

No matter how many stars I come within touching distance of, no matter how many times I hear that they put their pants on one leg at a time like the rest of us, no matter how many times I get the chance to be a small-time celebrity myself, there is

something magical about a Mohammed Ali. Standing right
beside him, I thought of how magical the name Mohammed Ali
must have appeared to the aspiring boxers whom Harold Rossfields Smith planned to turn into tomorrow's champions through
his two organizations—Mohammed Ali Amateur Sports and
Mohammed Ali Professional Sports. Smith had picked a powerful symbol when he bought the right to use Ali's name, and he
was not at all hesitant to capitalize on his acquisition.

Harold was a man who dealt in dreams, often promising
more than he could deliver. As Ali and I returned to court to hear
Smith's attempt to avoid imprisonment, it was clear that his
latest dreams had turned nightmarish. All of Ali's magic and all
the hopes of Smith's other supporters couldn't change a bit of it.
Harold Rossfields Smith was about to go away for a while. His
effort to become the leading force in professional boxing was to
be stalled, if not abandoned, by a change of address and lifestyle,
compliments of the federal government.

LITTLE CORRUPTIONS AT THE
WELLS FARGO BANK

Early in 1976, Harold Smith was trying to cash a check. A
recent arrival in the rich and showy Marina del Rey area of Los
Angeles, he tried the Marina branch of the Wells Fargo bank. He
spoke with Sammie Marshall, a young black up-and-coming
banking and services officer. At trial, Marshall recalled his
initial contact with Smith:

> He . . . had been in track and field himself in college. And he had been
> a part of the civil rights movement throughout. And he had worked with
> [Mohammed] Ali and become friends with Ali. . . . One of his goals was
> to put together a track team for underprivileged kids . . . academically not
> qualified to be admitted . . . to various colleges around the United States.
> So he wanted to gather the kids and put them in one situation where they
> could compete on a national and international level.

Smith explained that he needed to cash an out-of-state
check to attend a track meet in New York. Marshall said no.

About two weeks later, Smith returned to the bank, accompanied by track star Houston McTear. Again Smith wanted a check cashed, and again Marshall said no.

But they kept talking. Smith told Marshall that Mohammed Ali had taken an interest in McTear because of his poverty. The runner's father, felled by a stroke, lived with eight children in a two-room house. Harold was in the process of getting McTear a tutor so he could enroll in junior college. As they spoke more, Marshall's attitude changed.

"I just felt good—had good vibes about him," Marshall testified.

Marshall's business decision changed too. Smith got the money.

Smith (as his attorney was to argue to the jury much later), "was a man with a dream." The track team he was putting together was to be no penny-ante pick-up squad scratching in the dirt pretending they were somebodies. It bore the name of Mohammed Ali, as did several of Smith's enterprises. Having bought the right to use the name, Smith ran Mohammed Ali Amateur Sports (MAAS) and Mohammed Ali Professional Sports, (MAPS). The amateur sport group sought out and found a number of the nation's best amateur boxers, offering them television exposure, training, and a taste of celebrity—maybe even a sparring session with "The Greatest" himself. Smith planned to become the dominant force in professional boxing. The amateurs would win, bring home medals and publicity from the 1980 Olympics, and establish a dynasty to last for quite some time.

But you need a bankroll if you want to run a business that can become "The Greatest." When you use the name Mohammed Ali, and you want to dominate the promotion of boxing matches and other sporting events in the United States, you can't go around acting like a pauper. Airplanes, a yacht, a trip to Australia with 40 people in the entourage and $400,000 worth of unpaid bills—that's what it takes to make an impression in the inflationary late-70's.

It was important for Harold Smith to bank where he was well liked. Marshall filled the bill. After Marshall's help with the out-of-state check, Smith began to bank with him.

In late 1976, Sammie Marshall transferred to the Beverly Drive office of the Wells Fargo bank "in order to further my career," he testified. He started handling more sophisticated loans involving real estate and commerce. When he transferred to Beverly Drive, Marshall resumed his friendship with Ben Lewis, the operations manager there. Marshall and Lewis spent a good deal of time together, going to lunch almost every day, playing on the Wells Fargo basketball team, watching football at Marshall's house.

In October 1977, Smith opened an account at Beverly Drive. Marshall took the occasion to introduce him to Lewis. Lewis appears to have been impressed with Smith, testifying that he knew of Smith through newspaper articles about him.

In July 1978, Lewis took a honeymoon tour. It was a bargain trip, two tickets for the price of one, provided through Tommy Bole's travel agency. Harold Smith had arranged it with Bole. Lewis had told Marshall that he wanted to take a honeymoon trip, and Marshall had told Smith.

As Ben Lewis was visiting London, Paris, and Amsterdam, Harold Smith was having trouble keeping his accounts out of the red. Sammie Marshall was patient with Harold's frequent overdrafts, but the company's finances didn't improve. Soon after Ben Lewis returned from his honeymoon, Smith's financial situation grew worse. First Lewis had cashed a $3,000 check from Tommy Bole for Smith, then a $5,800 check from Mitre Corporation. Wells Fargo could not collect on either of these checks, and bank procedures called for Smith's account to be charged with them and debited $8,800. Lewis sent the checks to Marshall, but Marshall knew there wasn't enough money in Smith's account to cover them. Marshall called Lewis and asked him to give their friend Harold a bit more time to cover the checks. Marshall promised Lewis that "Harold is good for it."

Soon Lewis got a call from Mr. Two-for-One Honeymoon himself.

"I need a favor," Harold Smith said. He wanted Lewis to hold on to the checks for a little while. Lewis agreed.

Not much later, Smith called again. He asked if Lewis (a man who, according to his boss, Brian Feeley, lived, ate, and breathed boxing) would like to go see the Mohammed Ali-Leon

Spinks fight in New Orleans. (Fans will no doubt remember this return engagement which allowed Ali to regain his crown for an unprecedented third time.) Smith promised Lewis plane fare, tickets to the fight, hotel reservations, and a Mohammed Ali warm-up suit.

So on September 14, 1978, Ben Lewis joined the party and flew to New Orleans. He carried along a robe for Mohammed Ali that a friend had sent from Florida. Harold Smith brought Ben Lewis to Ali's room to meet the champ and deliver this special gift. En route home after the fight, Smith explained how he was dealing with the financial difficulties MAPS faced. He told Nancy Carter, who sat next to him, about his relationship to the Wells Fargo bank, describing Sammie Marshall as "his banker." Smith said that Marshall might come to work for him at Mohammed Ali Amateur Sports, but at this time it was more advantageous to keep him in his place at the bank. Smith also explained that the Wells Fargo bank was holding his overdrafts for him.

Back in Los Angeles after the fight, Ben Lewis still had some bouncing checks to deal with. The Bole and the Mitre checks had been on his desk for almost two weeks. He sent them back to Marshall. But on October 11, Marshall again sent them back to Lewis. While the two were playing ping-pong with the checks, Marshall decided to take a leave of absense from the Wells Fargo bank and go to work for Smith.

In late 1977, Smith had offered Marshall a job in MAPS, Smith's professional sports company. Marshall had turned the job down because he knew nothing about boxing, nothing about track and field, and nothing about negotiating TV contracts. Marshall changed his mind after Gene Kawakami, his supervisor at Wells Fargo, told Marshall that he didn't want Marshall in the office. (Kawakami was later to plead guilty to embezzlement in another case concerning Smith's accounts.)

And now, at what the prosecution called a critical juncture of the case, Marshall and Lewis engaged in an important phone conversation. Before Marshall left Wells Fargo, he performed a transaction for Smith. On October 4, Marshall had issued a $19,000 cashier's check to Tel-Star for Smith without receiving any funds. Though Marshall was supposed to send a copy of the check through bank channels for processing, he held that copy until the 16th of the month. At that time he sent both the check and the debit half of a branch settlement form through the branch settlement system, as if he were transferring funds from one branch to another. At the same time, he sent the credit half of the same branch settlement form to Ben Lewis. Confused? So was Lewis. He asked Marshall what he was supposed to do with the credit half of the bank settlement form that Marshall sent him. Marshall said he was doing Harold Smith a favor and didn't have time to clear it up. He wanted to know if Lewis would take care of it for him. Lewis agreed.

At trial Lewis testified: "I had no account to debit or anything. I asked Sam how I was supposed to clear this. He told me I could just roll it over and code one-half of the branch settlement [form] with the account number at Miracle Mile, which he gave me in that conversation, and that it would go through."

Lewis questioned whether this would work since "it wasn't the right way to do it." Marshall said it would go through okay.

If you were on the jury at the trial later, you would have heard prosecutor Dean Allison explain how the system worked in his opening statement. The explanation follows:

> The branch settlement system is basically an accounting or a bookkeeping system that the bank uses to transfer money between one branch office of the bank and another branch office of the bank.
>
> The bank uses a bookkeeping system for this purpose because there are so many of these interbranch transfers every day that it would be physically impossible to send little messengers running back and forth with bags of money.
>
> Now, the bank used a computer located up in San Francisco to keep track of all these transfers between branches going on every day.
>
> To make one of these transfers the bank used a standard form for entries telling the computer what to do. The standard form was called a "branch settlement letter." You may also hear it referred to during this trial as a "branch settlement form" or a "branch settlement ticket. . . ."
>
> As the first step in the scheme, Lewis, the inside man at the bank, would pay money out to the defendants, to Smith, to Marshall, or to one of their companies . . .
>
> [As] the next step, Lewis would send the debit half of a branch settlement form into the computer, just like in the normal transaction,

telling the computer in effect, "Charge the branch settlement system for this money I paid out to Smith, Marshall, MAPS, and MAAS."

Within 10 days after sending in the first half, though, instead of sending the credit half of the ticket over to Miracle Mile like he was supposed to, Lewis would put the credit half into the computer himself, violating the . . . principle . . . that one branch is never supposed to send both halves of the ticket into the computer.

To fool the computer into thinking that the credit half of the form had come from Miracle Mile, which it hadn't, Lewis misencodes the credit half. He puts Miracle Mile's special code number in magnetic numbers on the bottom of the credit half, violating the second principle I mentioned: One branch is never supposed to use another branch's code number.

At this point Lewis had done enough to prevent a tracer from going out because the computer has gotten both halves of the form within 10 days. And he succeeded in fooling the computer into thinking that the two different halves of the form have come in from two different branches because the debit half has Beverly Drive's code number on it and the credit half has been misencoded with Miracle Mile's number.

But Lewis has one additional problem to solve. The books [had to] balance.

If you look at this transaction so far, you will see that there are two credits and only one debit. The reason you are a debit short is that there is no real money being put into the system. No customer's account is being charged to make up for the money paid out to Smith and Marshall over here.

So what does Lewis do to solve this additional problem? To supply the missing debit Lewis takes another branch settlement ticket and he takes the debit half of this new branch settlement ticket, and at the time he sends in the credit half of the first ticket he sends in a new debit with it. So that what the computer sees up to this point is: credit, debit; credit, debit; and everything is balanced. The computer has gotten both halves of this ticket within 10 days with two different code numbers, and the computer gives Lewis another 10 days to get the credit half of the second ticket in.

The trial transcript is silent concerning what went through Ben Lewis's mind as Sammie Marshall told him about the rollover method. Within a couple of weeks, though, $47,000 worth of transfers were made using this ploy. In explaining himself at trial, Lewis testified, "It started out with Sammie Marshall being a friend of mine and he introduced me to Harold Smith. And I trusted Sammie Marshall, and I saw no reason not to trust Harold when Sammie verified the fact that Harold always made things good."

In addition, Lewis liked Smith's Youth Amateur program, he was very fond of Mohammed Ali, and he said, "at this point, I was—so deep into it, I couldn't get out anyway."

Once he plunged in, Lewis was consistent. On October 27, Lewis made out a new branch settlement ticket. He offset the credit ticket he had received from Marshall with a new debit ticket and he held the new credit ticket under the blotter on his desk. Ten days later he offset the credit with a new debit, and put its corresponding credit under the blotter. He kept scrupulous account of how much he took, clinging to the hope that Smith would strike it rich and pay off his debt to the Wells Fargo bank. Every few weeks he would talk to Smith about how much the debt was, and Smith would always assure him that it was no problem, that the money would be coming.

Smith promised each upcoming event would turn the tide. January '79 was a banner month. The Mohammed Ali Invitational Track Meet and a Marvin Gaye concert were supposed to produce enough funds to repay all the debt Lewis was carrying. But the Marvin Gaye event was cancelled and the track meet netted much less than hoped. Lewis asked Smith where the money was and once again Smith assured him not to worry.

Not long afterwards, Smith invited Lewis to join the entourage going on the "Down Under Tour" of Australia and New Zealand featuring Mohammed Ali. But by February 13, 1979, the Down Under Tour was in danger. Smith told Lewis at an urgent meeting in the Beverly Drive parking lot that unless Mohammed Ali received $223,000 up front, he would not go. No Ali, no tour. So Lewis went inside the bank and cut a check for $223,000. This check was concealed through the same use of the branch settlement procedure. Suddenly the stakes had grown. Up to this point, Lewis had rolled over numerous checks to keep Smith's account afloat, but none much larger than the $19,000 cashier's check Marshall had cut to pay Tel-Star.

With the payment of $223,000 to Ali, Lewis almost doubled the amount that had been stolen from the bank since August 17, when he and Marshall began bouncing the $5,800 Mitre check between them.

Within a month of the parking lot meeting, Lewis added another $300,000 to the theft. By April 1979, the bank was out almost a million dollars.

For Lewis, the criminal's life was not a happy one. Any unfamiliar car in the Beverly Drive parking lot frightened him. He feared it might belong to an auditor who would discover the fraud.

Smith appeared unfazed by the growing crime. In mid-1979, Smith visited Lewis at the apartment Lewis had moved to after separating from his wife. Smith, ever-generous with Wells Fargo's money, was paying Lewis's rent there. "Look at this" Lewis told Smith showing him the running total of their theft. "Don't worry" Smith replied.

Smith continued to spend. In February 1980, he purchased a jet for $350,000. In March 1980 he told Lewis to pay out $145,000 from the same branch settlement system for the house he had bought.

When asked where he got money to finance his many fights, Smith had more answers than Ali had moves. His explanations included "middle eastern investors," "people in the oil or gold industry," his wife's recently departed relatives, and his wife's relatives (still alive in truth and in this alternate version of his fundraising sources).

On January 14, 1981, the bankroll ended. Ben Lewis doesn't know what happened—whether he forgot to send in a debit ticket, or if it was lost in the mail. At any rate, a credit Lewis sent had not been offset by a corresponding debit for 10 days.

On January 14, Judy MacLardie, operations manager at the Miracle Mile branch, received a "tracer" asking why the imbalance still existed. On checking, she learned that the credit actually had originated from Ben Lewis's Beverly Drive branch and not Miracle Mile. MacLardie called Brian Feeley, Ben Lewis's supervisor, and expressed her confusion to him. "Send me a copy of the tracer," he said. Still not aware what she had chanced upon, MacLardie accompanied the tracer with a light note:

My Dear Brian—

I grew 4,927 grey hairs, bit my nails to the elbow, wet my pants *twice*, had three fainting spells, tried (unsuccessfully) to swallow my tongue, and am on the verge of a nervous breakdown because I got this tracer. I am currently in enough trouble with R-E-G-I-O-N (and others) to last a lifetime *plus*. This type of thing makes me sweat a lot and my teeth shake. I would appreciate *any* help you can give me because if I don't get this cleared *quick* God and others will be out to get me . . .

Funny —not *"everyone"* thinks I'm hilarious . . . (scratch head) . . . I *just don't understand* it . . .

Jude

When the tracer arrived at Beverly Drive, Brian Feeley took it and the note and put them on Ben Lewis's desk, adding a note of his own that said simply, "Ben, take a look at this when you have a chance." Shortly thereafter, Lewis called MacLardie and asked her to make up a substitute branch settlement to clear the tracer. (That is, to reverse the entry in the branch settlement system by originating another branch settlement letter.) Judy MacLardie thought this "kind of funny." She agreed to do so, but didn't do what Lewis had requested. Instead she called Feeley and expressed her fears to him. He said, "Yeah, well maybe it might be funny, and maybe it might not be."

The next week Lewis was still concerned about the tracer. He asked Feeley what was up. Feeley said nothing. Then Lewis called MacLardie and asked, "Have you cleared the tracer yet?" MacLardie dodged the question. She ordered copies of background documents to explain the transaction. On January 23, MacLardie finally got the details. They showed quite clearly that Lewis was at fault. When MacLardie told Brian Feeley, there was no choice but to involve higher management. Feeley called branch manager Bob Smith and together they confronted Ben Lewis.

"How could you do this . . . advance these funds and use Miracle Mile's Office number?" Feeley asked Lewis. There was little Lewis could do but acknowledge that he had done it.

While Lewis was at the meeting, Auditor Lloyd Gassway called. Gassway suggested that he should come meet with Ben

Lewis at the Beverly Drive branch. Lewis said that he would rather not talk there. Gassway asked, "What about meeting at Region [the regional Wells Fargo headquarters]?" Lewis rejected that suggestion as well, saying that it was too embarrassing. Finally Gassway suggested El Monte, where he worked. He said, "Why don't you come at one o'clock, that will give you time for lunch." Lewis agreed.

Lunch was probably a low priority to Lewis. After leaving the bank, he called Harold Smith, repeatedly, trying to warn him and make plans. Finally, he went to Smith's office, upset and worried. There, behind closed doors, he spoke with Smith.

Smith was quick to mobilize. He called up Terry Kaye, his bookkeeper, and told her to retrieve all his financial records. At 1 P.M., Lewis called Lloyd Gassway and told him that he was too upset to come out to El Monte just then. Gassway, seemingly the model of total restraint and patience, replied, "Okay, what about 3?" Lewis agreed. At 3, Lewis called Feeley. Feeley encouraged Lewis to get out to El Monte, telling him that by delaying his trip there he was only going to make himself look worse. Then Feeley said, "Listen, I talked to Lloyd, and he told me that there was another $250,000 branch settlement on Monday the 19th." Ben replied, "No, there weren't any others."

FEELEY:

Ben, he told me he researched it.

LEWIS:

No, there weren't any other ones, just the ones I told you about.

FEELEY:

Come on, level with me.

LEWIS:

[After hemming and hawing] Well, yeah, maybe, maybe there was.

FEELEY:

Gees, Ben, how could you forget that? It just happened Monday, you know.

LEWIS:

Well, ah, I don't know.

Shortly thereafter, Lloyd Gassway froze all the accounts that had been controlled by Harold Smith.

Meanwhile, Smith and Lewis checked in under false names at the hotel on the Queen Mary in Long Beach. The two considered their options, realizing that their plan had fallen apart. "Why don't we tell the bank everything, and ask them to just let us go till after the This Is It fight, to see if we can make it all back," Lewis suggested.

"No way, man, they're gonna come down on us," Smith replied.

"Do you think I should run?" Lewis asked Smith.

"It's a hard life, man," he replied. Smith had done his share of evading the Law. As the conversation progressed, running seemed more and more attractive.

Smith suggested that Lewis go to San Diego to hide out while Smith attempted to obtain false passports for himself, Lewis, and Smith's wife. Lewis had his picture taken, and a man named Bruce Barrett picked up passport applications. Then Lewis changed his mind. He turned himself in to the FBI February 3, 1981.

THE INVESTIGATION AND TRIAL

There was no shortage of evidence of how the theft from Wells Fargo was committed. Once Lloyd Gassway began unraveling the transactions, one clearly led to another. When he called Brian Feeley to report on the extent of the loss, Gassway said: "You'd better get a piece of paper—a very big piece of paper."

Still, the process of ferreting out all the documentation took considerable effort. After it was completed, it took the FBI several weeks just to make summaries of the evidence to be used at trial.

Volume rather than lack of evidence created a problem. Assistant U.S. Attorney Dean Allison had to communicate what had happened without losing the jury's attention and without letting the vastness of the evidence overwhelm them.

Howard Moore, Smith's attorney, was faced with perhaps even a more formidable problem—defending Smith. Moore decided that an aggressive defense was needed. He challenged Lewis's credibility. It was Lewis's desire to live a "high life," he claimed, not directions from Smith, that led Lewis to steal. Moore also attacked the bank's security, suggesting that Wells Fargo's failings somehow reduced Smith's culpability.

Questioning Ben Lewis's supervisor, Brian Feeley, Moore suggested that Wells Fargo was so poorly run that it was unfair to blame Smith for this one of the many illegalities the bank was involved in. To say that this argument failed is to exaggerate its sophistication. Nonetheless, the facts elicited by Moore do present a frightening lesson in how not to supervise.

Smith and Marshall were found guilty of most of the charges against them after a 37-day trial. Lewis had already pleaded guilty and agreed to cooperate with the prosecution. Each was sent to prison.

AWARENESS—THE KEY TO SECURITY

The story of Harold Rossfields Smith proves that not all computer criminals are young, bright, qualified people willing to accept a technical challenge. The tall, affable Smith had his own eccentricities, but no one ever accused him of computer freakdom. When interviewed on television, Smith exclaimed, "Commit a computer crime? I can't even type."

Yet perhaps the key message in the Wells Fargo case is that with collusion, all things are possible. Smith, a consistent con man, had no trouble finding people who knew what he didn't know. Like any con, he went slowly and traded on both the idealism and on the greed of others. Thus, his first meeting with Marshall was one in which he made a modest request for the slightest variance of bank rules, and when he failed, he managed to leave a good impression with Marshall. The next time he met Marshall he further endeared himself to the point of getting Marshall to vary just a bit from the norm. From there, with patience and friendship, Smith quickly gained Marshall's confidence. Before long, Smith had a number of people pulling for him within the bank. Each, it would appear, was drawn by the dazzle of Smith's connections to Mohammed Ali and the world of big money. Each was in a position to help Harold get what he wanted. The only kind of genius this computer criminal needed was a genius in associating with the right people. This Harold Smith had in spades.

BEWARE OF ON-THE-JOB TRAINING IN COMPUTER CRIME

Employees trusted with access to company accounts have always been able to steal. With computing and the accompanying dispersion of access to company accounts, the number of potential embezzlers grows dramatically.

When you train employees to work with your computer, you may be giving them the tools to commit computer crime. Neither Marshall nor Lewis had to go to night school to figure out how to outsmart Wells Fargo's computerized accounting system. Marshall had worked in the bank computer center. Both he and Lewis had to learn how the branch settlement system worked to do their jobs.

Apparently they knew what would cause the issue of a tracer, and they had good cause to believe that unless a tracer was issued no human would scrutinize their scam. (Ironically, Wells Fargo was scheduled to implement another control soon which would have brought the theft to light.) Lewis made sure that no branch settlement amount exceeded $1 million and that every 10 days the old transactions were replaced by new ones. Once these accounting matters were taken care of, it was easy to cut cashier's checks or credit Smith's accounts.

If you cannot keep employees from gaining access to valuable information, as was the case here, you can at least keep the information they get from remaining valuable. Good security procedures are usually designed from the premise that "the enemy" will eventually learn what the procedures are. Thus changing the procedures or varying the triggers that cause the security procedures to go into effect are two ways that a business can reduce its vulnerability to employee computer crime.

A FOOLISH CONSISTENCY IN
INVESTIGATION IS ANOTHER INVITATION
TO CRIME

One observation stemming from the Wells Fargo case, most easily made in retrospect, is that parameters for investigation should occasionally be altered. Instead of always investigating imbalances of more than a million dollars or always waiting 10 days before sending a tracer, a sophisticated system could easily alter its operating parameters from time to time. In addition, more sophisticated tests for the distribution or frequency of transactions or other patterns could be performed with currently available software. These would make it much more difficult for the would-be embezzler to predict if he or she would be detected.

Also, the parameters used can be much more cautiously drawn then was the case here. To wait 10 days for the resolution of an imbalance is an inordinate cost, one which few banks will allow. According to Stephen Ross, former data security officer for Irving Trust Company, "In some banks, if there is an imbalance in the settlements one day, it goes to the branch manager the next, and if there is an imbalance that day, it goes to a higher level of management. There aren't many imbalances where that kind of situation applies, you can be quite sure."

AUTHORITY DEGRADED IS
AUTHORITY DENIED

In viewing the relationship between Lewis and his boss, Brian Feeley, we can see an all-too-common degradation of authority. The controls that originally called for Feeley to supervise Lewis's work enforcing the security of the Beverly Drive branch were allowed to deteriorate. Lewis was delegated the function of overseeing branch security because of Feeley's misplaced trust in him.

"I had a lot of confidence in Ben, I trusted him. I felt that we had a very good close working relationship," Feeley testified at the trial.

It may be a little difficult to square Feeley's view of Lewis with that expressed by Harold Smith's attorney, Howard Moore: "Mr. Lewis was . . . what we call a 'high signer.' He lived a high life."

In retrospect, Feeley seems to have been unusually unsuspicious. He was aware of an entity called Lewis & Smith Enterprises. He testified that it was a name Smith had decided to do business under to promote concerts.

Testimony showed that at the very least, Ben Lewis had something to gain if Lewis & Smith Enterprises did well. Feeley believed that if Smith was successful in starting the business, "later on up the road, there would be an opportunity perhaps for Ben to go to work with him at that time."

However, Feeley also testified that he believed Lewis was not part of the organization because that was what Lewis told him.

However, the plates on Ben Lewis's car (which was paid for with funds embezzled from the Wells Fargo Bank) read LSENT, for Lewis & Smith Enterprises. Lewis actively sold tickets to a Shirley Bassey concert that Feeley attended and that Lewis & Smith Enterprises promoted. Feeley himself even worked for Smith on the Cuevas-Herns fight in July 1980. (He made a grand total of $50 plus a warm-up suit.)

Thus Feeley found himself in the embarrassing position of testifying to possible violations of bank procedures by Lewis, his trusted subordinate.

The bank had rules to prevent conflicts of interest. An officer responsible for a particular customer's account could not have any outside interest in that customer's affairs, Feeley testified.

His conclusions about Lewis's lack of conflict of interest seems questionable. Feeley admitted that Lewis violated another bank rule requiring a two-week vacation each year. (Again, hindsight tells us why. Lewis had to keep submitting new branch settlement forms to the computer every 10 days.)

ETERNAL VIGILANCE IS THE PRICE OF COMPUTER SECURITY

As differential association theorists would predict, this $21.3 million crime began with acts that were only slightly less legitimate than what everyone else was doing. Cashing a check on an out-of-state bank is not an unheard of practice. Holding off on collecting a debt from a regular customer is also within the norm. But, as we have seen, however legitimate the favors to Smith were in mid-1976, they had become wildly illegitimate by late 1978.

Closer observation of Smith's affairs as they teetered near disaster for quite some time might have substantially reduced the bank's ultimate losses. Another kind of vigilance is required and that is vigilance against petty corruption, or even the appearance of possible petty corruption. It seems reasonable to assume that Harold Smith knew the value of granting favors. He seemed to always tie a new request to a new favor. Ben Lewis was given a two-for-one honeymoon before Smith asked for his first favor and a trip to New Orleans after Lewis agreed to hold a bouncing check.

Lewis may have understood the value of doing favors, too. He had offered Feeley a position in Lewis & Smith Enterprises. Lewis had said that once the boxing business was going better this would be a possibility.

Feeley testified he didn't take the offer too seriously: "I thought he [Lewis] was kind of 'B-Sing' me. Until I heard it from Smith . . . Then I might think about it."

One must wonder whether Lewis's offers of employment to Feeley, MAPS' hiring Feeley to work at the Cuevas-Herns fight, and even Brian Feeley's attendance at the Shirley Bassie concert reduced Feeley's ability to be vigilant in enforcing the rules at the Wells Fargo bank. Ever since Jesus enunciated the principle, it has been noted that those who are not themselves guiltless may find it hard to react to others' guilt. Admittedly, implementing this insight in modern business is not an easy task.

EPILOGUE: THE CON CONTINUES

Time does not seem to have diminished Harold Rossfields Smith's ability to make friends and influence influential people. He was paroled from the federal prison at Boron, California in November 1988 after serving slightly more than half of his 10-year sentence. Quickly and quietly Smith obtained a California boxing manager's license. Though there is no evidence that he violated any laws in obtaining the license, the convicted felon's ability to gain the license without even a public hearing has embarrassed the California Boxing Commission and tarnished the reputation of Ken Gray, executive officer of the Commission staff.

Assistant Attorney General Ron Russo represents the State Athletic Commission as one of his tasks in the Consumer Protection Division of his office. Russo says that "generally there is a public review of any application for a boxing license submitted by a person convicted of a crime."

Raoul Silva, chairman of the Boxing Commission, admitted that there is "a lot of loose enforcement of regulations" by the Commission. He had little doubt that if Smith's application "had come before the Commission, he would have been turned down."

Smith denied that there was any impropriety in his receipt of a license. "They took me through more [procedures] than the average guy off the street applying for a manager's license," he told Earl Gutskey of the *Los Angeles Times*. "I had to write letters. It took a lot of work. I've done my time. I'm still fighting my case, but I want to get on with my life."

CHAPTER 7

TECHNOLOGY

DONALD BURLESON: THE COMPUTER INSECURITY DIRECTOR

Responsible computer security requires more than employee awareness. Careful, security-minded attention in the choice of employees is one key. Technological controls to channel the efforts of employees are also critical. The Texas computer crime prosecution of Donald Burleson provides a close-up view of the difficulties faced by one company trying to secure a mid-range size computer against an employee who was in charge of computer security. (It also shows how media attention can seriously distort the significance of one incident.)

Technologies as simple as door keys and as complex as mainframe access control packages are available to every computer user. When Donald Burleson decided to get revenge on the Fort Worth securities-trading firm of USPA & IRA, he demonstrated just what a difficult responsibility it is to choose the right mix of products and people to keep computer operations secure.

THE BATTLE ZONE

For Donald Burleson, the computer room at USPA & IRA must have felt like the "battle zone" described in Chapter 3. And every time he got a paycheck it must have felt like an assault. Burleson was a man committed to an unpopular point of view, a follower of (now-jailed) tax protestor Irwin Schiff. As computer operations manager and computer security officer, Burleson was responsible for assuring that the company's password system worked properly. This position made his commitment crucial to the security of USPA & IRA. That commitment was apparently clouded by his belief in tax protest.

Burleson argued with his superiors over the tax issue, appearing "fanatical" to fellow employee Patricia Hayden. Burleson believed, after having studied Schiff's works, that he was exempt form the withholding of federal income tax on his paycheck. But he had not been able to convince his employers at the securities-trading firm.

Burleson kept trying. The Schiff organization had sent out tapes, books, videotapes, and other materials to assist its followers in persuading their employers not to withhold taxes. Using these materials, Burleson had sent an affidavit to USPA & IRA arguing that he was exempt and giving the reasons why.

On September 18, 1985, Burleson was taking the next step in his battle for tax freedom. He was at his terminal preparing papers to sue USPA & IRA to force them to stop withholding taxes on his pay. Burleson did not want his employers to know about the lawsuit he planned. He had told fellow worker Duane Benson that he hoped no one saw the petition. But he accidentally caused his computer to send instructions to the laser printer and print a copy. Bill Hugenberg, Burleson's supervisor, saw that copy and confronted him. "You are not supposed to be doing this work," Hugenberg said. Burleson was fired shortly afterwards and told to give up his keys.

Saturday morning, September 21, the consequences of Burleson's beliefs and actions came to light. Martin Durbin, the director of commission accounting, began his work at 7 A.M. The end of the month was coming, and before the company sent out its September commission checks, Durbin had to review the preliminary listing of all the commissions.

USPA & IRA is a nationally licensed life insurance agency and a registered securities broker. It sells insurance and securities as part of the financial planning services it offers to career officers of the U.S. military. The sales are made through 450 different independent agents who receive about $2 million every month. USPA & IRA would receive most of its information on magnetic tapes from other insurance companies and securities firms and then store the information in the commission records. Calculating the commissions from these records was a lengthy and critical job, with hundreds of thousands of files involved.

The printout Martin Durbin reviewed ran 5,000 pages. It looked accurate. This month, Durbin had time to do some spot checks directly on the computer. He tried to access a commission record and he couldn't. He tried again. Same result. Durbin knew enough about the computer to be concerned.

Durbin went to George Jimenez and told him about the trouble he'd had. George Jimenez confirmed Durbin's worst fears. Ultimately it turned out that some 168,000 records no longer existed on the computer—they had been deleted from the system! Without the records it would be impossible to produce the September payroll. This would not make USPA & IRA appear reliable and trustworthy in the eyes of the agents, to say the least.

George Jimenez had been having problems of his own with the system. Some of the programs he used to accomplish his main task, monitoring the computer's operation, were not functioning.

Jimenez needed to find out what had happened on the computer, so he caused the computer to print out a history log showing the computer's activities since 1 A.M., when the preliminary commission report began to run. The log showed the accounts that had been used, the passwords of the people who had used them, and the time of each use.

At 3:30 P.M., the preliminary commission program had completed its operation. That explained why Durbin had received the accurate preliminary report.

George Jimenez didn't recognize the job that started seven minutes later. But he suspected it had something to do with the missing records. The fact that someone unknown to him had signed on the system at 3:04 A.M. increased his suspicion. An operator on the graveyard shift usually knows all the people working on the system.

The problem was growing more serious. Senior Systems Administrator Duane Benson was called to the site right away. Benson ordered that a back-up copy be made of everything in the computer at the time. Then he started looking at the history log George Jimenez had printed, scrutinizing it for much more detail.

The unknown person George Jimenez had noticed on the log had used an account unknown to anyone else. Benson knew the accounts in use, and they were all listed elsewhere in the computer. To a systems analyst, the strange account's name was a giveaway. It was named QCNM. Benson knew that accounts beginning with Q are supposed to be accounts provided to a computer user by IBM. This account, however, clearly was not from Big Blue, as industry types affectionately refer to the computer giant.

Whoever used the account signed off after four minutes, but not before attempting to use unauthorized security functions on the computer.

At 3:08, someone signed on at the same terminal, using a password that identified its user as the security officer. Benson wasn't sure how this could have happened, since access to this password was limited to three people. He couldn't imagine the department head or another programmer using the security officer's password. The only person who might have used it would be Burleson, but he'd been canned three days earlier, and the security account password had been changed. Two minutes later, the unknown person started some programs running and then signed off.

At 3:12 there was unusual activity at another terminal, this one located in a more deserted part of the building: Al Wynn's account was accessed. Wynn, the company's newest programmer, didn't usually come in during the early morning hours. He had no reason to. Benson wondered if the person who made the 3:04 and 3:08 accesses to the computer had then moved to this location.

Two minutes later, someone signed on the security officer account. At 3:19, Wynn's account signed off: then at 3:25, the security officer's account also signed off. During the same minute, Wynn's account was signed on again. Not much showed up on the log to explain what happened between 3:14 and 3:25.

As Benson knew, the preliminary commission report was listed on the log as ending at 3:30. Seven minutes later, three unfamiliar programs ran. They were named CMRCSS, CMRCSW, and CMRCSR, and no one in the programming staff had heard of them.

At 3:47, the programmer's account signed off. Whoever was using this account had turned off several communication lines.

The three programs that started with the letters CMR ran until 4:36, 4:37, and 6:07 A.M. The CMR programs were like traffic directors. Each directed a program to one of three commission detail files, which between them contained the records that had been printed out for the report Durbin had been reviewing. The programs the CMR programs sent to the detail files were the culprits that had destroyed them. These programs, each of which began with a *Q,* were designed to delete large sections of the files.

Benson could see that the *Q* programs had been created at 3:24. They were copied from a preexisting program Benson identified as ARRARF. The name may have been a computer hacker joke, short for Arf Arf Arf, but Benson wasn't laughing. He found that the ARRARF program had been created as early as September 2 at Donald Burleson's terminal, under his account.

ARRARF was one of a group of programs Benson called the ARFARF system. Together their role was to delete records from designated files, to produce new copies of themselves, and to disguise their names and locations in the computer so that they could not be easily identified. They were what security experts call worms.

The programs had done their jobs. For the next three days, employees reconstructed the commission detail records and reentered them into the computer. Some had been backed up, requiring only computer operations. These records were reconstructed through the use of journal files, backups, and manual reentry of certain records. Some, however, had been copied onto defective tape and had to be retrieved from paper records and input by hand. Benson and some others also went through the computer system removing destructive programs such as those in the ARFARF system. The computer could not be used for its usual functions while the recovery operation was in process.

According to Duane Benson, Burleson confessed that the programs and plan were his. Benson said Burleson was at his home on September 28, 1985. Burleson was really excited,

Benson recalled, admitting that he had caused the deletion of the commission records. Burleson said that he'd created a system of programs that could move through the computer, the programs Benson had called the ARFARF system. "He said he'd be remembered a long, long time," Benson said.

TRIALS

It is unlikely that Donald Burleson knew how many people would remember him for the program he had created. The odds are, if Burleson had just gone about finding a new job after USPA & IRA fired him, he would have been remembered by only a handful of workers there. But he brought suit in the Justice of the Peace Court in Fort Worth, the Texas court where small claims are handled, and started a series of events that would ultimately make him international news.

Rather than fight Burleson in small claims court, where anything can happen, USPA & IRA consented to a judgment against them at that level and litigated the issue by appealing to the County Court. As long as they were in court already answering Burleson's charges, USPA & IRA decided to file a counterclaim, suing him for making an unauthorized entry into their premises and interfering with the use of their computer system. On July 4, 1986, the jury of six found for USPA & IRA in the amount of $11,226, plus $561.30 interest.

USPA & IRA went to the district attorney shortly after responding to Burleson's crime. To Davis McCown's knowledge, Burleson's was the first computer crime prosecution in Texas. McCown was the deputy district attorney who first indicted Burleson for computer crime on December 10, 1985. The papers in the case are a treasure trove for anyone wondering why criminal lawyers seldom seem to smile. They include an indictment, two superceding indictments, motions to quash, discovery motions, motions to dismiss, answers to all motions, amendments, briefs in support of the arguments, and the stipulation which ultimately allowed the case to proceed to trial in September 1988.

At trial, the People presented the evidence that is summarized above. The defendant denied entering the USPA & IRA building on September 21, 1985, and denied ever making the ARFARF programs that destroyed USPA & IRA's records. He also denied making the statements Benson attributed to him, and suggested that he was the victim of a cover-up, blamed for someone else's failures because he was the last person to leave before the records were destroyed.

Burleson lied. He said he and his son had been over 200 miles away in Bryan, Texas visiting Burleson's father when the ARFARF programs had been created on his computer. He produced a Texaco credit card receipt which showed he had paid cash on that date at a station near Bryan to have a flat tire fixed. He didn't lie well. McCown brought school records showing that Burleson's son had been in school on September 3, the first day of the term. He brought an expert from Texaco to identify the credit slip as a type not printed until 1987, two years after Burleson said he'd gotten it.

The jury found Burleson guilty, but the judge sentenced him leniently. Burleson was ordered to pay $11,800 to USPA & IRA and was put on seven years probation. The amount of the restitution was the amount of the judgment against him handed down two years earlier in the County Court. In the intervening two years, he had made one $100 payment.

LEARNING RESPONSIBLE COMPUTING THE HARD WAY

In retrospect, the executives at USPA & IRA probably have a much better understanding of computer security. They probably now understand the importance, for starters, of an employee key policy. When Burleson was fired, his department head testified, he returned his key to the office. But there was no policy in place preventing Burleson from making a copy of the key he'd been given. Several of the USPA & IRA employees believed that Burleson had an extra key. The absence of signs of forced entry into the USPA & IRA building on September 21 was certainly one factor leading to this belief.

When USPA & IRA terminated Burleson, they removed his account from the computer and changed the password for the security officer. The Q account Benson found seemed to be

Burleson's secret "trap door." Following a common practice among some programmers, he had created it in case he needed to enter the system sometime after his authorization had ended. It wasn't clear which method he used, but Benson believed that Burleson used the Q account to give himself the clearances that came with a security officer password. It is necessary to clear a security officer to many parts of the computer so that the officer can do her or his job. But USPA & IRA learned that this means particular care must be taken in choosing a trustworthy security officer.

MEDIA MADNESS

Burleson was arrested in 1985, but defense discovery motions capitalizing on the complexity of his case kept it bouncing around the Tarrant County District Attorney's office for the next two years without anyone taking much notice. In August 1988 *Business Week* made Burleson the lead in its cover story on computer security. "The Burleson caper," wrote *Business Week* reporter Katherine Hafner, "is just one in a string of recent events that point to the alarming vulnerability of computer systems—and the businesses and government agencies that rely on them."

To understand why this case became so celebrated, it is necessary to consider its timing. In December 1987, the Christmas Tree virus had embarrassed IBM and introduced a few readers to the concept of viruses as a type of computer crime. But it wasn't until March 1988 when the topic really began to take off. When copies of Aldus's Freehand program were found to contain the World Peace virus, computing had the equivalent of a "Tylenol" scare. If off-the-shelf, shrink-wrapped programs designed for personal computer users could be contaminated with viruses, computer crime was becoming an issue related to the computer community's "public health." Between March and November, the media scrambled to try to explain the new concept of computer viruses to a curious audience. All they lacked was an example of a computer virus prosecution. When UPI discovered the Burleson case, they thought they had a winner.

Oddly enough, Davis McCown never called the programs Burleson used "viruses." He knew better. As he understood the computer science of the time, a virus was a program which could only reproduce itself if it was activated by another computer program. What Burleson had created was more like a worm, since it operated only within the USPA & IRA system and didn't replicate itself. But the articles and the cover stories were all about computer viruses, and the reporters had enough trouble understanding what viruses were without trying to figure out what a worm was.

As the concept of a "hacker" progressed from computer wizard to teenage electronic vandal to computer criminal, so the concept of a "computer virus" has progressed from the careful scientific definition Professor Fred Cohen first gave it in his doctoral thesis to programming crime, as the Burleson case coverage has redefined it. Perhaps the term will next become synonymous with computer crime.

According to Dr. Cohen, whose research began the academic study of computer viruses, a virus is "a program that can 'infect' other programs by modifying them to include a possibly evolved copy of itself." The key to this definition, Cohen has stated, is the infection property. "With the infection property," he writes, "a virus can spread throughout a computer system or network using the authorization of every user using it to infect their programs."

USA Today quoted Tarrant County prosecutor Davis Mc-Cown at length about his conviction of Burleson in the "first computer virus case." McCown has consistently denied that his prosecution involved a virus. "This was not a contagious computer program," he told me. "It was designed for this computer system only and did not replicate outside it. As I understand it, that means it was not a virus."

It bothered me at the time. "If we're going to have reporters for UPI and *USA Today* defining the terms of computer science, we're in a terrible mess," I fumed in an opinion piece rejected by *Computerworld*. In retrospect I must agree with their decision. The same opportunism which led UPI to call Burleson's program what it thought the public wanted to hear about seems to have led the NSA to call Robert Morris's program (the subject of Chapter 18) a virus. Had the indictment resulting from Morris's effort occurred earlier, it, and not Burleson's case, would have been the illustration used when the media wanted to talk about viruses before the majesty of the law.

I guess there is not much of a lobby for linguistic purity in reporting on the computer industry these days. Those who care about computer security seem to be the last ones to look to for assistance. They seem to prefer exaggeration, so long as it boosts public awareness of the need for security. I got a full dose of this ends-justifies-the-means cynicism as I spoke recently with a computer security professional who works in a large company.

"Our executives care only about the bottom line," he explained. "Computer security is simply not important to them unless it is going to impact profits in the forseeable future. Our only hope, therefore, is taking advantage of anything that catches their attention." Viruses, of course, are the ideal vehicle. "If Ted Koppel has a show about viruses tonight, someone from upstairs may call me tomorrow and ask if we're covered," my informant continued. "That's when I have an opening. If I need uninterrupted power supply, I'll call it antiviral hardware. If I want a new training film, authorization to attend a conference, or another body to audit our computers, I'll justify it as antivirus and maybe it will fly. That," he smiled, "is how you play the game."

Since Burleson's case ended, several other prosecutions have come to the attention of the National Center for Computer Crime Data. The media has played the virus story nearly to death, however, so these cases rest in the obscurity they probably deserve.

Laws will not substitute for the security technology that Burleson was able to evade in this case. Also, it is hard to look at Burleson's punishment and see his case as a deterrent. Being ordered by a criminal court to pay money you have already been ordered to pay by a civil court is hardly a hardship. On the contrary, the case suggests that computer crime is a good strategy. With the criminal courts punishing this lightly, the criminal is told: Try crime. If you don't get caught, you come out ahead. If you do get caught, you break even. Attacking this logic is more important to fighting computer crime than drafting a passel of new laws. USPA & IRA is doing its part. As this book went to press, its attorneys were pressing Burleson to pay the money he owes the firm. Clay Humphries, their attorney, has scheduled a contempt motion to compel Burleson to explain why he has not yet paid his debt.

Meanwhile, at USPA & IRA, Burleson has left his mark. Six months after his destruction, the company moved to a new building. During off-hours a guard patrols the computer center. Current users of the computer system are reminded of the consequences of unauthorized access every time they log on. A message warns: "The unauthorized use of this Computer System or its contents and/or the attempt to gain unauthorized access thereto constitutes a violation of the Texas Penal Code."

CHAPTER 8

LAW

LAURENCE OLSON: THE COMPUTERIZED "ROGUE" COP

When security awareness and technology do not prevent computer crime, the threat of criminal prosecution is often considered the major deterrent. Credible prosecution, however, requires computer crime laws adequate to the task. The case of Laurence Olson demonstrates one of the difficulties in applying the concepts of the criminal law to computer technologies.

THE ROGUES' GALLERY

Officer Laurence Olson's problems surfaced on August 16, 1984, when a conscientious fellow-officer tried to help him out. Officer Ernest Salotti of the University of Washington Police Department discovered five computer printouts and five small photographs of young women when he relieved Olson that morning at the department's communication center. The printouts were on regular communication center computer paper, so Salotti assumed that the information was part of a current investigation. He turned the pictures and the printouts in to a superior, Sergeant Scott Drown.

Drown noticed that the information had been printed out more than a month before, on July 8. Unable to identify a case for which the printouts might have been generated, Drown referred the matter to his superior, Lieutenant Randy Stegmeier. A check of the communication center logs showed

Officer Olson had been the dispatcher working at the communication center between 3:47 and 4:17 that morning.

The next day Stegmeier showed Olson the photos and printouts and asked him about their purpose. Olson admitted that they were his. He claimed he had only collected the photos and printouts, but hadn't called any of the women. He said he'd gotten the photographs, all of them showing University of Washington students, from a University publication and admitted knowing that his actions in retrieving the printouts were a misuse of the police department's equipment. When asked what the material was for, Olson replied that it was his own "rogues' gallery."

Four days after the confrontation, Olson asked Stegmeier and Assistant Chief of the University of Washington Police Serra to come to his locker to see that he had no more printouts. The officers said it was not necessary, but Olson insisted. The locker contained a large number of *Playboy* and *Penthouse* magazines and many loose nude foldouts. Olson opened his briefcase while at the locker and leafed through a yellow pad that had been inside. At the back of the pad he found 27 printouts, pictures of University students, and a list of numbers indicating police contacts with the school's sororities. Olson said he had forgotten about these materials.

Lieutenant Stegmeier carefully contacted three of the women about whom Olson had gathered information most recently. They were very upset to learn that someone had collected information about them.

The investigation had turned up a total of 37 printouts. In addition, while taking a lie-detector test, Olson admitted to destroying another 50 to 100 printouts. He had placed checkmarks next to the pictures of 336 women shown in a school publication and added other comments. The comments included both vital statistics and Olson's opinions. Next to one woman's information, Olson had typed in, "With friend with cheek-high cut-offs and visible tush." He used a symbol, "xx," to signify women who were especially pretty.

The University police department decided to prosecute Olson, perhaps motivated by the growing awareness of feminism on campus and the consequent concern for the privacy of the women whose pictures wound up in Olson's private collection. The offense report provided to the King County prosecutor's office stated, "There is no indication that any of this material is connected to any investigation being conducted by UWPD nor to any investigation we have conducted in the recent past."

Washington, one of the first states to pass computer crime laws, has a computer trespass law under which Olson was prosecuted. On June 14, 1985, Judge Herbert Stephens found Olson guilty of first-degree computer trespass. In the words of the statute, "a person is guilty of computer trespass in the first degree if the person, without authorization, intentionally gains access to a computer system or electronic data base of another; and . . . the violation involves a computer or data base maintained by a government agency."

Almost two years later, Olson's conviction was overturned. The Washington Court of Appeals found that Olson did not violate the Washington statute, even if he used the data in the police department's files without authorization.

In reaching its conclusion, the court drew heavily on the analogy to a case involving joyriding. In this case, a man named Clark had gotten permission to use a man named Dennis Noll's car to run some errands around Seattle for a few hours and to return around noon. Instead, Clark drove to Colorado. The Supreme Court of Washington found that Clark could not be charged with joyriding under those facts and Washington law. "Otherwise," the Court noted, "the theft statute and the joyriding statute would prescribe the same conduct, yet a defendant potentially could suffer a different penalty depending on which crime was charged."

So, in finding Olson's conviction improper, the Court of Appeal likened his situation to Clark's. "The actus reus [improper act] of the joyriding statute is the taking or driving away of the vehicle without permission," wrote Court of Appeals Justice Grosse. "The actus reus of the computer trespass statute is accessing a computer without authorization," the Justice continued. "At the time Clark drove away the car he had permission. At the time Olson retrieved data he had authorization. It was the personal use of this data after access that was against departmental policy."

Anne Bremner, the prosecutor arguing in favor of the trial court's decision, suggested that the Court of Appeals look to the Washington cases dealing with burglary rather than those dealing with theft. In burglary cases, she argued, "whether an entry is unlawful . . . depends on the *scope of permission* extended by the possessor of the premises [emphasis in the original]." Bremner argued that Olson "had no authority to access information for his personal use."

Perhaps the weakness in Bremner's argument helps explain why the State lost. It is one thing to say that someone has permission to enter a building, but not to enter a locked office in that building which has a sign saying "Keep Out." It is quite another to say that one has permission to enter the building and the locked office in the building as long as the entry into the office is for the right purpose.

The evidence before the court was that Olson had authorization to access student records through the University of Washington's computer system. He had an access code which enabled him to access those records. The Court of Appeals, however, could find no evidence that his authorization was limited to proper use of the system. Justice Grosse wrote: "While the evidence shows that certain uses of retrieved data were against governmental policy, it did not show that permission to access the computer was conditioned on the uses made of the data." What the court left unaddressed was the question of whether any legal principles prohibited the unauthorized use of data the court found that Olson had made.

COMPUTER TRESPASS LAW:
A TOOTHLESS TIGER?

The problem of abuse of police files is in no way limited to the case of Officer Olson. A number of cases of unauthorized police officer access to governmental data have come to the attention of the National Center for Computer Crime Data over the years. The cases suggest that the problem is a real one, one the law needs to address. As will be seen in the following brief summary, in some cases the law has proved adequate and in others it has not. Where the law offers no protection, however, other sanctions may still be brought to bear, as Officer Olson was to learn.

In 1987 the *St. Petersburg Times* reported that the Indian Rocks Beach Police Department had begun an internal affairs investigation in early August to determine whether one of its sergeants had used a police computer to gather information on women he found attractive.

Richard Cook had been suspended for four days in 1983 for using a police computer to find the name and address of a woman he saw in a supermarket parking lot, according to Indian Rocks Police Chief Sam Heath. A resident of Pinellas Park complained that Cook stopped by her house and told her he'd seen her at a local Kash 'n' Karry, where he took down her license plate number. He explained that he was able to obtain her name and address from the license number. He asked her for a date. Though the woman said she wasn't interested in dating, Cook returned to her house two more times. After the third visit, she complained to the police. When confronted by then Police Chief Ed Bulger, Cook reportedly admitted the visits, explaining that the woman was attractive and he was single.

In 1984, a man complained that Cook had flirted with his wife and tried to make a date with her when he stopped her for a traffic ticket. An internal affairs investigation uncovered two notebooks in Cook's handwriting, one of which contained the name of the man's wife. The notebooks also contained the names, and usually birthdates, addresses, and license plate numbers of 179 other women as well. Cook apparently annotated these entries with comments like "wow," "white sexy dress," "slinky black dress," "must have—10" and "didn't give ticket—sharp." The 1984 investigation was closed when the woman who complained declined to pursue the matter.

In 1985, a woman complained to Chief Heath that Cook had, according to an internal affairs report quoted in the *St. Petersburg Times*, "called on the phone, parked in front of her house, followed her in a police cruiser, and . . . stopped her while in a police cruiser for no apparent reason." This complaint was called "unsubstantiated" because, in the words of the internal affairs report, the woman "did not at any time actually inform Officer Cook that she did not want to have a personal relationship, nor did she at any time advise Officer Cook that she did not want to be harassed in any way." The investigator recommended that Cook have professional psychiatric counseling "due to past incidents involving females."

Cook underwent psychiatric counseling. Chief Heath would not disclose the results of the counseling, but he did tell the *St. Petersburg Times,* "Basically there was nothing wrong. He was just a healthy male."

Cook resigned while an internal affairs investigation into the charges against him was underway. Chief Heath and three other city officials wrote letters of recommendation for him and he was hired by the Charlotte County, Florida Sheriff's Department.

Though charges of sexual harassment touch some of our deepest fears of violation of privacy, they are not the only sort of abuses of computerized law enforcement records the Center has seen.

In 1982, Ralph Davenport, a former Los Angeles County deputy sheriff, was sent to jail for six months after pleading guilty to a violation of the California computer crime law for making 287 unauthorized accesses to the L.A. Sheriff's Department criminal history system. Davenport, who had been fired from the sheriff's department shortly before his conviction in a federal fraud case, was working as a private investigator. He regularly queried the sheriff's system for charges pending, arrests, and convictions.

At the sentencing, Davenport's attorney urged the court's mercy, claiming that his client had "a problem of zeal and certain unauthorized techniques," but had simply "short circuited" the common process followed by "most other people in the investigative community [on a] daily basis."

Davenport's method was simplicity itself: he used names of other sheriff's deputies he had worked with. But this simplicity was his undoing. A deputy receiving one of Davenport's calls sent the information he requested to the deputy whose name Davenport had used.

Another deputy sheriff was suspended from the Los Angeles County Sheriff's Department for allegedly using the Department's computer system to gain information about a burglary involving more than $1 million in currency, jewelry, firearms, and silverware. Sergeant Gordon Barrett was suspended after Imperial County authorities inquired of the Los Angeles County Sheriff about Barrett's interest in the burglary, which was being investigated by another sheriff's station. The next year Barrett retired from the sheriff's department at age 42.

CAN THE LAW PROTECT POLICE FILES FROM POLICE PRYING?

One significant difference appears between the Washington cases involving joyriding and computer trespass. The Supreme Court left no doubt that a prosecutor could have charged Clark with theft and gained a conviction. No specific charge appears to be available in Washington when someone with authorization to enter a computer system abuses that authorization to take information to which he or she is not entitled.

Those who struggled through law school classes on the history of the law would find a case like this quite familiar, with depressingly ancient lineage. It's like "deja vu all over again" (as Yogi Berra might say). Centuries ago only the law of larceny protected property. To prosecute someone for larceny it was necessary to show that the person accused had formed the intent to take something before he or she received it. Thus, if a servant was given a load of grain to deliver to a mill, and halfway along the journey decided to trade the grain for a few pints of ale, the servant could not be charged with larceny.

Clearly this was not a situation which could be tolerated forever. Perhaps when the law of larceny was first formed, the social fabric was sufficiently strong to keep most servants honest. A servant who stole from a master was not the most employable of individuals, and mobility wasn't what it is now. But as feudal bonds weakened, the temptation grew for underlings to take what was entrusted to them. Eventually it became evident that a legal punishment would help persuade servants to honor the trust that was placed in them. Thus the stage was set for the development of the law of embezzlement. Unlike larceny, this crime could be committed by someone who had been given an item in trust and only decided to steal it afterwards.

As the common law eventually did, so the law of computer crime needs to attend more closely to the issue of violation of trust. The reasoning of the Court of Appeals in the Olson case demonstrates that we have a way to go before our computer crime laws reflect this attention. As Robert Morris, the subject of Chapter 18, awaits trial, the question of authorized access may weigh heavily on his attorney's mind. Morris is charged with unauthorized access to a computer system. But as Olson was an authorized user of the University of Washington computer system who simply abused his authority, Morris may be able to argue that he was an authorized user of the Internet network into which he injected the worm program that caused enormous damages. If so, the law of computer crime may get a much-needed boost when the public realizes the need for strong, enforceable computer crime laws.

ADMINISTRATIVE SANCTION

Olson did not emerge victorious from his brush with the Washington computer-crime law. Before his conviction was overturned, administrative proceedings ended in his termination from the university police. Like Barrett and Cook, Olson learned that there are sanctions available against computer abuse even when the law is inadequate. Unfortunately for computer security, these sanctions are seldom discussed and thus result in far less deterrence than they might.

PART 3

RESPONDING TO IRRESPONSIBLE COMPUTING

As the first eight chapters of this book have demonstrated, computer security doesn't always work. Computers crimes occur despite the best efforts to prevent, detect, and deter them. Victims of computer crime, both individuals and organizations, have more strategies available than is commonly known. Prosecutors around the country are bringing computer crime prosecutions with increasing frequency. As the case of Laurence Olson in Chapter 8 showed, the law, and occasionally the judges, may not always be up to the task. Walter Moore's case, the focus of Chapter 9, makes the same point.

For most victims of computer crime, however, the biggest problem with prosecution will be the one that Bill Christison experienced when he tried to interest authorities in New Mexico in prosecuting the "contagious consultant" discussed in Chapter 10. These authorities would not take any action, having "bigger fish to fry." Christison's relatively cost-effective use of civil litigation under the Electronic Communications Privacy Act points to the possibility that any individual with a valid gripe and a modicum of money can go after a computer criminal and win.

Corporate victims of computer crime have long been the focus of considerable dismay on the part of computer security consultants. We have bewailed the fact that so few corporate victims will bring their computer crime losses to the attention of prosecutors. Without victims, there are no prosecutions. Without prosecutions, the computer crime laws will deter no one. US Sprint's litigation against Frederick Mason DeNeffe III, the subject of Chapter 11, may be a harbinger of change. Choosing disclosure over secrecy, Sprint brought several lawsuits against individuals and companies that were stealing and selling Sprint access codes. Unlike Christison, Sprint was able to get law enforcement support for its efforts. The result was a two-barreled offensive, with both criminal and civil proceedings.

In our enthusiasm over fighting computer crime, it may be tempting to ignore the rights of the accused criminals. The authoritarian solution to any problem is more force, and less solicitude for the rights of those who present the problem, and computer crime prosecutions are not immune to the excesses of this point of view. Thus, in the final chapter in this section, I question whether the jailing of Kevin Mitnick for seven months without bail was ethical behavior on the part of the U.S. Attorney's Office. It is but one example of what I see as a growing trend towards unprincipled strategies in the fight against computer crime.

Our concern for the rights of victims of computer crime is also crucial. This book has been written to demonstrate that the chances of becoming a victim are much higher than most individuals—and too many businesses—are aware. But the novelty and significance of computer crime as a problem should not blind us to the need to be ethical.

When the government reacts to individual wrongdoing with official wrongdoing, the result is a net loss. No computer crime-fighting strategy can be effective, I suggest, if it ignores this principle. We are still trying to develop an effective deterrent to computer crime. If the acts of government prosecutors are seen as unjust, the law's deterrence loses much of its effect. With millions of computer users in constant communication, we can ill afford to lose the moral high ground. We need these users to believe, as Bill Christison and US Sprint did, that our legal system will be applied in the best interests of society.

Litigation is just beginning to appear as a multidimensional strategy to react to computer crime. I hope this section shows a few of the key issues in using the courts as effectively as possible to communicate society's commitment to responsible computing.

CHAPTER 9

PROSECUTION

WALTER MOORE: THE STREET COMPUTER CRIMINAL

Walter Moore's case had all the qualities that would normally make it forgettable, the kind of petty crime a prosecutor brings to court between important cases or when filling in for someone else. The defendant was poor and had had previous brushes with the law. He was charged with theft from the Bay Area Rapid Transit (BART) ticket machines, normally not a very heavy offense.

But Moore, unemployed and unaccustomed to being considered a computer genius, was charged with computer crime. Suddenly Deputy District Attorney Joan Cartwright was faced with technical, practical, and psychological issues that are the challenge of trial practice.

With computer crime laws in place in every state except Vermont as of 1989 (and one likely to pass in that state sometime during 1990,) cases like Moore's are likely to be popping up in the assignment bins of an increasing number of prosecutors. Without an understanding of the vagaries of computer crime trials, prosecutors (and consequently those they represent) are likely to lose cases that should be won.

Deputy District Attorney Joan Cartwright was assigned to represent the people of California in a preliminary hearing held in the courtroom of the Honorable Roderic Duncan Oakland in 1981.

Cartwright called BART Police Officer Mistner to testify to the events leading to Walter Moore's arrest. As Mistner recalled: "After he accepted a $5 bill which returned to him [from the

BART ticket machine], he looked around him to see what was around him, and he reinserted the $5 bill. The amount indicator lit up and increased by $5, and went to $10, and the $5 bill came back again."

"I saw him repeat it again after looking around," Mistner continued. "When the amount indicator was $20 and he received the $5 bill back for the fourth time, he pushed for a ticket—a $20 ticket is the maximum you can buy from BART machines. He pushed for the ticket, inserted the ticket in his right rear pants pocket and he stood away from the machine for a few seconds to allow passing patrons to move on."

Still Walter was not done. Officer Mistner continued: "After there was nobody in the area, he returned to the machine and repeated everything I just testified to and pushed for another $20 BART ticket, still holding on to the original $5 bill that he had started with." In all, Mistner and his fellow officer testified that they saw Moore put 11 $20 tickets in his pocket before they stepped in and arrested him.

Mr. Fairwell, Moore's Public Defender, tried to cast doubt on the officer's ability to clearly observe what Moore was doing. He elicited testimony that Mistner was some 40 feet away from Moore, behind a wall and peering through a crack.

Exactly what had Moore done to rob the ticket machine? Robert Buckley, a specialist with BART, explained how the ticket machine in question had been fooled. It was at this point that Cartwright's job became difficult.

"The bill is inserted into a bill validator," Buckley began. "[It] is scanned first for its thickness and its magnetic contents. It is scanned for a gritting pattern, and it is checked for length."

The problem Moore exploited had to do with "anti jam" features of the machine. These features allowed the machine to reverse the direction of money flow and return bills instead of attempting to deposit them in the machine's vault.

If another bill is inserted before the first has cleared, Buckley explained, "the machine automatically will go into reverse and will send the bill back, trying to clear any potential jams." Moore had exploited this feature by using a specially designed $5 bill.

Prosecutor Cartwright took the $5 bill the officers had taken from Moore on his arrest and showed it to Buckley. It was marked People's No. 12. The bill that had been cut and folded back, a space of approximately three quarters of an inch appearing a bit less than one-third the bill's length from the upper right corner, and above the serial number.

Cartwright asked, "If this particular bill were inserted in this machine . . . what would happen?"

Buckley replied: "The scanning portion . . . would go down this edge of the bill . . . and as the scanner sees the bill progress down here [pointing to the space in the bill] it's gone beyond the two-thirds length [that it requires before accepting a bill], it will see this opening and the machine will issue a pay pulse . . . As the bill continues, it [the machine] will see the last part here [pointing to the part of the bill after the space] as if somebody put something in front of the bill and thinking it was starting a new bill . . . it will reverse the motor and send the bill back."

Faced with this testimony, Public Defender Fairwell engaged in a bit of advocacy (or showmanship, depending on one's perspective) targeted, it seems, to touch popular discontent with computers applications like BART's.

Fairwell began his cross-examination by asking, "Mr. Buckley, is this machine incredibly stupid or is this a design defect?"

Buckley was not jarred. "I don't think the machine is incredibly stupid," he replied. "It's an unfortunate situation of timing characteristics that is forced by the manufacturer."

Buckley admitted that BART had been aware of the problem for several years, and that some $330,000 was being spent to correct this bug. But Judge Duncan found there was enough evidence to believe a violation of the computer crime law had been committed. He ordered Moore to appear for arraignment and trial.

But Moore went free. David Anderson, an assistant public defender, secured Moore's acquittal with a classic defense. In a short but effective argument, Anderson urged: "This vending machine [for BART tickets] is only a fancy Coke machine, and hence does not come within the meaning of section 502 [the computer crime provision of the California Penal Code]."

Anderson continued: "According to the testimony before the magistrate, the machine in question does only a couple of things. It accepts money, determines its value, and then issues a ticket for that value. A Coke machine performs this function as well. . . . It then dispenses a Coke for that value *and even makes change!!!* [emphasis in the original] However, this hardly makes every Coke or other vending machine a computer."

Anderson made the less colorful but more legally effective argument that the prosecution had failed in making a required proof. He quoted the California Penal Code's definition of a "computer system" (which has since been changed): "A 'computer system' means a machine . . . that performs functions including but not limited to logic, arithmetic, data storage and retrieval, communication and control. The machine itself," Anderson argued, "is not described as possessing a computer program or data, and hence is not a computer system."

His conclusion was stirring and short: "This case is petty theft and to characterize it as anything else is ludicrous."

Anderson's argument carried the day. The judge reviewing Judge Duncan's decision reversed it and dismissed the case.

THE DEMOCRATIZATION OF COMPUTER CRIME

Cases like Moore's are far more common fare for most prosecutors than the spectacular cases like those of Robert Morris, Stanley Mark Rifkin, or Harold Rossfields Smith. This fact reflects what might be called democratization of computer crime. For the last several years, we at the National Center for Computer Crime Data have been conducting a continuing computer crime census to determine the kinds of cases actually being prosecuted around the country and the implications of these cases in the continuing effort to achieve better computer security. In 1986, we accompanied our first report of the census results with the following summary comments: "One major conclusion stands clear. The 'democratization' of computer crime is evident. The 'computer criminals' in our sample include recidivist street thugs, petty office embezzlers, vindictive employees, and bank tellers who had run up debts."

Nothing could be a less surprising consequence of the spread of computing to our schools, offices, government agencies, and homes at a breakneck pace. With so many people gaining more access to computers, the opportunities for computer crime grow like Topsy. The worst thing about the computer crime myths is the extent to which they keep us from sizing up our problems realistically. The prosecution of dozens of Walter Moores requires different planning, education, and budgeting than the prosecution of an occasional Kevin Mitnick.

This, of course, is not the problem of prosecutors alone. All of us who are potential victims of computer crime need to recognize that the simplest criminology says that increased opportunity to commit crime will tend to result in increased incidence of that crime.

Commitment To Security, our most recent publication of the computer-crime census results, indicates that the trend toward democratization is continuing, apparently even picking up speed. The data from California, though more extreme than the data from other jurisdictions, suggest that the demographics of computer crime are very quickly approaching those for crime in general. People who would be inclined to commit crimes for whatever reason are now more likely to commit computer crime because computers, in Willie Sutton's memorable phrase, are increasingly seen as "where the money is." Almost one-third of the California computer-crime arrestees since 1986 have been women. Members of minority racial or national groups comprise 45 percent of those arrested. Students have played a small part in the problem, and employees with access to computer systems play the greatest role.

We can also see the democratization of computer crime in the degree to which people with previous criminal records find themselves involved in computer crime. Ray Houston, Walter Moore, and Harold Rossfields Smith were opportunistic criminals. Computers merely presented an exploitable environment for their criminal schemes.

Criminals read *Time* magazine and watch *60 Minutes,* just like the rest of us. If computer professionals like Stanley Mark

Rifkin are vulnerable to the myth of computer crime, should it surprise us that ordinary criminals fall prey to it too?

Two questions haunt me about the Moore case: How many people knew how to rip off BART? And how many did it? Moore was one of three individuals prosecuted for the same sort of theft. (The other two were found guilty.) I'm sure that Moore and his friends talked, and that there were many others who knew about the vulnerability of the ticket machine but did not exploit it. The more people use computers, the more the computers' vulnerabilities will be discovered. Discovering the vulnerabilities first is one challenge that should keep our computer security professionals increasingly busy as more and more computer criminals come from "the street."

CHAPTER 10

CIVIL LITIGATION

BILL CHRISTISON VERSUS THE CONTAGIOUS CONSULTANT

You may be the victim of a computer crime. As we saw in Chapter 4, victims come in all sizes, sexes, and organizational structures.

Imagine how computer crime might victimize you. Your computer disk suddenly crashes; a malicious program was the cause. A policeman has been harassing you. He obtained your name and unlisted phone number from police records. You just got a bill for $123,456 because your telephone credit card number was posted on a hacker bulletin board. A vengeful employee took your most valuable computer files and left.

Do you think you'd want to sue? If you came to me, I'd try to dissuade you, if only to test your mettle.

First I'd tell you about the costs. "Justice isn't cheap, and it isn't easy," I'd say. The costs include time, anxiety, the possibility of an embarrassing and even costlier loss, and the terror and tedium of spending an emotional eternity dealing with lawyers, a fate often far more painful than death.

When someone sues you, it can be even worse. You may share the heartaches of the person who sued you without the pleasure of having made a choice.

Then I'd warn you about the danger of being too dependent on a specific outcome. I once had the good fortune to speak with a genuine litigious paranoid. This was a person whose life revolved around the misery of her many legal battles. To hear her tell it, life had dealt her an enormously bad hand. And yet each time she reacted to her plight she only seemed to make it worse.

"Beware," I told myself, "this could be you." And this could be *you*. The worst thing about litigation, really, is its potential to make your life miserable, particularly if you let your life revolve around it and you can't bear not to win. So here I just finished telling you that you have to be ready for great sacrifice, and now I'm telling you not to seek great gain.

I'd nail the point down by challenging you to sue only if you wanted justice, and not just victory.

It is hard, in times as dominated by materialism and selfishness as these, to go into a lawsuit seeking justice rather than the annihilation of the opponent. Melvin Belli is said to have quipped, "My clients do not want justice, they want freedom." But psychologically, and even tactically, I would try to get you to agree that justice is the more advantageous goal.

As I tried my best to sober you with the challenges a litigant must deal with, I might find myself hoping you would start to resist. Sometimes justice requires a lawsuit, and the belief that, although flawed, our legal system can sometimes provide valuable redress for those who have been harmed. Lawsuits change history. Heroic plaintiffs accept the costs of litigation because they have a cause that seems worth fighting for almost regardless of cost. What lawyer doesn't dream of representing heroic clients, engaged in battles of principle to establish right?

My sense is that Bill Christison was seeking justice, and my delight is that he found it.

IS THIS BOOK REALLY ABOUT COMPUTER CRIME?

This is a book that mixes autobiography, short stories, essays, and reportage. It is designed to lure you into caring about computer security, even working to bring about change in it. That's why it's great to turn to a sweet and simple story of success in the face of adversity, the kind of success it's often hard to believe in.

This is the story of one bulletin board operator who took a technical trespasser to court, and was victorious. The victory wasn't won without cost and uncertainty, but Bill Christison can now tell a tale of simple justice amidst the complexities of the computer age.

THE SANTA FE MESSAGE

Every morning at about 5:45, Bill Christison goes to his computer room and does maintenance on the Santa Fe Message bulletin board. He and his wife, Kathy, have operated the board since 1985, primarily to engage in political debates with a group of largely unknown colleagues ranging in age from their early teens to their 60s (which is where Bill finds himself). "Kathy and I have always been interested in world affairs and lively debate," Bill explains. "We met in Vietnam when we both worked for the CIA, and haven't stopped debating since. We've set this bulletin board up largely to be an intellectual bulletin board. There are 50 or so hard-core callers who regularly engage in hot-and-heavy debates on topics such as Star Wars, Nicaragua, defense spending, and Dan Quayle."

On May 4, 1988, Bill learned firsthand what it means to become the victim of a Trojan horse. Three days before Christmas that same year, he learned what it means to use the law to obtain justice from his attacker.

Much of the activity on bulletin boards is nocturnal. Trying to minimize the bite that telephone connection time can put into the devoted bulletin board user's pocketbook, many devotees work in the middle of the night. Bulletin boards can be run without an operator present, so this works out just fine.

Bill's normal procedure on rising is to answer messages left by people using the bulletin board the previous night. Then he tests and releases new files and programs left for possible distribution through the board. Finally he prints out a log of the previous day's activities. On average, his bulletin board gets 36 calls each day.

"I felt violated," the former CIA employee explained, describing his reaction to the events of May 4. "I was sitting in front of my computer. I had taken programs off the hard disk which were left the night before. I put them on a floppy disk, and put that disk in my A drive." (This was one of the four portals, A, B, C, and D drives through which data could be entered into his system.) "I began to run the program, and right away I knew there was something seriously wrong. The light went on, indicating that my C drive was running." Since the C drive was used only for his hard disk, Bill became nervous. He figured that a command in the program on his floppy disk had somehow activated the hard disk. Ten tense seconds passed. Then the light went on in the D drive. "Oh, Christ, there it goes," was Bill's only response. The program came to an end, and Bill attempted to see what it had done.

"I tried to use the C drive and tried to get to the directory of programs and files, knowing it probably wouldn't work." He was right. "The FAT [file allocation table] was really screwed up. I tried to copy or rename files, and nothing happened. I tested to see if the operating system had been destroyed and found that it had been erased. I tried the D drive, and the same damage had been done there."

Bill was relatively lucky. Even though the program had wiped out his operating system file allocation tables, and thus access to all the files, it only took him five hours to put things back together. This is because through pure coincidence he had backed up all data and programs on his hard disks 24 hours before. "How many people would have been so fortunate?" Christison asked me much later. Few, I agreed. His backup consisted of copies of the data and programs that resided on tape cartridges. Still, to return his system to where it had been before the intrusion, Bill had to reformat both of his hard disks—a lengthy process. Then he painstakingly copied files from the several tapes back to those hard disks. By the time he was finished, he was mad.

Since Bill's bulletin board system is sophisticated in its assignment of access codes, it seemed it would be a simple matter to confront the person responsible for Bill's inconvenience. The program in question had been submitted by one Carter Pruett. Bill looked Pruett up in the phone book and called him, ready to give him "what for" for messing with his favorite hobby bulletin board. "It was an embarrassing two minutes for me," Christison recalled. "I started off real angry to someone who identified herself as Pruett's wife. She told me that she was still grieving her husband's death, and that neither of them had ever used a computer."

Realizing that he had been deceived, Christison decided to find out who had been responsible. Every day after May 5, "Mr. Pruett" called to find out if his program had been made part of the Santa Fe Message bulletin board's library of programs. Christison went to the chief of security at the local telephone company and convinced them to install a trace on his bulletin board's phone to check where the calls from "Pruett" were actually coming from. "Pruett," like the Greeks of old, had sent a destructive program hidden in one that looked innocuous.

Shortly after his first effort, "Pruett" submitted the Trojan horse program to the Santa Fe Message bulletin board once again. This time Christison was ready for him. With phone company cooperation, he was able to document that the program was sent to his machine by someone using a specific phone number. The phone company would not release the name of the registered owner of the phone to which that number was assigned, but was willing to tell the police. Christison says that without the phone company's aid, his case could never have been brought to a successful conclusion. "I'm eternally grateful that the telephone security office really pitched in and helped. No law said they had to help but they did."

During the same time period, Christison found that another local bulletin board had been the unwilling recipient of the same program. The name used by the person planting it was not "Pruett," but the phone number was the same as that from which Bill's bulletin board had been called. Copies of both programs were sent to Ross Greenberg, who is active in the business of analyzing viruses and writing preventive and curative software. Greenberg identified the programs as Trojan horse programs.

Feeling violated, Christison decided that the case was appropriate for criminal prosecution. Realizing that his loss was not great, he still felt that he wanted to "mete some punishment out to this person, and to publicize what the person had done."

He quickly learned "you don't get things done just by having a crime committed against you."

Christison started with the district attorney's office in Santa Fe. "We're far too busy with crimes of passion and violence," said Assistant District Attorney Robert Sena, though taking an hour and a half to talk with Bill and his wife. "We also don't understand computers all that well," Sena added. Sena didn't close the door to prosecution, however. "Our decision is based largely on the police report which we receive," he told the couple.

To get a police report on file, Christison called the local sheriff's department on the day of the crime. He quickly saw that he had "a big education problem." "A deputy sheriff came out," Christison recalled. "Nice enough, in his 20s, even interested in what I had to say. He walked into the room where Kathy and I keep our four computers and was impressed. 'My gosh,' he said." Christison continued: "There were the computers, buffer devices, and three printers whirring away. 'This is just fascinating,' the deputy said. 'But how can someone put something in your computer and damage it?' "

For the next 45 minutes, Christison tutored the deputy on modems, telephone connections, and the essentials of personal computer communications.

The report was written, but Assistant District Attorney Sena found it insufficient. He encouraged Christison to get a better report. Christison was able to convince a detective from the sheriff's department to come speak with him.

"She was a smart one, very cooperative, but she admitted she was no computer expert." The detective visited the suspect, took a statement, and made a report.

Meanwhile, Bill contacted people at the state and federal levels without success. A friend in the local FBI office told him, "God, Bill, don't ask me to help you. We have bigger fish to fry."

While recognizing that his injury was not world-class, Bill was bothered by the law enforcement response. "We are small peanuts," he says, "but Los Alamos and Sandia Labs, two of the nation's foremost nuclear research centers, are right near here. If either of them were hit by a Trojan horse there would certainly be great interest." (Readers may remember the fuss when Los Alamos lab was visited by members of the 414 gang in 1983.)

Frustrated by the difficulties of trying to get a criminal prosecution going, Bill spoke with Ann Yalman, a friend who is a local Santa Fe lawyer. "She told me that at the very best I might break even and get damages sufficient to pay her fees." At worst, he could face a countersuit requiring even greater expenses, and the possibility of an adverse judgment. After calculating the amount they could afford to spend on this matter of principle, Bill and Kathy decided to go ahead.

Looking through the records Bill keeps of all past correspondence on his bulletin board, Bill was able to find old messages coming from Michael Dagg, who left the Trojan horse. "He used the bulletin board for about nine months, with his true name. He advertised himself as a programmer and said he knew about Trojan horse programs and how to prevent them. He also would leave information about other systems having been hit by these sorts of programs." Bill suspects that Dagg may have planted the Trojan horses either to encourage business or as pure and simple vandalism.

The Christisons filed suit in mid-August in the federal court in Albuquerque under sections 2701 and 2707 of title 18 of the U.S. Code. They argued that Dagg had committed a violation of the Electronic Communications Privacy Act. A criminal provision of this act calls for punishment of anyone who "intentionally accesses without authorization a facility through which an electronic communication service is provided; or . . . intentionally exceeds an authorization to access that facility; and thereby obtains, alters, or prevents authorized access to a wire or electronic communication while it is in electronic storage in such system." The Act specifically allows for civil suits by "any provider of electronic communication service, subscriber, or customer aggrieved by any violation."

Bill Christison was pleasant but low-key when I last spoke with him. "We won," he said simply. "The guy did nothing. He sent us a check for $2,700 and has never done anything else." The $2,700 represented $1,000 minimum statutory damages for each of the times Dagg was alleged to have left a Trojan horse program in Bill's system, $700 in attorney's fees, and court costs. Had Dagg refused to stop planting Trojan horses, Christison could have obtained an injunction as well under the provisions of the Act.

I wondered what steps Bill had taken to publicize the result of his lawsuit, since he'd mentioned that goal when I spoke with him before. "I was on an Albuquerque TV news show," he said proudly, "and the local papers wrote up stuff before the default." But Bill wasn't pushing things. "I felt it would be a bit of overkill to push for publicity. We won our suit, he paid the judgment. That's all we have a right to expect."

USE IT OR LOSE IT

Our legal system seems like the instrument of others' oppression, far too often and too seldom an instrument of our own vindication. Yet many states have passed provisions similar to that in the Electronic Communications Privacy Act which allow for civil suits in cases of computer crime. The priorities of prosecutors and the police may not match yours if you have been victimized by computer crime. You can make someone stop, you can force them to pay damages, and you may even be able to obtain some restitution in special hearings after a finding of guilt in a criminal case.

Yet as Goldwyn said of verbal contracts, these provisions are not worth the paper they're written on if no one uses them in court to vindicate the violated rights of computer crime victims. It's the fear of a lawsuit, far more than the experience of losing one, that we rely on to try to deter illegal conduct. But unless a few computer criminals lose civil lawsuits, as Michael Dagg did, we can't expect those who contemplate committing computer crimes to worry about us suing them.

CHAPTER 11

CIVIL LITIGATION II

US SPRINT VERSUS THE LITTLE O ORGANIZED COMPUTER CRIMINAL

Criminal entrepreneurship has not been slow to flower in this era of telephone service deregulation. Now, not only college kids calling home and teenagers trying to locate abuser-friendly computers steal phone services; businesses have been setup which do nothing else. Toll fraud has snowballed into what the Communications Fraud Control Association estimates to be a half-billion-dollar-a-year problem for the phone companies.

Their problem is our problem, since we are all consumers of telephone services. No one wants to experience the shock Flo Selfman got when she received a 10-page bill from Pacific Bell totalling $8,143. Selfman learned that the calls on her bill were made from pay phones in filling stations in Los Angeles. All of the calls were directed to Mexico. The longest was an astonishing four-and-a-half-hour call to Mexico City which cost $631.13.

Selfman's next bill was more worldly, including calls to Romania, Germany, Sweden, Hungary, and Yugoslavia. She moved (presumably for other reasons), changed her phone number, and put the matter behind her. US Sprint and the other carriers must continue to fight the growing abuse of telephone access codes every day. Sprint is the first company to take an aggressive and well-publicized approach to fighting this problem, using a combination of civil and criminal lawsuits to demonstrate that serious punishment will be dealt out to anyone who is caught engaging in massive toll fraud. As the story of Sprint's prosecution of Frederick Deneffe makes clear, stealing access codes and selling them to unsuspecting (or greedy) consumers is a high-tech cottage industry offering significant payoffs—unless one is caught. It shows how small criminal organizations like Deneffe's can quickly cause big problems.

INVESTIGATING A CELL OF HACKERS

Sandy Sandquist is a security officer who worked on the investigation leading to the arrest of Frederick Deneffe. "We knew we had a cell of people very active in hacking in the Northwest," Sandquist said. Sprint's monitoring of its switches indicated unusual activity in the Portland area, and the company decided to investigate. They traced the calls back to their origin, and contracted the local Lake Oswego police department, which prepared a little search warrant to take a look at the place from which the calls to the Portland switch were coming.

Later, Bales spoke with Robert Hamlin, a hacker who had worked for Frederick Deneffe explained his involvement in stealing access codes. "It was the best money I've made in a while," Hamlin said. Deneffe paid him to hack US Sprint access codes. Hacking the codes meant buying a Commodore computer, setting it up with software, and letting it run. The software was an autodial program that automatically generated a series of numbers with the same number of digits as a US Sprint access code every 15 to 20 seconds.

After gaining access to a computerized long-distance switch within the Sprint network, the computer program would dial a random number in the format of a US Sprint authorization code. If the circuit was completed and the code was accepted by the switch, the personal computer would then record the "captured" Sprint authorization code and move on to search for another. Once captured, the codes were disseminated and sold throughout the United States.

As US Sprint would later allege in its lawsuit against him, Deneffe "entered into a conspiracy" to develop and design computer hardware and software systems to obtain authorization codes and to sell both the systems and the codes. Though not the Colonel Sanders of access code hacking, Deneffe was willing, for a price, to set individuals up with their own access code hacking operations.

The key, Sandquist heard, was keeping a step ahead of telephone company security and the police. Deneffe spent a while in Chatanooga, Tennessee, and when investigators there got too close to his operation he moved to the Northwest.

In October 1986 Deneffe was in Lake Oswego, Oregon, running a business called Hello America. He and a man named Burton Andrews were operating a Commodore SX-64 personal computer to access the computerized Sprint long-distance switch in Portland, Oregon.

On the 16th of the month, the Lake Oswego police officers executed the first search warrant against Deneffe. They found 155 authorization codes at 8 Yorick, the residence rented by Deneffe at the time. By January 12, 1987, Sprint had been able to document a total loss of $3,018,818 from the unauthorized use of some of the 155 codes.

Frederick Deneffe may have been bothered by the raid, but it does not seem to have stopped his business efforts. A customer of Hello America received a letter dated November 21, 1986, and postmarked Tacoma, Washington. It contained four Sprint authorization codes which had not been among the 155 seized in mid-October. The investigators were pleased. Deneffe's continued activity allowed them to gather the kind of evidence that would make a much stronger case.

The Secret Service entered the case and worked with the Lake Oswego Central Office of the Pacific Northwest Bell Telephone Company to place trap-and-trace equipment on the Sprint access switch in Portland. Between April 16 and April 21, 1987, the equipment recorded over 1,000 calls to the Sprint switch from a phone number listed to Rick Deneffe doing business as "Hello America." Investigators noted that the calls were between 14 and 19 seconds apart, about the time it took for an autodial program to dial them. The telephone line on which the calls were made came from 8 Yorick. Alas for Deneffe, the Lake Oswego police knew Yorick well from the search made the previous October.

This time, the residence was equipped with a Commodore 64 personal computer, a Code-A-Phone Model 2540 telephone answering machine with an added circuit board, and a Commodore model 1541 disk drive. There was a diskette in the drive with a handwritten label that read "Snuff Copy."

The next month, Homer Elrod told U.S. Secret Service investigators that he had purchased a hacking system from Deneffe. He told them that Deneffe had moved to Vancouver, Washington, where he continued his illegal business of hacking Sprint codes under the business name Prepaid Legal.

Sprint investigators worked with Pacific Northwest Bell to install trap-and-trace equipment to monitor Deneffe's Vancouver phone and its contact with the Sprint computerized telephone switch for the Vancouver area. Following the pattern of the earlier investigation, Sprint concluded that automated accessing of its Vancouver switch was occurring from Deneffe's phone. The accesses between June 10 and June 12 came in bursts 16 to 18 seconds apart and were voluminous.

The Secret Service searched Deneffe's Washington residence on June 16, finding over 15 new US Sprint authorization codes. After this search Deneffe was arrested. The next month the investigators were back in Portland, searching Robert Hamlin's trailer, when they found David Cox. Cox said he'd been set up with the hacking system in use at that location by Deneffe. Cox said he would forward Sprint codes by telephone to a number in California. From there they were distributed through a voice mail box.

In August 1987, Sprint sued Deneffe and Burton Andrews in the U.S. District Court for Western Washington. The civil suit charged violations of the federal RICO law, the Communications Act, the Electronic Communications Privacy Act, and fraud in connection with access devices.

The suit sought money damages for lost revenues in excess of $3.5 million, for other damages, and for injunctive relief to prohibit Deneffe from, as Sprint's complaint phrased it, "engaging in the use of or the obtaining of US Sprint authorization codes; and . . . offering, disseminating, transferring, or selling any US Sprint authorization codes or any computer or other system for obtaining these codes."

The same complaint alleged that Sprint had suffered numerous damages including payments to the Bell Operating Companies and other companies for access services, and the loss of revenues "which defendants' and their customers' long-distance calls would have generated had they paid for the services which they obtained by illegal means." Sprint also had to bear the expenses of correcting legitimate customers' billings, cancelling the compromised numbers, and issuing new authorization codes to legitimate customers.

Bernard Bianchino, who supervised the suit for Sprint's legal department, considers the suit very important. "Sprint has decided to pursue civil remedies because we want injunctions as well as damages. People cannot violate our rights with impunity," he says. "They ought not think they will get away with it."

Deneffe, sentenced to three years in prison based on the criminal case arising out of Sprint's investigation, is probably not too concerned with the civil judgment which also hangs over his head.

USING THE CIVIL LAW AGAINST COMPUTER CRIMINALS

As the Sprint investigation demonstrates, it is no longer necessary to wait for a prosecutor to act to punish an alleged computer criminal. A number of novel civil remedies have been written into law, each offering alternatives that computer users may want to use in appropriate cases.

As suggested in the previous chapter, civil law remedies are useful only if they are used. A general understanding of the types of remedies offered by the civil law may help convince you that you, too, can use the civil law to combat computer crime, whether to protect an individual, a business, or a government agency.

Civil Suits. Even without special legislation, victims of computer crime are often entitled to sue the perpetrator under common law. If I steal your property, or that of your business, you can sue me. In some states, the law is unclear about the protection offered for intangible property like computer programs or the use of computer services. The computer crime laws offer added help to protect these kinds of property.

Added to the traditional remedies, there are now new causes of action that allow the victims of computer crime to file suits. These new types of suits are often valuable because they allow the recovery of far greater damages than traditional law would allow.

Connecticut, for example, provides for damage suits alleging computer crime. Where there is proof of "willful and malicious conduct" on the part of the defendant, the victim may be awarded treble damages. Similar to special provisions for private antitrust lawsuits, this provision is intended to increase the motivation of computer crime victims to bring suit.

California's Penal Code addresses two practical problems of civil suits in its computer crime law. It allows for suits against parents of minors who are alleged to have committed computer crimes. It also defines injury to include "any expenditure reasonably and necessarily incurred by the owner or lessee [of a computer] to verify that a computer system . . . was not altered, deleted, damaged, or destroyed" by any illegal access of the computer. As most evident in the Internet worm case described in Chapter 18, the expense of this sort of verification could easily exceed the costs of any other damages.

Injunctive Relief.   Like the federal law US Sprint relied on in its action against Deneffe, the state computer-crime laws of Connecticut, New Jersey, and Delaware provide that an individual or business believing itself the victim of a computer crime can apply to a court for injunctive relief to stop the crime immediately.

Restitution Hearings.   A third important remedy available to victims of computer crime is a cross between civil and criminal litigation. After a computer criminal has been found guilty or has entered a plea, a court in Connecticut or Delaware can award the victim up to twice the defendant's gain from committing the offense. The court may hold a hearing to determine the amount of the gain.

A solution to the problem of computer crime will come from a partnership between civil and criminal actions, private security and law enforcement investigators, and, ultimately, victims willing to bear the expense of publicizing their victimization and undergoing the costs of litigation for the benefits it offers in return.

A LITTLE ORGANIZATION IS A DANGEROUS THING

Like Roy Houston, the computerized conman described in Chapter 4, Deneffe was involved in multi-level marketing before he began to steal access codes. Sandy Sandquist notes that such businesses are a serious concern to US Sprint. Their need for telephone services makes buying and selling access codes very attractive to them. Deneffe knew little about computers, relying on Hamlin's technical expertise. Nonetheless, he has the arrogance of a Jerry Schneider or a Star Zifkin, having offered to work for Sprint after his plea of guilty. He claimed to have great skills, and suggested he could be useful in Sprint's education program. US Spring has shown no interest in Deneffe's aid.

CHAPTER 12:

ETHICS

KEVIN MITNICK: THE WILLIE HORTON OF COMPUTER CRIME?

In the waning days of 1989 I sat in The Bicycle Club, a gambling club in Bell, California, sipping on a coke and listening to Susie Thunder tell me about Kevin Mitnick. Thunder, one of the few women hackers to surface in the last decade, had turned her skills and will to playing poker professionally. We spoke a few hours before a tournament in which she planned to compete.

In 1982, when I first heard of Thunder, she was part of a group that met at a Los Angeles Shakey's Pizza Parlor and planned ways to compromise Pacific Telephone's computer and communication systems. Kevin Mitnick and Leonard DeDicco were members as well. Phone phreaks with computer science sophistication, these teenagers studied communication systems and mastered their complexities. Computer systems are not the only kind of systems that interest people like Thunder (or Jerry Schneider or Robert Morris). Whether they involve calculating the odds on a winning hand, loopholes in the international banking system, or flaws in communication network software, systems-savvy people can often exploit any system they can understand. Susie understood the mathematics of poker, she explained, so now she had changed her focus from computer systems to gambling.

Intriguingly dressed from her feather earrings to her cowgirl boots, Thunder was willing to admit to a variety of "psychological subversion" techniques she had used to gain information about computer systems. She was the kind of woman, she told me, who would go to Kansas City on a whim and concoct a scheme of disinformation. She picked a man at random out of the phone book and circulated information suggesting he was guilty of a serious crime. She assured me she stopped before the man was arrested, but not before some information had circulated which could have been incriminating.

"Kevin's not like me," she explained. He's *really* crazy." I asked her about his being held without bail and she approved. "Any punishment he gets is ok with me," she said. "He's dangerous."

Speaking before a chapter of the Association for Computing Machinery I met a woman whose view of Mitnick paralleled Thunder. "I had to clean up the mess that little twirp made," she told me angrily "and I don't care if they throw the book at him."

In all, five people have told me how evil they think Kevin Mitnick is, and how happy they are that he has been punished. None has expressed an interest in considering whether his constitutional rights have been violated. As I read the reports of Kevin Mitnick's journey through the criminal justice system, I wondered where is Clarence Darrow now that unpopular computer criminals like Kevin Mitnick need him?

"The right to bail is illusory these days," says Jerry Kaplan, a Los Angeles defense attorney with a heavy federal caseload. Kaplan, whose clients are often charged with murder or cocaine offenses, has seen drug dealers detained a number of times. But even Kaplan considers Mitnick's case unique. "It is unusual for someone to be held without bail unless the case involves a presumption of dangerousness."

The federal law creates a presumption that someone arrested should be detained as dangerous if that person is charged with a violent crime, a capital crime, or a drug crime involving more than a 10 year sentence. Mitnick's case fits none of these criteria. Instead, it would seem to be brought under language in the Act allowing for pretrial detention whenever release of the accused "will endanger the safety of any other person or the community." Ironically, Mitnick could not have been detained under this law if his case had been brought in Massachusetts, where Digita Equipment Corporation maintains offices. In the case of U.S. v. Ploof, the U.S. Court of Appeals, First Circuit, ruled that detention for dangerousness is only permissible in those cases meeting the specific criteria listed above.

Clearly this language offers little precise guidance. Instead, it invests the judicial officer considering bail with considerable discretion. Since the decisions are discretionary, they are unlikely to be reversed on appeal. Appellate courts generally limit their reversals to mistakes of law, overturning only the most extreme abuses of discretion. Mitnick's case suggests very strongly that the vague language of our bail laws can be used to punish an unpopular defendant.

If the bail laws can be abused in this way, the example of this abuse also presents an ethical challenge to the prosecutor. Unlike the defense attorney, whose only responsibility is to the client, the prosecutor is obliged to work for justice, as well as for guilty verdicts. The prosecutor has the responsibility of presenting evidence under the bail laws and choosing those cases in which they will argue for pre-trial detention. I have serious doubts about the ethical behavior of the prosecutors who chose to argue for Mitnick's detention based on the evidence they presented to the court.

THE CHARGES

In contrast to the sweeping attacks on Mitnick's character that I heard, and which were widely repeated in the press, the charges filed against Kevin Mitnick at the end of 1988 were narrowly drawn. On December 15, 1988 Mitnick was charged with two counts of computer crime, a violation of federal law.

On December 8, 1988, (according to legal papers he filed) FBI Special Agent Christopher Headrick met with Leonard DeCicco. DeCicco had first called Chuck Bushey, Manager of Investigative Services and Corporate Security, at Digital Equipment Corporation (DEC), to warn him that Kevin Mitnick had been illegally accessing DEC computer systems.

DeCicco, a computer operator at Voluntary Plan Assistance (VPA) in Calabasas, California, told Headrick that he'd been letting Kevin Mitnick use a terminal at VPA. DeCicco and Mitnick had known each other for several years. Mitnick, DeCicco said, used the terminal to gain unauthorized access to DEC facilities in the United States and abroad. DeCicco also claimed that Kevin arranged it so that DeCicco's employer never had to pay for the calls. DeCicco claimed that his friend Kevin changed the telephone charges from VPA's MCI account to other accounts, or to non-existent ones.

Shortly after DeCicco turned Mitnick in, DEC installed a device to monitor and record Mitnick's activities. At one time, as Mitnick hacked away, FBI Special Agent Gerald Harman, DEC Systems Support Engineer Richard Mautz, and Kent Anderson, head of DEC European Security, observed that Mitnick was accessing a computer system located at Leeds University in England. Mitnick was examining lists of people with access to the Leeds computer system and their access codes. He charged the MCI costs incurred in accessing the Leeds computer to a different account.

Bushey told the FBI that DEC had developed a copyrighted internal security software package. Access to the package was limited to authorized DEC employees. Bushey said the program, called the "Security Software System," had cost more than $1 million to develop. It had not been released to the public or the University of Southern California. The Security Software System had been accessed without authorization four times in 1988. Bushey estimated that reacting to those intrusions and others in the past 14 months had cost DEC over $4 million in computer time lost while machines were not working, employee time spent reacting to the security breaches, and time spent rebuilding certain DEC files.

Tipped off by DeCicco, Bushey found that a copy of the Security Software System had been stored in the University of Southern California computer system. DeCicco assisted Bushey in retrieving it.

The day after his hacking was monitored, Mitnick was arrested. Investigators located a blue bag in his trunk. DeCicco had already told Headrick that Mitnick's blue bag contained disks, notes and other documentation which Mitnick used to access various computer systems.

FBI Agent Headrick directed that Mitnick's two-door black Nissan Pulsar be impounded at the FBI garage in West Los Angeles, and prepared a search warrant. Once the warrant was ready, on December 14, Headrick searched the blue bag. He found a summary of the law on computer break-ins. More interesting to him were notes pertaining to the DEC Security Software System which Kevin Mitnick was accused of stealing. There were also other documents and proprietary information available only to authorized DEC employees. When Mitnick was searched he had 14 MCI access codes in his purse.

Based on these allegations, Mitnick was charged with two counts of computer crime. One count was for defrauding MCI by using MCI's long distance lines without charge. The other count was based on the charge that he stole the Security Software System. Later a third charge was added based on Kevin's possession of the MCI access codes.

THE DETENTION

Mitnick was denied bail under the provisions of the so-called Bail Reform Act passed in 1984. This act allows for detention in those cases where the judicial officer "finds that no condition or combination of conditions of release will reasonably assure the . . . safety of any other person and the community." Prior law already allowed for detention where someone represented a threat to flee the jurisdiction. However, the comments of those judicial officers denying Mitnick bail suggest that preventing future crimes, not preventing Mitnick's flight, was the major basis for their actions. As such, the decision calls into question the ability of a judge or magistrate to predict future behavior.

In the first hearing after Mitnick's arrest, United States Magistrate Venetta Tassopulos ordered him held without bail, ruling that when "armed" with a keyboard he posed a danger to the community. In addition, the Magistrate granted a prosecution request restricting Mitnick's telephone calls from jail. He was allowed to call his lawyers or three members of his family, and only under jail officials' supervision.

Assistant United States Attorney Leon Weidman argued in favor of Mitnick's detention. "This thing is so massive, we're just running around trying to figure out what he did," the prosecutor admitted. Despite the inconclusive nature of the investigation,

Weidman expressed no doubt about Mitnick's threat. "This person," he said, "is very, very dangerous, and he needs to be detained and kept away from a computer."

Two weeks after Magistrate Tassopulos detained Mitnick, Magistrate Robert Stone heard an appeal from the detention order. Assistant United States Attorney Leon Weidman said investigators believed that Mitnick might have been the instigator of a false report released by a news service in April 1988 that Security Pacific National Bank lost $400 million in the first quarter of that year.

He also said that Mitnick penetrated a National Security Agency computer and obtained billing data for the agency and several of its employees.

Based on these arguments, and other allegations of past wrongdoings, U.S. Magistrate Robert Stone rejected Mitnick's appeal.

"I don't think there's any conditions the court could set up based upon which the court would be convinced that the defendant would be anything other than a danger to the community," Stone said.

Mitnick's attorney argued that house arrest and the removal of all of Mitnick's computers and telephone connections from his home would adequately protect society. Stone disagreed. He noted that while most criminals might be controlled by requiring them to remain in their homes, this was not the case with Mitnick. "This really sounds very different," Stone said. "It sounds like the defendant could commit major crimes no matter where he is."

After he pleaded not guilty before United States District Judge Mariana Pfaelzer, Mitnick once more requested bail. Again he was turned down. Judge Pfaelzer seemed convinced by the arguments of Assistant United States Attorney Weidman, saying Mitnick was "a very, very great danger to the community."

By April 1989, the prosecutor's office had reduced its estimate of the seriousness of Mitnick's offense. Arguing in favor of a plea bargain worked out between prosecution and defense, Assistant United States Attorney James Sanders told Judge Pfaelzer that Mitnick had neither damaged DEC's computer system nor attempted to make money from the software he copied from DEC. Sanders also revised the government's estimate of the damage Mitnick had done to DEC. Instead of $4 million, Sanders put DEC's cost at $160,000 in "downtime" to trace the security breach Kevin was charged with.

Pfaelzer took the unusual step of rejecting the plea bargain, saying, "look at Mr. Mitnick's background. He is a person who has engaged in this conduct before—rather consistently before."

Three months later, in July 1989, Judge Pfaelzer accepted Mitnick's guilty plea. The plea varied in one respect from the one rejected earlier. In addition to one year's incarceration, the sentence agreed upon called for Mitnick to spend six months in a rehabilitation program to deal with what has been called his "computer addiction."

Within a week of Mitnick's sentencing, significant evidence became available further suggesting that his detention had been unfair. In July 1989, Assistant U.S. Attorney James Asperger admitted that there was no evidence to tie Mitnick to the problem experienced by the Security Pacific Bank. He also admitted that there was no evidence that Mitnick had ever compromised the security of the National Security Agency. The National Security Agency itself absolutely denied that its computer security was breached at the time Mitnick was alleged to have broken in. Asperger, the prosecutor whose office was responsible for presenting evidence in support of these untrue allegations, and using them to influence the court, simply acknowledged: "A lot of the stories we originally heard just didn't pan out, so we had to give him the benefit of the doubt."

Other widely circulated stories which influenced the Magistrate's decision to deny Mitnick bail included the unproven allegation that he changed the TRW credit report of a judge who sentenced him to serve time for a juvenile computer offense, and that he disconnected the telephones of Actress Kristi McNichol. These charges, Asperger also admitted, could not be proven.

IS PRE-TRIAL DETENTION FOR DANGEROUSNESS FAIR?

Still incarcerated in July 1989, Kevin Mitnick must have taken rather hollow satisfaction in hearing Assistant United States

Attorney James Asperger's admission that much of the evidence used to keep him behind bars had turned out to be invalid. Correct or incorrect, the evidence had been used, and seven months passed before Mitnick was given the rights allowed every other prisoner, no matter how vile those other prisoners' crimes.

Mitnick's case suggests three problems in the operation of our pre-trial detention laws. First, can we predict dangerousness? Second, how much evidence should be required before denying someone bail? Third, how do we keep detention laws from being used as punishment?

Can We Predict Dangerousness?

Those who object to pretrial detention laws suggest that it is impossible to predict future dangerousness. Chappel and Monahan, two criminologists studying the issue, concluded that predictions are usually wrong. They found that in three studies, percentages of false predictions of future violent behavior were 86 percent, 95 percent, and 99.7 percent. A study of preventive detention by David Jett appearing in the 1985 American Criminal Law Review concludes that statistics like these refute the logic of denying bail. "The paucity of support for the government's position that violent or dangerous behavior can be predicted brings into question the legitimacy of the 1984 [Bail Reform] Act's method of achieving its goal of protecting society from dangerous individuals."

How Much Evidence Should Be Required before Denying Someone Bail?

One of the most glaring problems in the denial of Kevin Mitnick's requests for bail is the degree to which the three decisions denying bail were based on incorrect information. The bail law does not require proof of the facts presented beyond a reasonable doubt. On the contrary, the bail laws do not require that a person faced with pretrial incarceration be informed of information the government will use to support the claim of dangerousness. The right to confront one's accusers, a major part of the protections in criminal trials, is not found in bail hearings. Kevin Mitnick had no opportunity to confront those who supposedly could have proven the charges that were used to argue against his getting bail. The government was able to use hearsay by merely summarizing what might be proven by competent witnesses without identifying those witnesses.

Most significantly, the prosecutors need only to establish probable cause to believe someone is dangerous for the court to support their motions to deny bail. Later admissions by the United States Attorney's Office established that the facts used to support the motions were false. The limitations on Mitnick's procedural rights allowed the prosecutors to argue from unsubstantiated rumors. Whatever the intent, the result of the prosecution's argument was to deprive Kevin Mitnick of his liberty unfairly.

How Do We Keep the Detention Laws from Being Used for Punishment?

Our Constitution and the rights it protects in the Bill of Rights, are designed to make sure that governmental power is not used unfairly to punish those whose views or behavior are unpopular. In Kevin Mitnick's case, the likelihood seems high that punishment, not just protection of the public were involved in the decision to deny bail.

The courts have often declared that it is impermissible to punish someone before that person is found guilty of a crime. Following that rationale, it is important to ask whether the pretrial detention of an unpopular defendant like Mitnick was punitive. There are two types of punitive application of the bail laws that might be considered. One is the use of detention itself; the other is the imposition of conditions of confinement substantially worse than would be faced after confinement. In Mitnick's case, both seem to have occurred.

Based on my unrepresentative sample, and on conversations with several attorneys and former prosecutors, I have little doubt that one of the main reasons Kevin Mitnick was kept in prison was the widespread opinion that he was, as one colleague put it "a little shit." "They're not supposed to use the law to punish people," one lawyer told me, "but they do."

The novel condition of Mitnick's detention, severely limited telephone use, had the effect of seriously punishing him. Because of administrative problems in enforcing this unusual condition, Mitnick was kept in solitary confinement 23 hours a day. His treatment was similar to those who have violated serious prison rules. He had not violated any of these rules. The reason for his additional punishment was said to be that there weren't enough staff people to keep him from getting access to telephones So prison authorities just kept him in solitary. Mitnick's attorney, Alan Rubin, alerted Judge Pfaelzer to his client's extra punishment. The Judge took no action, treating Mitnick's punishment as an administrative detail not worth her attention. Some federal courts have ruled that it is impermissible punishment to subject a detainee to conditions of confinement substantially worse than he or she would face upon conviction. Since Kevin would have been kept in solitary confinement only if he violated serious prison rules, the condition of no telephone access, when implemented in the way it was, would certainly seem to be punitive.

I may be unfair in suggesting that the prosecutor, Judge, and jail officials who kept Kevin Mitnick in solitary confinement 23 hours a day were punitive. They may just have been inept. Computer crime is still a spectacular occurrence in the minds of many of those who make the criminal justice system what it is. (Some suggest that it is neither just nor a system, in short a double oxymoron.) If no one was able to figure out a way to protect our society from Kevin Mitnick's making collect calls from jailhouse pay telephones, we are facing a technological time warp of frightening dimension.

A bit of hysteria which attributed near-mythical powers to Kevin Mitnick may explain this over-reaction rather than an intent to do him harm. Such abuse of discretion, however, certainly suggests irresponsibility, if not unethical behavior. Most likely, however, Mitnick's treatment is merely another evidence that far too many in political power at this time prefer to deal with symbols of crime than its substance, whether the crime involved is computer crime, murder, or drug trafficking.

KEVIN MITNICK AND WILLIE HORTON

Any doubt that our society would prefer to deal with symbols of the crime problem rather than the realities should have been dispelled by the election of George "No-More-Willie-Hortons" Bush. The Bush campaign was able to brainwash a large part of the electorate into allowing Horton to serve as a symbol of Michael Dukakis' failure to fight crime effectively. So Mitnick served as a symbol of the federal government's commitment to fight computer crime. This symbol, however, threatens to encourage an end to thinking about the dangers of networks that allow Robert Morrises to send viruses careening through them. Mitnick's case also at least slowed the conversation about the dangers of educational systems that allow thousands of Robert Morrises to career through them, gaining technological power far outstripping their juvenile sense of responsibility.

MITNICK AND MORRIS: TWO SYMBOLS INSTEAD OF SUBSTANCE?

To Bonnie Mitnick, her husband's case seemed to have been the perfect distraction. "It has to do with Morris," she said. "His father is a big shot at the NSA, [Chief Scientist] and they want to take the heat off his case and put it on this case instead. Look—Morris Sr. is on a security committee [for the National Institute of Science and Technology] and they propose to analyze Kevin's case. Why aren't they looking at his son's case?"

Bonnie Mitnick doesn't put on airs. She doesn't have a finely wrought conspiracy theory. She probably couldn't tell you who she suspects is responsible for her husband's treatment before the law. But she looks at the allegations which appeared in the papers, which were argued in denying her husband bail, and which were well-known by the time sentencing was under discussion. "There's got to be more to it than that," she says. "Kevin just isn't the worst computer criminal ever. So why is he getting the strictest sentence ever?"

I look at Bonnie, try to smile understandingly, and confess that I have no answer. I know that her husband has alienated a lot of people, some of whom I quoted earlier in this chapter. In my own contacts with him, I've found him polite, friendly and deferential. Of course those that hate him would warn me not to be taken in. Many told me Kevin's skill includes manipulating people as well as computer systems. Should I believe my own impression of him, or should I rely on others' experience instead? My answer to this question will affect only the tone of this chapter. The answer provided by the judicial officers and prosecutors who cooperated to deny him bail had much more impact. I have to wonder if they had any more basis for their view than I for mine.

Next to Robert Morris, the "Sorcerer's Apprentice" discussed in Chapter 18, Kevin Mitnick was the most written-about computer criminal of 1989. Mitnick's journey through the criminal justice system, however, bore little resemblance to Morris's.

Morris was acknowledged as the author of the Internet worm in early November 1988. This program spread through a large network of computers used by academics and researchers throughout the United States, causing damage estimated at anywhere from $100,000 to $100,000,000. Morris was not arrested or incarcerated as the U.S. Attorney's Office considered what charges if any to bring against him.

Morris could contemplate the gravity of his situation at home with his family. Academics and professionals debated whether he should be prosecuted for irresponsibility costing hundreds of thousands—if not millions—of dollars. During the same time period, Kevin Mitnick sat in jail.

Arrested in December 1988, just one month after Morris's activity, Mitnick provided the media with the perfect story to capitalize on the interest in Morris's case. He also presented an ethical challenge to those assigned to prosecute him, a challenge that they were not able to meet.

NEEDED: PROSECUTORIAL ETHICS

This chapter has been the hardest chapter to write, the one which requires telling the least comfortable truths. As a former prosecutor, it grieves me to have to write about my former colleagues in less than flattering terms. I identify with the Los Angeles District Attorney's office, the first home of the National Center for Computer Crime Data, though it has been nine years since I left. And I identify with the federal prosecutors who handled the Mitnick prosecution. Their job is not much different than mine was for many years—their importance to public safety undeniable.

But I'm afraid that prosecutors follow the election returns, and reflect public sentiment, at its worst as well as its best. It appears that the Department of Justice's reading of public sentiment was similar to my little survey. Kevin Mitnick was the perfect scapegoat to satisfy the demands of a public getting more and more concerned with computer crime, and less and less convinced that the federal government is doing anything about it.

I'm haunted by Assistant United States Attorney James Asperger's admission that much of the argument used to keep Mitnick behind bars was based on rumors which didn't pan out. It was bad enough that the charges prosecutors made in court were spread to millions of readers by newspapers around the country. But it is much worse that these untrue allegations were a large part of the basis for keeping Mitnick behind bars without the possibility of posting bail! Prosecutors always have an ethical and legal duty to do justice, not just fight to convict all defendants.

The inherent unfairness of the pretrial detention statutes can only be tempered by prosecutors' wisdom in using the laws. Instead of acting as a safeguard to keep the wrong type of cases from being brought, the prosecutors in this case seem to have been all too eager to follow the public prejudices of the moment and abandon their responsibility to work for fairness.

The prosecutor's rigor must begin with conscientious consideration of the appropriateness of pretrial detention. At a minimum, it seems that the ethical prosecutor will be rigorous before deciding to argue that someone accused of computer crime be detained without bail. Where there is no presumption of dangerousness, the rule should be to avoid attempts to detain someone. Since it is difficult to predict future behavior, prosecutors need to have excellent reason to argue in favor of denying someone bail. Criminologists, psychologists, and even parents can agree about how hard it is to predict a person's dangerousness. Humility would dictate more care before depriving people of their freedom.

Prosecutors also need to be rigorous in collecting the information on which they base their arguments in favor of detention. The prosecutors' bail arguments are less subject to the protections of confrontation and proof beyond a reasonable doubt than their arguments at trial. Thus, their own obligation to present only reliable information must be very high.

Finally they must be rigorous in resisting the urge to punish "little shits" just because many people do not like them. With the growing public resistance to constitutional protections for those arrested of crimes, prosecutors have an increasing importance in the criminal justice system. Many of the judicial protections of our constitutional rights have been diminished in the 80's based on the argument that prosecutors and investigators will exercise their discretion to protect these rights.

Most notable of these rights is the right to be free from unreasonable search and seizure. Under current law, evidence seized in an unconstitutional way can be used against someone accused of crime as long as the officer seizing the evidence made a "good faith" effort to follow the law. This rule is clearly based on the expectation that law enforcement personnel will operate in good faith. Failing to operate in good faith is unethical. It is also imprudent, since it could result in the reinstituting of previous sanctions against illegal searches and seizures like the suppression of evidence they produce. In the same way, use of pretrial detention for punitive instead of preventive purposes will eventually convince the public that pretrial detention is a bad idea.

PRETRIAL PUNISHMENT

Mitnick is only the latest of several computer crime suspects punished without due process by law enforcement and prosecution officials. The most common tactic it appears, is to seize suspects' computers. Since 1983, FBI agents and other Justice Department officials have commented favorably on this practice. The federal government seldom jails juveniles, one official noted.

"But there are a lot of other possibilities: some kind of commit-ment on the part of the parents, maybe a monetary penalty. Heck, just our keeping their equipment has got to be a hardship."

The seizure of equipment is supposed to be investigative rather than punitive. This precept seems to have mattered as little to the quoted official as it did to the attorneys arguing that Kevin Mitnick should be denied his freedom based on rumor.

SENTENCING

Mitnick's case suggests that the false allegations used to keep him in custody also prejudiced the court's consideration of a fair sentence. After prosecutors and defense lawyers agreed to a plea bargain calling for him to spend one year in jail, the U.S. District Judge hearing his case, Mariana Pfaelzer rejected the agreement.

Finally, three months later, a disposition was reached. Mitnick was sentenced to serve one year in jail, being credited for the seven-and-a-half months he spent incarcerated before his plea. He was then to enter a rehabilitation program in Los Angeles to be treated as a computer addict.

The concept of computer addiction, discussed in chapter 3, is a novel one for the courts to consider. Perhaps it will gain favor. Maybe we have come up with a concept which will allow us to distinguish between "good" computer irresponsibility, the kind committed by nice upper-class kids, like Robert Morris, and "bad" computer irresponsibility, the kind committed by obnoxious lower-class kids: all we need to do is call the latter group addicts. Then, whenever we need to have a symbol of evil computing, we can focus on the addicts and leave the nice kids alone.

WHERE IS THE DIGITAL DEFENDER?

As consumer protection has yet to catch up with the computer revolution, so too has the criminal defense bar left the field of computer crime defense without any champions. Kevin Mitnick seems to have served as a convenient target for much of the frustration of the public and prosecutors over the increasing dangers of computer crime. Rather than for crimes he committed, it seems Kevin was punished for crimes the court feared he might commit. This fear is not an appropriate basis for judicial decisions, particularly when it reflects ignorance about the technology involved and distaste for a sometimes obnoxious personality more than it does a careful analysis of the facts.

Perhaps Mitnick's attorneys said what they were supposed to, pointing out the unproven nature of most of the charges against their client. Perhaps they were just doing their jobs without much concern about the outcome. In any case, they were not able to be heard. If we are to protect the rights of computer users, the unfairness Mitnick experienced should be recognized.

All computer users will want to rest easy that they will never be thrown in jail for seven months based on untrue rumors about their alleged computer prowess. All citizens concerned that a proper balance be maintained between state power and individual rights may wonder how many other cases of unfamiliarity with technology—or ethics—have put undeserving individuals behind bars. Computer ethics is the basis of computer security. If those who investigate and prosecute computer crimes show no ethical leadership, their job in fighting computer crime will be much tougher. Justice, not arbitrary punishment, must be the key to our efforts against computer crime.

PART 4

THE ROAD TO RESPONSIBLE COMPUTING

It is tempting to get caught up in the cops-and-robbers, spy-versus-spy quality of computer crime. It's fun, it's fast, and it's spectacular. But what if you weren't just a spectator?

It's relatively easy to talk about crime, because by definition crime is what people like "us" don't do. We define crime, except in unusual circumstances, as extremes of behavior that society will not tolerate. Killing someone is unacceptable. Yelling at someone and wishing them dead, though unpleasant, is not crime in the eyes of the law.

If I focus on the extremes of criminal law, I don't have to confront the harder questions of my responsibility in the computer age. Criminology may be the study of other people's problems, but politics and economics are not. The issues raised in this section are political and economic ones. The villains are not so clearly defined as those who have violated the law.

This section is designed to tempt you to ask some of these harder questions of responsibility. In the first three chapters, I discuss the question of taking responsibility for what you believe are the government's mistakes. In the next two chapters, which focus on piracy, I ask what your responsibility is when you are confronted with an unresolved relationship between economics, law, technology, and values. In the final chapter, I suggest that irresponsible computing represents a call to community.

Imagine yourself involved in Solidarity, like Jan Hanasz; at the core of "Contragate," like Oliver North; or in Berkeley protesting American defense policies, like Katya Komisaruk. Like the soapbox category of computer criminals discussed in Chapter 3, you would find that computers could play a major part in your communication strategy, either as messenger or message. (Sometimes it is difficult to separate the two, as Marshall McLuhan noted decades ago when he wrote *Understanding Media*.)

Jan Hanasz, Katya Komisaruk, and Colonel Oliver North used computers to communicate. But while Hanasz and Komisaruk were trying to reach as many people as possible, North was concerned with reaching a few key people and avoiding all others attention. Using a computer helped Jan Hanasz gain attention. Destroying one did the same for Katya Komisaruk. From their individual perspectives, each was acting in his or her country's best interests. Yet each was acting against his or her country's policies, and against its laws.

When would I use a computer to foster some political goal? When would I refuse to use a computer because of some political belief? Whether we consider them heroic or harebrained, dangerous or deserving of praise, Hanasz, North, and Komisaruk used computers to demonstrate commitment to their beliefs.

Commitment to one's beliefs is one important aspect of responsibility, but not the only one. The hard question posed by these cases is how we can protest responsibly when we believe our government is doing something seriously wrong. Would you want to be remembered for having done what any of these three did? That question focuses far more on their purposes and the depth of analysis in the choices they made than on their use of specific tools or their choices of specific targets. But to understand the types of computer crimes we might be tempted to commit, and to better judge the computer crimes of these others, it is a good idea to consider the issues of personal and social responsibility their choices raise.

Responsible computing, as I see it, is a sensitivity to the human consequences of all types of computer uses. As such, the important thing is not just the technology used, but the humanity the user brings to it.

The two chapters in this section dealing with piracy raise difficult economic and moral questions. Right now there is less of a serious deterrent to individual acts of computer piracy, or unauthorized copying of computer programs, than there is to other acts of computer crime. Piracy is more widespread and most likely, more costly than other computer crimes. Yet the social concensus necessary to really combat piracy is lacking.

I would be willing to bet that for every reader who has committed a computer crime other than piracy, there are a dozen of you who have copied someone else's copyrighted software.

What is the solution to piracy? The two chapters on this problem don't answer that question directly, but they do suggest the direction in which hope may lie. Technology, civil litigation, and legislative lobbying are three weapons which have yet to prove effective. The entry of user groups into political action is perhaps the best hope. This communitywide expression of responsibility may provide the mix of activism and stability necessary to resolve the question of how to best share the fruits of our progress in programming with the entire computing community.

This part concludes with a summary and comment on the Internet worm case, certainly the most talked about computer crime for several years. In demonstrating how closely our nation's computers are linked and how vulnerable that linkage is, Robert Morris challenged the suggestions of many security consultants that the dangers of computer viruses have been overblown. If nothing else, this section demonstrates how many difficult questions await our consideration and response. The road to responsible computing will be a long one, but one we cannot turn away from.

CHAPTER 13

POLITICS

KATYA KOMISARUK: THE "PRINCESS" OF COMPUTING

THE PRINCESS IN COURT

In a forest-green jumper, white roses clutched in hand, Katya Komisaruk was the perfect symbol of innocence betrayed. The 28-year-old Berkeley MBA had destroyed a $1.2 million IBM 3301 mainframe computer at Vandenberg Air Force Base in June 1987. It was the latest of 31 personal protest actions Komisaruk had taken over the last four years. All were expressions of her commitment to steer the United States away from nuclear war. "I want so much to have a baby," she had said, "and I didn't feel I could legitimately become a parent unless I made a serious attempt at making the world safer for my child."

Now, in October 1987, Komisaruk was hoping Justice William Rea would allow her a "fair" trial. Fairness, she said, required that she be given the opportunity to tell the jury why she had destroyed the computer, and to argue that she had done it to prevent a greater crime (if it isn't a trivialization to use no more harsh a word than *crime* to denote nuclear war). She wanted to argue that the computer was a weapon designed for a first strike attack against the Soviet Union and that such an attack would contravene international law.

Unless the ruling went her way, Komisaruk's trial for sabotage and destruction of government property was not going to be much of a competition. She had called a press conference the day after she wrecked the computer and described and explained her actions in detail. Since her admission of guilt was clear, justification of her actions was her only hope to avoid five years or more in federal prison.

Central casting could have done no better in picking the opposing attorneys. Assistant U.S. Attorney Nora Manella, in sharp red suit and austere, straight blond hair, opposed the casual and somber Leonard Weinglass. "The defendant is not seeking to present any legal defense," Manella said. She characterized Komisaruk's argument as an attempt to "sway the jury by the sincerity of her beliefs."

Classic extras completed the scene. Along with a couple of dozen reporters, the peace movement lived still, filling the rest of the courtroom's 75 seats. Katya's supporters held white roses and occasionally gasped at pro-prosecution rulings.

Lest the symbolism go unnoticed, the White Rose Collective had distributed press materials on the Los Angeles Federal Courthouse steps at a press conference before the hearing began. "During the Third Reich," the group's statement read, "a small group of gentile students, calling themselves 'The White Rose,' chose to resist Hitler. They tried to tell their fellow citizens what horrors were being committed in their name." Katya had long admired the White Rose group, first learning about them at the age of 14.

WITH COOKIES AND WIRE CUTTERS

Hitchhiking down through the middle of California the evening of June 1, 1987, Katya Komisaruk didn't make much small talk with the truck drivers who gave her rides. "I was going over what I would say to the soldiers [at Vandenberg] to avoid getting shot," she explained, "and I don't think the truck drivers would have been too sympathetic." In her knapsack Komisaruk carried a hammer, a crowbar, wire cutters, a cordless drill, a bicycle lock, fast-drying epoxy, cans of spray paint, topographic maps, a box of Mrs. Fields cookies, a bouquet of red, white, and blue flowers, her penny whistle, and her teddy bear, Judas Maccabeas. Her thoughts, when not on survival, turned to the possibility of embarrassment. She agonized over being caught before she had the chance to do anything. "I'd have to pay the price and wouldn't even get much attention for my position about nuclear weapons."

"The hardest thing about the truck rides was explaining why I wanted to be let off next to Vandenberg Air Force Base," Katya recalled. She said she was going hiking, and her driver didn't react.

Arriving at the base near Santa Barbara, California in the early evening, Katya waited for dark in the bushes nearby. She climbed over a barbed wire fence to enter the base and began walking up the road. "They weren't expecting me," she explained, "and anyway, the bushes seemed to be crawling with mutant poison oak." When an occasional searchlight or car passed, Katya simply dove into the shadows. She worried about infrared surveillance, but found none. She opined that the deer on the base grounds rendered the system useless and led to the decision to turn it off.

The road Katya followed led to the NAVSTAR complex, which was her target. It wasn't hard to identify, she told me. "The government issues excellent topographic maps. They don't tell you what the buildings are used for, but they do show you where they are." The complex of buildings was ringed by a barbed wire fence, but the gate was open. Katya simply went through the gate, closed it from inside, and locked it with the bicycle lock she'd brought, squeezing epoxy into the lock to slow down the security personnel she was sure would soon be coming.

Then Katya took the flowers, pushed them through the gate, and perched her box of cookies and a poem where they could easily be seen. "I was worried about getting shot," she explained. "If nothing else, it would take them an extra 10 minutes to defuse the box of cookies before going any further."

Later, Katya explained the logic of her activities a bit more bitterly:

> I was afraid that the guards would respond to an alarm—that there might be these soldiers dashing in with their automatic weapons, and it would be like Kent State, where young panicky men who had been through boot

camp and had a lot of brainwashing were suddenly faced with an emergency and did what they were trained to do, which was pull the trigger. I didn't want to be the target. I thought one way to get around that was to have them come across the flowers, poem, and cookies first, anything to distract them and make them stop and think for a few minutes before they went swarming in there.

Fearing she had very little time, maybe no more than three minutes, Katya Komisaruk set to work. "The computer system I trashed was in five wardrobe-sized cabinets. I used my crowbar to haul out all the chips. I piled them on the floor, jumped up and down, and did a dance over them."

One cabinet presented more of a problem. As she thought about filling a wastebasket with water to dump over it, Katya spied four fire extinguishers. She started emptying them onto the remaining machine. When she threw the switch on, "it sizzled and popped and shorted everything," Katya said.

Before she began her destruction, Komisaruk had attempted to communicate the motivations that would form her defense. "I had priorities," she explained. She took the spray paint she had brought and began painting "First strike," "Nuremberg", "International Law" and "Geneva Convention" over all the surfaces of the machines. "This will probably be the most litigiously grounded crime in your book," Katya later told me from jail in Spokane, Washington. "It was designed with the intent and expectation that it would go to court." This purpose explained the references to the Nuremberg Principles and other international law concepts Katya was busily spray painting. "I believed it would be very important to prove my state of mind as I destroyed these machines," she explained. "I thought it was a very clever strategy. I knew they would be taking pictures of all the machines to show the destruction, and I was trying to make sure they couldn't take a picture like that without getting some of my writing. . . . Out of over 150 photographs," Katya continued, "only 6 or 8 avoided my writing about the Nuremberg Principles. Those, of course, were the ones the prosecution sent to the jury."

Komisaruk finally stopped when she was exhausted, walked away from Vandenberg, and hitchhiked back home to San

Francisco. She was a mess. "I was utterly sweaty and disheveled," she recalled. "Although I've recovered somewhat from being a 'Princess'—my nails were ruined! The thing I wanted most was a shower and breakfast."

The next day a press release appeared announcing, "Peace Activist Destroys Satellite Control Center, Gives Self Up, Press Conference Noon Wednesday, San Francisco Federal Building."

The release summarized Katya's motives, saying that she "explains her actions by invoking the Nuremberg Principles of individual responsibility for government policies." Katya had chosen the NAVSTAR system as her target because "the NAVSTAR satellites, as part of the U.S. first-strike weapon system, make possible the deliberate killing of millions of people." She was quoted further as saying, "You're a party to mass murder if you don't get out there and try to stop it. It's better to destroy a few machines than to let those machines destroy millions of people."

"This was not a symbolic protest," Katya told me when I asked about the role the computer system played in her action. "I'm not a technophobe pleading with generals not to burn my baby. My reaction is not an emotional one based on the fear of destruction, but the result of analysis," the Berkeley MBA said. "I'm a strategic planner, I've studied programming, and worked with programmers. I was playing with a computer just before I came to speak with you," she added.

"The computer did not represent technology, the military, or computers in general. I was attacking NAVSTAR," she continued. Following the lead of Plowshares originator, Father Daniel Berrigan, Katya's commitment was to destroying instruments of war. "That computer is the equivalent of a sword," she explained. The Bible talks of beating swords into plowshares and pursuing war no more.

Though not symbolic, the action was certainly dramatic. "By turning myself in," Katya told an Australian reporter, "it reached some people who wouldn't otherwise listen if they didn't perceive that someone felt seriously enough to risk getting locked up for 20 years. They may think, 'Oh, the poor girl, such a nice young thing. She is going to be old by the time she gets out. I wonder what it was she cared about so much.'"

THE PRINCESS AND THE EMPEROR

When she appeared in court on October 25, Katya knew she faced a key motion possibly more important than her trial. If she lost this motion, there would be little hope of escaping jail and not even much opportunity to express her reasons for destroying the computer. At the very least, the hearing would provide an opportunity to educate the media and, in turn, the public about the dangers NAVSTAR represented.

Outside the Los Angeles Federal Courthouse, Leonard Weinglass, Katya, and several other lawyers and law clerks held a press conference for the 50 or so supporters and members of the media gathered on the steps. "Essentially, our argument is one of crime abatement," Weinglass explained. "There is a conspiracy going on to engage in the threat of first-strike war. Katya's acts were an attempt to abate that crime." Members of the group cheered at the end of the press conference, then filed peacefully into the courtroom of Judge Rea.

"We can no longer bring [military systems like NAVSTAR] under control," Weinglass argued to Judge Rea, claiming that NAVSTAR was the linchpin of a governmental strategy for first-strike capability in nuclear war. Katya had read *First Strike* by Richard Aldridge and found his work convincing and important. Aldridge, who retired from the military after many years of work on nuclear weapons systems, argued that NAVSTAR is essential to a first strike because of the accuracy with which it allows the system to pinpoint the location of Soviet missile silos.

The NAVSTAR system relies on 18 orbiting satellites to broadcast signals to users on Earth. The Air Force is reportedly planning to buy as many as 26,000 terminals for use aboard ships, airplanes, submarines, helicopters, and tanks with troops in the field.

U.S. Attorney Manella rejected the defense arguments, claiming that NAVSTAR was a navigational system used by aviators and sailors as well as by troops wanting to pinpoint their own locations. She dismissed the argument that the system was a weapon of aggression which needed to be destroyed. "That's like calling a typewriter a weapon of destruction because it can be used to write the attack order."

Judge Rea was unwilling to allow Katya Komisaruk to present evidence to explain that she had destroyed the NAVSTAR computer to prevent greater crime. A four-day trial ended November 16, 1987, with the jury finding Katya guilty of one count of destroying government property. (The sabotage count had been dismissed by the government, making it harder for Katya to introduce evidence of her motivations.)

Beaten but unbowed, Katya appeared in January for sentencing and challenged Judge Rea's fairness and that of the legal system.

As she stood to address the court, Katya knew that she was about to receive a lengthy sentence. She decided to follow the Ghandian idea of "speaking truth to power." "Sometimes, if you are vulnerable in the face of someone with power over you," she explained to me, "the conscience of that power wakes up."

Even if she could not bring about a change in Judge Rea's attitude, Katya felt it important to tell the truth about her trial as she saw it. She felt silenced by court orders forbidding her to refer to international law, the Nuremberg principles, and other recognized bases for resistance to government actions one feels to be illegal.

Given the chance to make her statement, she said:

> I'm in a delicate position. I believe I am expected to plead for understanding, for mercy . . . and the stakes are very high. What does one say to ward off the nightmare of ten years in prison? . . .
>
> I don't think we can have an honest dialogue, because I stand here below your platform and I'm afraid of you . . . and my stomach hurts and my mouth is dry and my heart is pounding and I wish I were anywhere but your courtroom. Yet there's one thing that bothers me more than my fear of what punishment you're going to pronounce. And that's the fact that I made a coward's choice during my trial. Like the sycophants who assured their naked emperor that he was beautifully dressed, I pretended that the trial was a fair and just proceeding. I was so intimidated by this huge courtroom, by all the marshalls and officials, by the formal language and

ceremony, and by you, Your Honor, that I failed to speak the truth. I never really stated just how ludicrous a proceeding this was. . . .

Your robes and bench are transparent, Your Honor. They cannot cover up injustice. They can only hide it for a while.

The judge was not visibly moved, sentencing Katya to five years in federal prison and ordering $500,000 restitution for the wrecked computer.

IN JAIL

Though she is in jail, Katya's cause continues. The White Rose Collective, a group of citizens who formed in support of Katya after her White Rose action, corresponds with thousands of supporters around the world. "Perhaps it's poetic justice," one of their recent appeals for funds reads, "that the mail generated by destroying an Air Force computer makes us dependent on a computer to respond. . . . Our mailing list has grown to include almost 2,300 individuals and organizations."

While maintaining a "level of simmering indignation" at the humiliations she experiences daily in prison, Katya works to maintain a "conscious attitude." "The greatest tragedy of all," she believes, "is if you brainwash yourself. You have to remember that the real battle isn't the day-to-day struggle to get petty privileges from bureaucrats in uniform, it's to retain your integrity." She continues to urge others to take more activist roles. "People have got to go march, speak in churches, do what they can . . . we can reverse the arms race," she says, "if enough people will just stand up and say no."

Komisaruk plans to go to law school after her release in 1991. Presently she writes essays, speaks with media representatives, and corresponds with her supporters.

A letter sent to those supporters in March 1988 expresses the spirit which seems to buoy her:

It's easier now that I've been moved to this prison camp . . . but it's still full of guards and cameras and many rules. And they've cut down all the trees inside the compound. In every direction one has an unobstructed view of the fence and barbed wire which closes us in. It's ugly. So I don't look at it very much. Instead, I gaze upon the huge pile of letters all of you have sent. . . . The guards stalk up and back, counting us every few hours. I've ceased to look up as they go past. I have too much to do and better things to think about. I still wish I had someone to hold me, but words can go where arms cannot . . . and in your letters are all the attention and affection anyone could wish for. . . .

Thank you again for your letters and financial assistance. They cut through these fences like a good pair of boltcutters, allowing me to remain

Unconfined,

Katya.

CHAPTER 14

POLITICS II

JAN HANASZ: THE POLISH TV PIRATE

I went to Torun, Poland, one rainy morning a few years ago, to meet my favorite computer criminal: the astronomer and Polish television pirate, Jan Hanasz.

A paragraph in the *Los Angeles Times* had caught my eye more than a year before. The article related that Poland's leading space scientist, Jan Hanasz, and three colleagues went on trial, "accused of having interrupted a state television transmission . . . to urge voters to boycott elections . . . "

Suddenly the newspaper caught my attention.

"They allegedly used a home computer, a synchronizing circuit, and a transmitter to flash messages on television screens."

A Polish computer crime! An opportunity to visit a friend and colleague and imagine myself as an investigative reporter. This was the kind of story I could do something with.

And I had. Now, in the summer of 1987, I was on my way to interview Jan Hanasz as part of the research for a story on underground computing in Poland. His, I was to learn, was but one example of several ways that computers were making life easier for the Polish movement known as Solidarity.

Jacek, a man in his mid-30s, and droll, drove, talked, and pointed out the sights as we approached the city of Torun, the ancient home of Copernicus. Despite occasional jokes, Jacek was depressing, distressing, and deep in his gloom. He was cynical about the Soviet Union, doubtful about glasnost, despairing about Poland. "The only way to live in this system is to cheat," he said angrily. "The gas station attendant mixes ethyl and diesel gasoline. He sells the ethyl he has left over to people who have no government-issued ration coupons—at a premium, of course. The truck driver gets a broken part, replaces a good one with it, sells the good one, and brings his truck in for repair.

"The government creates rules," Jacek continued, "partly to control us. If you follow all the rules you're exhausted and poor. If you cheat, you're vulnerable to being co-opted. If you want to get meat, for instance, you'll find that there are extra ration books available for people who are in the government's favor."

The scenery was postcard-pretty as we drove. Horse-drawn carts loaded with great mounds of hay passed us on the road.

Jacek was amused that I was curious about computer crime in Poland. He laughed about Polish computing. "Yeah! They started getting them [computers] in the 70s. Part of the industrialization. I've heard about boxes of them sitting in the sun where the managers had no idea what to do with them. We borrowed up to our ears from the West, built things that didn't work, and wound up worse than before."

What a contrast from Jacek's dour driving to arrive at the office of Jan Hanasz and experience hospitality, grace, and hopefulness from this philosopher of political piracy.

A gentleness and calm surrounded this man. A friendly smile, a supportive glance, and Hanasz put me at ease. He was very open-faced and radiant. His thin, gray hair peeked around the red-framed glasses at his ears.

Hanasz's office at the Copernicus Astronomical Center in Torun was a bit larger and older than most I'd seen in the United States, but otherwise it was quite similar. Paper predominated, and two computers were on.

I'd come to Poland to learn about underground computer use, and the professor obliged me beyond my wildest dreams. He told me of DES (Data Encryption Standard) encryption for information going between Solidarity centers and individuals in Poland. He filled me in on the word processing programs used to prepare articles for publication , and on database programs used to organize Solidarity's files and make them easier to destroy. "I remember raids when I'd be eating files, everyone else would be eating, and the police were at the door." Now, Hanasz smiled, "I'd just press a disk to my chest and bend it."

Pacing at the blackboard, Hanasz proceeded to demonstrate his own contribution to the Solidarity effort, a spectacular computer crime. Twice within two weeks, he had sent a message to those of the 120,000-plus residents of Torun who were watching the evening news. "Enough price increases, lies, and repressions. Solidarity Torun," said the first message. The second read, "It is our duty to boycott the election," and then displayed the stylized version of the Solidarity name.

He had done it, Hanasz explained, by performing the equivalent of electronic hitchhiking on the Polish television network's airwaves. As an astronomer, he was more used to dealing with waves traveling through the air than the average computer user. After three months of planning, Hanasz and three colleagues had created an electronic system that could produce television signals, synchronize them with the signals of Polish state television, and aim them in the same path as the television network.

"There is a psychological phenomenon which allows us to join two different images we see on a television screen into a single picture," Hanasz told me. As a result, it was possible for the message to appear with much of the strength of the regular television program.

The key to his communication, Hanasz explained, was a form of synchronization. Unless the messages he was sending out were synchronized with the Polish TV station's signals, the plan would not work.

Hanasz, Zygmunt Turla, Leszek Zalewski, and Piotr Lukaszewski were charged with possession of an unlicensed radio transmitter and publication of materials that could cause public unrest.

The details of their action were summarized in the sentence handed down in Department 2 of the Regional Court of Torun:

> A picture transmitted by the official Polish television station was being received on a Neptune 150 television set. Vertical and horizontal synchro-

nization pulses were being input to a digital device controlling and working with a DX-spectrum microcomputer and a transmitter. The digital device caused the microcomputer to time its generation of signals in synchronization with those of the government station, allowing television viewers to receive both the government signal and the Solidarity signal at the same time.

Thus, while watching the evening news (jokingly referred to as the evening comedy hour by many Poles), many of the residents of a suburb of Torun saw the Solidarity message. The prosecutor claimed that as a result voting was much poorer in Torun than in the surrounding area. Hanasz would not take all the credit for the downturn in voting, noting that there were leaflets, speeches, and underground newspaper articles also urging Poles to boycott the elections. But this, he agreed, was the most spectacular action; and, he smiled, "People like spectacular actions."

Hanasz warmed to the task of explaining to me why he took the action he did. He was a strong advocate of taking one's political identity seriously, and he railed against those who voted when they did not approve of the elections or the government. "The government controls everything," he said. "If someone votes, he doesn't lose only for himself, he loses for the nation."

Hanasz estimated that more than 50 percent of the Poles had voted in the 1985 elections, despite efforts like his. He sternly characterized this percentage as "terrible". "If people don't believe in the government, they shouldn't vote", he said. The prosecutor would later argue that the text of Hanasz's message had been sent at "a time of great unrest for the city and the country." The question of voting was far from trivial, as American readers might easily assume.

Not everyone in Poland was willing to follow Hanasz's advice in the message. "People are frightened even of their shadow," Hanasz sighed. "People are always blaming 'them,' " he went on. "They complain about what 'they,' [the government] are doing, but they won't take action." For Hanasz, the situation was clear: "The government isn't worth supporting.

But people aren't used to having clear signals. They prefer to see mixed signals, which allow them to cooperate with the government."

As an example of why his fellow Poles resisted Solidarity's call for a vote boycott, Hanasz pointed to his own daughter's situation. Before the election, he said, his daughter wanted a passport to go abroad. Since the government lists those who vote, she was in a difficult situation. She knew of people who did not vote and then were denied passports. "No one tells you the reason you've been denied a passport is because you didn't vote," Hanasz explained. "You never know why these repressions take place. People vote just in case. It's the same thing if you want a building permit or a shop license."

In response to these fears, Hanasz urged his fellow Poles to act courageously. His daughter didn't vote, and she received her passport two weeks later. "I claim that in most cases this is true," Hanasz asserted.

Even when a citizen is sanctioned for failing to be sufficiently loyal, the astronomer suggested, the punishment is worth the price. "I feel much more free, resisting the government," he said. "I cannot go abroad, cannot go higher in my work, but I feel free. It depends on your attitude. If you want to have too much, you are never free."

Freedom is a revolutionary concept to Hanasz. "If many people were thinking this way, the government could do nothing." Instead, he found that people were constantly comparing themselves to those in Western Europe and wanting better standards of living. "This makes them support the government," he explained. Then he smiled and shrugged: "But these are normal people, I'm tolerant of them."

The first time he pirated the airwaves, Jan Hanasz was not frightened. "You don't think about consequences then," he explained. "I was frightened afterwards," he added, "knowing that sometime it had to end." He felt prepared. "There's no fighting without victims," he said.

Hanasz's fears were justified. The first time he and his colleagues transmitted their message, it was seen but they were not caught. Policeman Jozef Medzik saw it and read the text.

The next time, Hanasz and his associates were not so fortunate. Probably the victims of gossip about their unusual feat, Hanasz and the others were arrested September 14, 1985.

On that date, Polish police officers went to the flat from which they believed the transmissions were coming. "They knocked for quite some time at the door," Hanasz recalled, "and then decided to use force." This proved unnecessary. Hanasz opened the door, showing the officers several people packing electronic equipment and a television in plastic, one of them on the balcony taking apart a television antenna. The power supply for the transmissions was on a bed in another room, near a transformer plugged into the wall. A Sanyo computer and a tape recorder lay on a table nearby.

For the next three months, Hanasz was held in jail without being allowed any contact with his wife or attorney. He was questioned continually, as the authorities tried to find out if others had helped in his broadcast. After another month's delay, the case went to trial in January 1986. The pirates' lawyers, like lawyers dealing with a computer crime case anywhere, did their best. "At the start," Hanasz remembered, "it all looked obvious. However, the defense attorneys did a good job of complicating it."

However, all four men were found guilty. In determining their sentences, the judge noted that the defendants were well-respected scientists, each the author of several scientific achievements and the recipient of many prizes. Each received probation and was required to pay a fine of less than 100 U.S. dollars. Though much more onerous than a similar fine would be in the United States, the fines were considered fairly light.

"I didn't imagine the amount of noise our case would generate," Hanasz laughed. "Our colleagues worked on defending us, a Congress of intellectuals discussed it in January, and we began to get newspaper clippings from West Berlin, France, Great Britain, and Israel." Six months later, an amnesty was declared for all political offenders. Hanasz's case was considered political, so the punishment was ended and everyone's records expunged.

Returning to work at the University, Hanasz had to step down to a lower level of responsibility. (He had been the Principal

Investigator on a joint project with the Soviet Union involving experimentation with satellites.) Six months more passed, and in January 1987 he returned to his former position after "quite a fight in the Academy," as he described it. "People who officially say they don't support the government have a hard time being seen as loyal," he said without a trace of irony. However, although he was restored to his original post, Hanasz said the project was much smaller than it had been before his arrest.

WAS JAN HANASZ A HERO?

The last time we met, I was curious about the role that Jan Hanasz felt he had played. "I'm not a hero," he said. "In the underground there are people risking their lives all the time without being known. When they make a mistake and get attention—then they become heroes. This is a paradox." He reminded me of Father Jerzy Popieluszko, the priest who had been killed by the Polish police. "When you are working in the underground," Hanasz explained, "you are prepared that some-one can 'break your leg.'"

Returning from Torun with Jacek, I saw the bridge over the Vistula River from which the priest's body had been thrown by the Polish police. No more comment was necessary.

EPILOGUE

This chapter was written at a time of enormous change in Poland. Tasdeusz Mazowiecki, the first non-Communist to ever head a Communist nation, had just been chosen as Poland's Prime Minister. This was the latest of a series of revolutionary changes suggesting that Jan Hanasz was correct, if not pre-scient, in his prediction that the Communist government of Poland could not survive without the support of the Polish people. In 1987, no one I spoke with even hinted of a hope that such dramatic change could come with such speed. The under-ground is now part of the establishment, and I can't wait to go back to Poland and find out what that means for people like my companion Jacek and my favorite pirate, Jan Hanasz.

One thing is clear with the hindsight of history—Hanasz's feat has all the hallmarks of a classic computer crime. It mixed courage, impact, and significance, contributing in a spectacular way to Poland's evolution into a formerly Communist-controlled country. Before events in Hungary, East Germany, Bulgaria, Romania, and Czechoslovakia complemented the successes of Solidarity, this was a unique distinction in world politics. Hanasz's faith that even Communist governments can be toppled if they lack popular support has received spectacular vindication. His crime put one of the first cracks in the 'Iron Curtain', helping set the stage for the opening of the Berlin Wall.

CHAPTER 15

POLITICS III

OLIVER NORTH VERSUS TELL-TALE TECHNOLOGY

Like Jan Hanasz, Oliver North opposed Communism. As most of us saw on the evening news, the handsome yet vapid Marine, sat bolt upright and proud while he admitted having lied to keep his anti-Communist activities secret. Like Katya Komisaruk, North was willing to break the law for a cause he believed in. Fawn Hall, his secretary, expressed what seems to have been the reigning political philosophy in North's office when she responded to a question from Congressman Foley. She said, "sometimes you have to go above the written law."

North's relationship to computer technology differed from Komisaruk and Hanasz's in a crucial way. Hanasz and Komisaruk wanted to be heard; they took advantage of the spectacular capabilities of computers to communicate their political messages to a larger audience. However, Lt. Colonel Oliver North wanted to escape detection, so he took advantage of what he perceived to be the security of a computerized electronic mail system to shield his actions from public—or congressional—view. North sought deniability, not accessibility.

Although not focusing on his use of the PROFS computer system, a jury evaluated Lt. Colonel North's efforts to conceal his activities. North was found guilty of the criminal offense of "destroying, altering, or removing documents" along with two other charges in the trial that concluded in late 1989. His conviction demonstrates the importance of an information policy in our information age. Increasingly, computers are being used to create, store, and communicate documents like those North tried to conceal. Thus, his case can serve as a warning of the dangers of similar computer crimes looming in the future.

In short, North's crime was an attempt to steal history. It is significant for those who care about computer security because Lt. Colonel North attempted to use a computer to cover his tracks. Though only a part of North's unsuccessful cover-up, the PROFS computer system that North used demonstrates the key role that computerized communications play in the operation of government.

How can we protect these systems from being used improperly to destroy important information, yet use them to implement those valid governmental policies that require secrecy? The ongoing litigation over some of the information in the PROFS system suggests that these are long-term issues that will create challenging problems for those committed to defending the security of governmental information.

THE COVERUP BEGINS

In August 1985, congressional interest in the role Oliver North played on behalf of the Contras was mounting Lee Hamilton, chairman of the House Intelligence Committee and Congressman Michael Barnes addressed inquiries on the topic to the National Security Council. In the same month the Center for National Security Studies made a request under the Freedom of Information Act (FOIA) for "copies of all documents from October 1984 to the present concerning contacts of Colonel Oliver North and other staff members of the National Security Council (NSC) with the Nicaraguan Contras, including any documents concerning the propriety of such contacts." The NSC replied to the request claiming that a search of its "institutional files" did not produce any such documents.

These requests, made 15 months prior to the first revelation of the Iran Contra affair, did not go unnoticed. Lt. Colonel North told Congressional Investigator James Nields, "my name surfaced in connection with, in some cases half-way accurate, and in some cases wild and spurious allegations, about my role in support of the Nicaraguan resistance."

Beginning in August of 1985, North stopped writing documents relating to his support of the Contras. In his congressional testimony in response to questioning by James Nields, North explained the reason for his decision:

NIELDS:

I take it you stopped putting these memoranda in the system because of a problem that arose out of the fact that Congress had asked to look at the documents?

NORTH:

Exactly.

NIELDS:

And, you didn't want to show Congress the documents in the system?

NORTH:

I didn't want to show Congress a single word on this whole thing.

North did, however, communicate with his superiors, including John Poindexter and Robert McFarlane. He told Nields: "There came a time when I stopped sending up what we call 'in system memoranda.' I continued to communicate with my superiors using the PROF system. . . ."

North's use of the PROF system was facilitated by a Private Blank Check PROFS memo written by John Poindexter. "We . . . wanted to avoid more restrictive legislation," Poindexter testified in his deposition to the Select Committee to Investigate Covert Arms Transactions with Iran, "and so any activity that he would have been involved with on Central America, we wanted to keep very compartmented." (It appears, "compartmented" means known to as few people as possible.)

Poindexter had been involved in the installation of the PROFS system used to "compartment" North's communications. In a deposition, Poindexter testified: "When I came [to the NSC as military assistant to then National Security Advisor Richard Allen] we didn't have any computers. . . Eventually, practically every staff member on the NSC staff had a terminal."

The proliferation of terminals led to the need to restrict access to the national security advisor:

> We put some software into the system so that Mr. McFarlane and I could send out messages to anybody on the staff directly . . . The reverse was not true. Every staff member could not reply or send a message . . . directly to Mr. McFarlane or me. . . [But] if we sent a staff member a note directly, the system was designed in such a way that this staff member could reply directly and that note would not be intercepted by the executive secretary . . . Lt. Colonel North was working on some very sensitive issues for us, terrorism, hostages, Central America, the Iranian project eventually. So rather than change my direction as to who could communicate back, the way I got around the system that I installed, was to send Colonel North a PROF's note. The subject was "Private Blank Check." I said, if you want to respond directly to me or, if you want to send me a note directly and nobody else can see it, then respond to this note. So he kept that note in his system. When he wanted to reply directly, he sent it.

Asked whether the Private Blank Check was set up in response to the congressional inquiries from Barnes and Hamilton, Poindexter replied, "Well, indirectly, yes."

In addition to "compartmenting" North, Poindexter was involved in the destruction of incriminating documents. Poindexter told the congressional investigators of a key meeting leading to North's destruction of documents:

> Mr. DeGraffenreid, the special assistant to the President for intelligence affairs, came in to see me and to indicate his concern for Colonel North's exposure on Central America. At that time there were a lot of stories in the newspaper. He wanted to know if I recalled that there were several memoranda in System IV, which was our paperwork system, to keep track of intelligence matters and other sensitive issues on Central America that would be very damaging to the Administration, that talked about the details of supporting the Contras. I told him I didn't recall the memos specifically, but I did recall back in early '84 or '85 that Colonel North had sent some memos to Mr. McFarlane and laid out the status of funding of the Contras . . . The clear intent of Mr. DeGraffenreid's visit was to figure out a way to get rid of those memos. I told him . . . to go talk to Colonel North and see what you could work out . . . That was probably some time in October [1986] . . . after Hasenfus was shot down.

DeGraffenreid took steps to retrieve the memos. He asked June Barlett to retrieve six original System IV documents from the files. Barlett gave Brian Merchant a list of the documents that DeGraffenreid had requested. Merchant had become the supervisor of System IV documents in October 1986. Merchant testified to providing these documents to Oliver North. After North got them, they were never seen again.

Lt. Colonel Oliver North was found guilty of the destruction, alteration, or removal of four of the documents that Merchant had taken. The documents were among those requested by the Center for National Security Studies in its August 1985 Freedom of Information Act request. The National Security Archives [the Archives] claims, in court papers: ". . . [i]f these requests had been properly responded to, the controversy of Iran-Contra would have been revealed to the public much earlier than it was. Indeed, the very documents that Oliver North shredded and the files that he deleted from the PROFS computer system are precisely the documents that the Center had requested under the FOIA and that the NSC had claimed did not exist.

THE TELL-TALE TECHNOLOGY

PROFS is one of those ubiquitous acronyms which can keep nonusers of technology from understanding what users are talking about. PROFS is an abbreviation of IBM's Professional Office System. A PROFS system was installed for the National Security Council staff in 1982 and became fully operational in April 1985. Its electronic mail features allow staff members sitting at their computer terminals to create and transmit documents which became part of the computer's data base. As George von Eron, a government representative, pointed out:

> Over the past few years, NSC staff members have come to use electronic mail a great deal in their daily work. It is far quicker than regular interoffice mail, and it is less intrusive than a telephone call . . . Moreover, since the system is cleared to handle classified information, it often can be used to exchange information more easily than a 'secure' telephone call. It saves time and enhances efficiency of both the NSC professional staff and the NSC support staff.

In 1983, while then Vice President Bush's Chief Deputy, Craig Fuller wrote of the advantages of electronic mail in an office automation system:

> We schedule meetings, change schedules, announce agenda items, and distribute briefing papers, press guidance, talking points for speakers. Virtually everything we send needs to be received and acted upon quickly and so it is transmitted automatically.

The PROFS system not only covered important topics, but offered the NSC system users a technology that they believed was secure. This belief was mentioned in the Tower Commission's description of the PROFS notes as "conversations by computer, written at the time events occurred, and presumed by the writers to be protected from disclosure. In a sense, they provide a firsthand, contemporaneous account of events."

In his congressional testimony, North said: "We all sincerely believed that when we sent a PROF message to another party, and punched the button "delete" that it was gone forever. Wow, were we wrong." As described later, North confused erasing a table of contents with erasing the content of the computer system.

PROFS AS AN INSTRUMENT OF CRIME

The PROFS notes created by Oliver North, as part of his efforts to conceal violations of the Boland Amendment prohibiting aid to the Contras, made the PROFS system work like an instrument of crime. We can certainly look at his use of the system to consider the implications of sophisticated electronic mail systems for responsible computing by our government.

The PROFS system reminds me of "flash paper." When I first joined the Los Angeles District Attorney's office, I prosecuted my share of petty bookmakers. The administrative vice officers who investigated these cases knew they had to capture the flash paper on which bets were recorded before the bookies threw the paper in water, causing the betting evidence to dissolve without a trace. Unless I understood that flash paper was evidence of bookmaking I was not likely to win my betting cases.

I had long been comfortable with flash paper when I had to forget about it. Moving ahead with the times, the bookies of the late 80s use computers instead of flash paper. Keep the current bets in a word processing file, as soon as you hear the officers beating on your door press reset and all evidence of those bets disappears.

Just as the shift from flash paper to computers changed illegal gambling procedures, the shift to electronic media like the PROFS system has changed our government. As this chapter is written, the legal status of PROFS memoranda remains unresolved. Pending litigation questions the application of federal records laws to the PROFS memos. Like North's use of the PROFS as part of his cover-up, the litigation demonstrates that our government has not yet developed adequate information policies to reflect its use of electronic media.

Governmental information policies existed before the PROFS system was installed. Whether or not they were adequate at that time, the policies now need to be reexamined in light of the new uses to which electronic mail can be—and is—put.

When you consider the difference between electronic mail and a telephone, the need for new policies becomes clear. A PROFS system automatically captures the content of communications it transfers in a way that a telephone system does not. Information policies developed when telephones were used are likely to be silent on the question of what should be done with the stored communication data that a telephone system would not produce. Such policy is not only the concern of punctilious, modern librarian-types sometimes called archivists or record managers. It is crucial to the workings of historians and those working to hold government accountible for what it does.

As an example of the significance of information policy, consider the testimony of Robert McFarlane at North's criminal trial. Directed by Congress to look for records that would demonstrate whether Lt. Colonel North had any contacts with the Nicaraguan Contras in violation of the Boland amendment, NSC personnel searched only the "official files," not North's "personal files," McFarlane said.

The "personal files" left unsearched included, according to McFarlane, PROFS messages, copies of official memoranda, records of telephone contacts, schedules, and calendars. North would ultimately destroy 60 boxes of these "personal files" without sanction.

When asked why Colonel North's own files were not searched by the agency in response to Congress' request for information, McFarlane said: "I don't know. I think the staff officer who had made the judgment would probably tell you that it was a matter of FOI [Freedom of Information] precedent and a routine established over the years."

It was the policy of the National Security Council to respond to all FOIA requests for information by searching only its "institutional" files, much as it searched only the "official" files of Oliver North. Since most of the activities undertaken by the NSC did not generate information which wound up in institutional files, this policy allowed for a great deal of secrecy.

Consider the irony of it! The Freedom of Information Act has become a source of authority for withholding information that could bear on matters central to national security. Instead of serving as a populist tool to allow citizens to discover the previously hidden operations of government, the Act has become a bulwark of bureaucracy. Its multitude of exceptions provide a virtual handbook for achieving enormous degrees of governmental secrecy. It often takes organizations with the size, sophistication, and persistence of the National Security Archive to fight bureaucratic evasions such as these if any success under the FOIA is to be achieved.

Instead of providing a minimum level of compliance with request for information, the Freedom of Information Act was used as an excuse for failing to comply with critically important Congressional investigations. Governmental information policy should distinguish between Congressional inquiries and requests under the FOIA.

HOW TECHNOLOGY TRIPPED-UP OLIVER NORTH

At the risk of injecting undue levity into the discussion of this very important topic, the evidence of both Watergate and Contragate is that a knowledge of technology is essential to an effective coverup. Just as the tape recorder was Nixon's undoing, the PROFS memos proved to be more resilient than Oliver North had thought, providing key information about the Iran-Contra affair.

On November 25, the day that then Attorney General Meese announced the connection between the Iran initiative and the Contras, White House Communications Agency Master Sergeant Kelly Williams changed the password to Oliver North's PROFS account. Backup tapes for the dates of November 15, November 22, and November 29, 1986 were made shortly thereafter. Williams testified that according to the backup tapes, on November 15 there were 698 memos in North's file. On November 22 there were 737 memos. On November 29 there was one note—the Blank Check memo setting up direct communications between North and Poindexter. Somewhere between November 22 and November 25, it appears that Lt. Colonel North attempted to delete all of the PROFS notes remaining in his system except his "Blank Check."

Most of the PROFS notes recovered during the Iran-Contra investigation had never been printed out by North or anyone else. They were only preserved through the efforts of Congressional investigators. The Tower Committee had reconstructed several hundred of these notes by February 1987. Later that year, a "dump" of all of the information in the system led to the reconstruction of 96 additional PROFS notes. North's attempt to "erase" the PROFS notes had resulted only in erasing their address from the computer system. This meant that they could not be retrieved easily. But all those messages which had not been written over were still in the computer's memory. This allowed investigators to reconstruct the memos once they received the print-out of the entire contents of the memory.

The attempted destruction of a number of the PROFS notes is indicative of the belief that their publication would have been embarrassing to the administration, either because of resulting security exposures, evidence of wrongdoing on the part of the administration, or both. Fawn Hall clearly knew their importance. She had run into Colonel Earl's office in panic before the FBI came to search Oliver North's office. "I asked him if he would help me pull the PROFS notes" she told Congress, "and he did so . . . The PROFS notes were folded, and he was going to take them and put them in his jacket, and I turned to him and said, 'No, you shouldn't have to do this. I will do it' . . . I put them in my back . . . When I had completed putting the documents in my back I turned to him and asked if he could see any, and he said no."

WHAT THE PROFS PROVE

In a recent opinion concerning access to the PROFS notes, District Judge Charles Richey wrote:

> "The PROFS system achieved (and may continue to achieve) some notoriety in connection with the investigation and prosecution of the participants in the so-called Iran-Contra affair (some have referred to it as 'Iranamok'). It appears that certain participants sent PROFS messages containing the details of the scheme by which arms would be sold to Iran, with the proceeds diverted to the use of the Nicaraguan Contras. The exegesis of mysterious PROFS notes consumed much time during the congressional investigation of the matter as well as during the recently concluded criminal trial of Lt. Colonel Oliver North."

The first evidence, (albeit hearsay) the Congressional committees investigating the Iran-Contra Affair found concerning then Vice President Bush's position on the Iran initiative were found among 96 PROF notes which were reconstructed by the Joint Congressional Committee.

Another of the PROFS notes includes a comment from National Security Advisor John Poindexter. Poindexter stated in the note that even though the Secretaries of State and Defense opposed the Iran initiative, CIA Director Casey, Attorney General Meese, Chief of Staff Regan, and Poindexter were "fully on board this risky operation, but most importantly, President and VP are solid in taking the position that we have to try."

Those PROFS notes which have been recovered have been quite valuable to the many governmental investigations. More than a dozen chapters of the final Report of the Congressional Committees Investigating the Iran-Contra affair cited PROFS messages as key sources of information.

Gary Stern, an author of articles on the constitutional implications of the Iran-Contra affair, said in court papers that the PROFS notes produced as a result of an earlier lawsuit and from the Congressional investigations "showed . . . how the NSC engaged in the operational aspects of covert operations in Nicaragua, Iran, Central America, the Middle East, and other regions of the world."

LITIGATING INFORMATION POLICY

Stern, an ACLU lawyer, was but one of several litigants attempting to use the courts to compel our government to follow its information policies in a rational manner. The National Security Archive is the major organization currently involved in such litigation. Its efforts demonstrate the considerable resources, patience, and sophistication needed to litigate issues involving governmental information policy.

The National Security Archive describes itself as a "nonprofit, nonpartisan, public interest, scholarly research institute and library of declassified government documentation on national security policies and issues." The Archive's Iran-Contra Documentation Project has already collected, catalogued, and analyzed all of the PROFS notes released as a result of the Congressional and other investigations of the Iran-Contra affair. It produced a complete cross-referenced index to all the events and names mentioned in the notes and other Iran-Contra documents. In the beginning of 1989 the Archive published all of the Iran-Contra-related PROFS notes as part of a 30,000-page document set to be issued on microfiche with a two-volume catalog and index.

In the case of *Scott Armstrong et al. v. George Bush et al.*, the National Security Archive is trying to compel the NSC to preserve the PROFS notes that qualify as records in accordance with federal record laws. The Archive's papers describe its extensive use of the Freedom of Information Act. In the three and a half years of its existence up to February 1989 the Archive filed 2,500 FOIA requests to more than 150 different executive branch components. Documents resulting from these requests made up around 35 percent of their holdings at the beginning of 1989.

In the papers filed on the Archive's behalf, they argue that the National Security Council has made a "generic determination that information generated over the PROFS system does not constitute either a 'record' or a 'presidential record.' " The NSC has refused to specify whether various categories of documents such as interoffice mail, messages concerning the conduct of government business, calendars, schedules of meetings, drafts of documents, chronological lists of PROFS files, and distribution lists are considered records. Such a determination allows the NSC to avoid the Archive's demand that it comply with the relevant federal laws for these types of records. Governmental policy concerning governmental records is articulated in the Federal Records Act. The Presidential Records Act applies to records deemed "presidential records."

In September 1989, United States District Judge Charles Richey denied a government motion to dismiss the Archives' case. Instead, he granted the parties 90 days to engage in additional discovery, and ordered them to submit a joint memorandum by the beginning of 1990 with suggestions as to how to best proceed with the litigation.

HIDING BEHIND A COMPUTER

Robert McFarlane demonstrated his expectation that the record of the National Security Council's efforts in connection with the Contras would never come to light. In one of the deleted PROFS notes that was reconstructed, he wrote: "I hope to daylights that someone has been purging the [deleted] files on this episode."

Clearly the hopes of Robert McFarlane were not realized. The information policies of the National Security Council and other parts of the Executive Office of the President are still under judicial review. Thus the question of responsible computing by the government remains to be resolved. Writing on the implications of the Iran-Contra investigation for historians in a *Time* magazine essay, Walter Isaacson suggested that history is under attack: "Pity the poor historian," he wrote. "The wonders of modern technology have combined with the dynamics of government scandals to make his task next to impossible . . . Electronic memory shredders will, no doubt, be a feature of the next generation of DELETE keys."

Isaacson suggests that history needs our help. "One solution would be to make it once again respectable—perhaps even mandatory—to tape important discussions for the historical record." The advantages of recording our history have not been lost on those who investigated the Iran-Contra affair. The Tower Commission concluded that the decision-making process regarding the Iran initiative was lacking partly because it lacked a formal institutional record. The apparent failure to document NSC consultations and presidential decisions made it difficult to determine where the initiative stood, and to learn lessons from the record that could guide future actions." The Commission recommended: "the National Security Advisor must . . . ensure that adequate records are kept of NSC consultations and presidential decisions."

Isaacson would certainly agree. "Had the judgment of history been hovering over their shoulders, the architects of the Iran-Contra affair, for example, might have reflected a moment longer on the long-term implications of their actions," he suggests. "Indeed, the dulling of our historical sense could be the reason the U.S. needs so many special prosecutors these days."

At the same time, there is no question that certain government operations, deliberations, and overtures must be kept secret. History need not be immediately available, and reasonable delays before governmental records can be made public certainly make sense.

The generic refusal to separate information regarding crucial subjects from other information maintained in the PROFS materials files is a much less defensible position for the executive branch of our government to adopt. As our country attempts to develop safe and sane computer security policies through the Computer Security Act of 1987, the importance of this policy debate is heightened. It involves not only clarity about the application of laws like the Federal Records Act and the Presidential Records Act, but a strong commitment to having them observed.

John Poindexter demonstrated the practical problems in effectuating a historically sensitive information policy during his testimony before the Congress.

Congressman Jack Brooks noted that the Presidential Records Act says the President may dispose of presidential records that no longer have administrative, historical, informational or evidentiary value. It requires that the President obtain the views of the Archivist of the United States before disposing of presidential records. He asked Poindexter:

> "I wonder by chance, did you call the Archivist before ripping up [the December 5, 1985 finding signed by the President?]"
> Poindexter: Absolutely not, Mr. Brooks.
> Brooks: You didn't call him?
> Poindexter: The thought didn't even cross my mind.

I'm afraid it will take more than wise information policy to overcome the cynical embrace of "deniability" as the operating principle of covert governmental operations such as the Iran-Contra affair which is illustrated by Poindexter and North's actions.

A policy which encourages governmental employees to hide their activities from review ill serves a democratic nation. Accountability, not deniability, should be the advantage of using sophisticated computer systems like the PROFS system. Deniability is an abomination. Using computers to foster it is irresponsible computing.

CHAPTER 16

PIRACY

BERT VAN DEN BERG VERSUS THE PIRATES OF UCLA

Piracy puts the general problems of computer crime in perspective. It is probably the most spectacular form of computer crime in term of its widespread nature and economic impact. If Bert van den Berg is right, piracy is a $5-billion-a-year problem, making computer crime—at half a billion dollars a year—peanuts. Van den Berg calls an estimate of one illegal copy for every two legitimate copies conservative, since others put the number at thirty copies pirated for every one that's bought. As a small business owner, a big litigant, and a past pirate, van den Berg knows whereof he speaks.

Looking at van den Berg's experience will allow us not only a more inside view of the problem, but the opportunity to fashion a solution that will work. It is in the area of rights to software and data that our society is most confused. The forces for and against responsible computing are most evenly matched here, and consensus on a solution to the problem is farthest from being reached.

A SMALL BUSINESS OWNER EXPLAINS THE PIRACY TAX

To understand one aspect of the problem of computer program piracy, consider the mathematical analysis of Bert van den Berg. After five years of running BV Engineering, a software company primarily selling circuit analysis and graphics software to electronic engineers, van den Berg was pretty good at estimating his costs. He spent 69 percent of his sales revenues on advertising, labor, materials, rent, insurance, and other fixed costs.

If two illegal copies of his software were made for each paid copy, and if one quarter of those who copied it would have otherwise paid for it, van den Berg figured that he was losing a volume of customers equal to half of those he had. Were he able to sell those additional copies, he argued in a paper, he could "charge 23 percent less and still maintain the same level of profitability" his company already enjoyed.

The Computer and Business Equipment and Machine Association estimates the annual value of software sales in the United States at $20 billion. Applying van den Berg's calculations and assumptions, piracy within the U.S. becomes a $5 billion problem. The international price tag on piracy committed outside the U.S. is estimated at just a bit less—the International Trade Commission reported it as $4 billion. In an era when trade deficits and international economic competition are the most crucial types of competition around, losses to piracy play no small part in the difference between being a debtor and a creditor nation.

There is a growing call for action to resolve the problems of piracy on both the national and international levels, but little sign that anything has changed.

The problem may by deeper than pronouncements and even occasional lawsuits can address. It may be so pervasive that nothing short of a shift in values and a consequent shift in practice will make any impact at all. If slowness to change at home hampers our ability to fight piracy abroad, then those who most need the computer revolution to succeed should work toward solutions to the problem of piracy, rather than becoming part of the problem. In Bert van den Berg's case, the University of California did just the reverse by backing the apparent piracy of one of their employees. I wish they would heed the logic of van den Berg's call to responsibility.

His conclusion clearly states a value more evident in industry speech than action: "When someone copies a program illegally, they aren't just stealing from the rich like Robin Hood.

As likely they are stealing from small companies trying to make a decent profit for their efforts. Twenty-three cents on the dollar," van den Berg says, is "how much it costs you directly to support the people who steal our programs."

Van den Berg can speak from painful knowledge and subtle pride about a more hidden cost of computer piracy—the cost of trying to enforce one's rights to fight it.

At the time van den Berg sued UCLA, BV Engineering was a four-person operation. Two of those four people were Bert van den Berg and his wife Wilda. Bert designed the programs, hired the programmers to supplement his work, and made other executive decisions while his wife worked in the office. The other two members of the company were Ian James, van den Berg's director of marketing, and Steve Sauls, his software development and product support software person. BV had a product line that filled a 56-page catalog. The company grossed less than $250,000 that year.

In 1986, the company made two sales to UCLA that led to van den Berg's firsthand experience with the hidden costs of piracy. On January 29, 1986 UCLA bought two software programs and their documentation: ACNAP, a network analysis program, and LOCIPRO, a root locus program. About a week later, the university bought five additional programs and documentation.

As is common in the industry, van den Berg placed warnings on the programs indicating that they could only be used on a single computer at a single location. He also included registration cards featuring pledges that the users would not copy the software or documentation van den Berg had sold them. Additionally, van den Berg sent out applications for "site licenses" which would entitle the buyer of a program to make as many as 50 copies of a program. The site licenses cost $500.

On February 21, van den Berg received the registration cards for the programs they had purchased back from UCLA. He got a copy of an application for a site license, but not payment. Van den Berg was surprised. He knew from firsthand experience that UCLA would need more than one copy of each of his programs. Either they didn't realize they needed a site license, he thought, or they're planning to just make copies and not pay me. Van den

Berg sent a letter to UCLA reminding them of the requirements of the site licenses. He never heard back from UCLA.

But van den Berg did hear from the author of one of the programs he had sold to UCLA. The author had run across the program he had workea on and asked an electronic technician in the UCLA lab whether the lab had a site license for its use. He was told that they did.

Hearing this made Bert van den Berg mad. He called the technician who had signed the registration card and confronted him with the author's report. The technician denied having made any copies of the software from BV. In fact, "he was ranting and raving about greedy software writers," van den Berg recalled.

The situation allowed for no retreat, in van den Berg's mind. He sent a "nastygram" to the technician, informing the technician that he believed the program was being used at more than one site, that this was a violation of the license, and that UCLA had 30 days to pay and come into compliance with the license and the copyright law.

Receiving no reply, van den Berg then wrote to the university administration demanding payment for site licenses to his seven programs.

Still no action occurred. Van den Berg hired an attorney, filed suit, and began the painful and slow process of discovery. It was not without its rewards. Under oath, the technician testified that he had made 10 copies of each of the seven volumes of van den Berg's documentation, or 70 copies in all. He also admitted making 3 copies of each of the seven programs, or 21 in all.

Van den Berg's suit foundered on the provisions of the 11th Amendment. First the trial court then the appellate court for the Ninth Circuit ruled that he could not sue UCLA for damages for violation of his copyright to the seven programs. As a state entity, UCLA was able to take advantage of an apparent oversight in the drafting of the Copyright Act. Since there was no specific language in the act to allow damage suits against state instrumentalities like UCLA, the doctrine emerging in a number of copyright cases was that states could not be sued for damages if charged with violation of copyright. Since copyright suits can only be brought under federal law, the 11th Amendment means that the only remedy someone like van den Berg would have against piracy would be an injunction, and this would not gain him any damages, just prevent further copying.

After losing in the Ninth Circuit, van den Berg sought review by the U.S. Supreme Court. He had been joined by the Software Publishers Association, a trade group designed, among other reasons, to fight piracy. He also had help in the form of an *amicus curaii,* or friend-of-the-court brief. When the Supreme Court denied his request for a hearing, the anomaly of state immunity was left to Congress to resolve. In the words of the Ninth Circuit opinion, "We recognize that our holding will allow states to violate the federal copyright laws with virtual impunity. It is for Congress, however, to remedy this problem."

As I complete this chapter, H.R. 1131, a bill sponsored by Senators Kastenmeier and DeConcini, is pending in the Senate, having passed the House of Representatives. This bill would abolish state immunity from lawsuits seeking damages for violations of copyright.

Before attempting to gain Supreme Court review of his case in 1987, van den Berg estimated the total costs of his litigation at $50,000. The cost of responsible computing may be much higher.

THE GRAVER COST OF PIRACY

State immunity from software copyright violation damages is no trivial problem. Input, a data gathering and marketing research firm, put the size of the state and local government software market at $55 million in 1986 and $68 million in 1987. But UCLA's response to van den Berg's suit, I suggest, indicates a much graver problem—that of disregard for the principles of responsible computing. Such disregard by an institution of higher learning has even more serious implications when we consider that such institutions are training the computer scientists of tomorrow.

I am so vexed by this case that I challenge UCLA in print to justify its actions, with the publication of an open letter to UCLA:

Don't you teach ethics at UCLA?

In 1983 a high-school student named Ronald Mark Austin was convicted of computer crime for accessing computers at UCLA without permission. What message do you think you are sending to Mr. Austin when you show absolutely no respect for Bert van den Berg's software property rights?

Your employee acknowledged in a deposition that he made 10 copies of van den Berg's documentation and 3 copies of his programs without paying any site license fees. When a professor of computer science like UCLA's David Kay includes a section on ethics in his textbooks, do you expect his students to measure the actions of their university by the standards he is attempting to teach them? Or is there some new ethic developing, an ethic which says that what the business part of a university does is not to be judged by the rules taught students in the academic departments?

Don't you teach respect for the value of ideas?

Perhaps I'm aiming too high when I suggest that part of the goal of a university is to provide moral guidance to its students. Certainly in these paranoid and cynical times, one must consider the sensitivity of various political power groups before one attempts to influence the moral development of students. Behind the computer ethics crisis suggested by your apparent condonation of computer software piracy is a literacy crisis. It is bad enough that millions of Americans cannot read. It is worse if college students are getting the message that there may be little value in reading because their universities demonstrate no commitment to the value of intellectual property.

I don't think it is farfetched to say that the university as an institution shows less respect for the value of ideas than it used to. The growth of vocational curricula and the decline of the liberal arts curricula are well documented. The attitude that ignores the value of the literate underpinning of our culture also debases the value of all intellectual property, treating it as another product to be taken whenever one can get away with it. Wouldn't it have been shocking—and inspiring—if you had held a press conference after your lawyers told you about the 11th Amendment loophole, and you announced your intention to pay van den Berg anyway? Imagine the ripples of thought, discussion, debate, and possibly even moral action that might have occurred if you'd said, "We believe in the importance of copyright law. We know the importance of supporting the advancement of knowledge and ideas. The Copyright Act is designed to promote knowledge and ideas and we support that. We hope by our model to convince all other state agencies to also honor the Copyright Act by agreeing to be bound by it despite the loophole we could use. We do this because of our commitment to the importance of intellectual property." Wouldn't that have taken the world of copyright law by surprise! Wouldn't it have been wonderful to teach your students by example?

Even your business sense should have tempered your commitment to resisting Bert van den Berg's request for payment due. Before you decided to withhold the paltry $3,500 that Mr. van den Berg requested, did you ever talk with the people at University of California Press and ask them how much they would lose if other state agencies started copying their materials instead of buying them? Did you ask the folks in the computer science department how much the University of California makes on its own sales of software to state agencies? I'm willing to bet either figure is a lot more than $3,500. Have you noticed the wonderful irony here? Perhaps if, instead of trying to win the battle at hand, you had looked to the university's own financial, intellectual, and moral stake in the copyright law, you would not have been so quick to resist Mr. van den Berg's claim.

Do you teach the adversary system?

I realize that from a lawyer's perspective, what I'm saying seems like the most nonsensical of wimpery, a self-sacrificing ethic which could put many lawyers out of work. Giving the bar its due, I will concede that there are issues worth fighting for, even when settlement seems the more economical solution. But if it is suggested that the demands of the adversary system justify the nature of UCLA's resistance to Mr. van den Berg's claims, I must ask two questions.

First, I ask why this is an issue worth fighting for? Are you asserting some right to copy software in violation of the Copyright Act? Is there some higher good that is served by pirating programs when it is done on behalf of a state agency that is not served, when it is done on behalf of an individual, a corporation, or a federal agency doing the same work? Did you fight this case because your practice of piracy is so common that to pay Mr. van den Berg would be to invite hundreds of similar lawsuits by people whose software has been similarly ripped off?

If the answers to either of these questions is yes, the adversary system is not being served. These issues were left undecided when the courts based their rulings on the issue of sovereign immunity and did not even discuss the other points. If UCLA has a lot to lose by paying the people it pirates from, hadn't we better do something about making practice and preaching coincide?

Even if the goal of UCLA's resistance were to test the stretch of the 11th Amendment, why did it resist attempts to argue the issue by objecting to the *amicus curaii* briefs offered by representatives of the American Association of University Publishers (of which the University of California Press is a significant member)?

I assume that UCLA has put little or no thought into the questions I have raised in this letter. Lawyers are not taught much about restraining the power they might exercise, or about the ultimate benefits that may come from short-range "losses." This scares me. Making a federal case out of refusing to pay for pirating software scares me. I hope it is not too impertinent to suggest that a decision to exploit a loophole rather than address the merits of this case is behavior our society finds distasteful when practiced by lawyers representing street criminals. Is there a double standard which finds it acceptable to exploit such a loophole on behalf of an institution that is supposed to stand for the best in our culture?

How can we hope for the emergence of responsible computing when an institution our future computer science professionals attend defends itself from charges not much different than simple theft by running up high legal fees, exploiting loopholes, and refusing to acknowledge and make amends for its mistakes? What example have you set for future professionals at UCLA?

A JOLLY ROGER PIRATE CONFESSES

To compound the complexity of this case, Bert van den Berg is himself a confessed pirate. In his paper on the costs of piracy, van den Berg wastes no time in admitting his culpability. "Most of us know that software piracy exists," he writes. "Some of us, including myself, have participated at one time or another, and the excuses for doing so are endless."

When I spoke with him, van den Berg expanded on the theme. "I knew they were pirating copies at UCLA. Everyone does it. When I was at General Dynamics, I was a member of the 'Jolly Roger Software Club.'" This informal arrangement was what van den Berg calls an "underground railroad for software." "We had a whole network set up to distribute the stuff, most of which we got from JPL." Like many computer buffs, van den Berg took many programs and only later decided which he wanted to use. When he started his own software business he made sure to purchase legitimate copies of all the software he was using.

There's no false self-righteousness about Bert van den Berg, just a sense of outrage that UCLA wouldn't treat him fairly.

More essentially, I mention van den Berg's piracy to illustrate the point that UCLA's case is notable because it is so unexceptional. It is only one example of a practice that extends across the breadth of computing. Technological, educational, litigious, and media solutions have been tried consistently at least since off-the-shelf software became an important economic fact of life. None will work, I suggest, until our society reaches concensus about the *values* which should underlie a solution to the problem. This case demonstrates that our society has not yet reached that agreement. The Quaid case discussed in the next chapter suggests, however, that it may not be as far in the future as one reading this chapter might fear.

CHAPTER 17

PIRACY II

JERRY SCHNEIDER: PROTECTOR OF USERS' RIGHTS

When I speak, I often end with a challenge from the Talmud. "If I'm not for myself, who will be? If I'm only for myself, what am I? If not now, when?" In the first chapter I considered the career of Jerry Schneider, a man who moved from irresponsible computing to irresponsible systems analysis. As lucky irony would have it, I can devote this next-to-last chapter to another person named Jerry Schneider—this one devoted to responsible computing.

(So that I don't drive you crazy, I'll only talk about the Jerry Schneider who stands for responsible computing in this chapter. If I have to refer to the other one, I'll use the name he now calls himself, Jerome.)

I'm afraid that I cast a bit of doubt on Jerry Schneider's credentials just by beginning to research this book. A letter I wrote to one of the personal-computer throwaway newspapers, *Computer Currents*, explained that I was doing a book about computer criminals and asked for information. This letter led several people to call Jerry Schneider and ask what his name was doing on the short list of people I was seeking information on. It had been a while since people asked Jerry about his infamous namesake, though he had had difficulties with past job applications as a result of Jerome Schneider's activities.

Jerry Schneider has been in the forefront of a small cadre of user group leaders who are actually moving their user groups to action. Many user groups are seen as nothing more than excuses for widespread computer software piracy. Most focus primarily on sharing information on the technical capabilities of hardware and software that group members might use.

While a number of individuals have fought for the rights of consumers of computer products, Schneider has been among the most effective at mobilizing computer users to work as a group on issues of social import. The first such effort to attract my attention was the *amicus curiai* brief the Capital PC User Group filed in the case of *Vault Corporation* v. *Quaid Software.*

Before describing this action, we must take a detour and describe the legislative strategy that purported to combat piracy, and the numerous individual and group efforts to counter that strategy. All of these created the climate for the Capital PC User Group's efforts.

It is invigorating, in this age of anomie, yuppies, and nuclear despair, to learn that there are people who not only care about computing, but who have been able to turn their concern into effective action.

In 1986, four men mobilized computer communities in three different states. Small-time operators using their own petty cash for expenses, they went up against a corporate lobbying effort and won every time. Where they were too late, Jerry Schneider was able to help.

The contests centered around a bill called the Software License Enforcement Act. Touted as an antipiracy bill, it was passed in Louisiana with great fanfare. W. Krag Brotby, president of Vault Corporation, predicted that the law would provide a model for the other 49 states. Vault, a Southern California company specializing in copy-protection software, had invested $50,000 (by Brotby's estimate) to push the bill. Alan Grogan, a respected computer lawyer whose firm represents Vault, drafted the bill. Donald Radoff, a publicist, had set up a "clearinghouse" for information about software protection legislation, particularly the bill that Vault was pushing. Press releases and interviews originating with Vault led the media to report that the bill had been introduced in Georgia, Texas, Maryland, California, Hawaii, and Arizona. Actually, the bill was only introduced in the last three of these states and was defeated in each. To understand the issues, a discussion of the law of contracts is necessary.

PIRACY AND CONTRACT LAW

It is astonishing to see the totemic effect of words in our supposedly sophisticated society. Call a bill a piece of "antipiracy" legislation, and normally sane people will choose not to challenge it lest they appear soft on what is now widely viewed as a crime.

Thus, just as these are difficult times to be in favor of legalizing drugs, many people seem to think that being soft on piracy is tantamount to losing all credibility in computing circles.

Piracy is wrong, if by piracy one means violations of the copyright law. How wrong it is, what the most effective ways to combat it are, how to protect the correlative rights of software consumers, and hosts of other equally vexing and complex questions remain open and widely discussed, as the last chapter and this one should demonstrate beyond doubt.

Despite the implications of misleading publicity and lobbying, the Software License Enforcement Act was not primarily an antipiracy measure. It was special interest legislation designed to improve the economic position of software manufacturers without doing anything of substance to challenge software piracy.

Hawaii's acting director of consumer protection in 1986 neatly dispatched the connection between piracy and the Act, which was then pending in his state: "The bill appears to be an antipiracy measure intended to protect the proprietary interests of the software manufacturers," Mark Nomura testified to the Hawaii Senate Committee on Consumer Protection and Commerce. "The bill doesn't appear to further deter piracy or address the primary problem of detecting the violator."

In its simplest terms the Software Licensing Enforcement Act attempted to validate "shrink-wrap" contracts. A look at the law and the equities of these so-called contracts demonstrates why this unusual effort to create new contract law was seen as necessary by the backers of the bill, and why consumers of computer goods and services who looked at the bill were almost unanimous in their opposition.

Virtually all software sold for personal computers at the retail level is accompanied by "shrink-wrap licenses." Usually, a document beneath the shrink-wrap on the software package warns the buyer that opening the package or using the software is deemed consent to the terms of a software license. These terms are a set of provisions written by a lawyer for the manufacturer.

The Software License Enforcement Act attempted to ensure that these documents would be recognized by state contract law as valid contracts. Often, contract law requires an active "meeting of the minds." In other words, unless you and I agree to the terms of an agreement, no agreement exists. I can't, for instance, put a label on this book and say that opening the book is deemed agreement to a "license" that prohibits you from reselling it or from giving it away. Yet that's the sort of agreement that the so-called software licenses seek to enforce. Whether the "licenses" themselves are binding remains an open question, one upon which only the courts in Louisiana have opined. The purpose of the Software License Enforcement Act was to get state legislatures to declare that these licenses were valid legal agreements and that buying or using software with these licenses attached to them did constitute an adequate "meeting of the minds" so that a buyer could be held responsible for the terms they contain.

I've never put much stock in these so-called licenses. As a lawyer, I believe that any such license should require more knowledgeable assent to its terms than just using a product that has a document attached to it containing one-sided legalese.

The terms of these "licenses" are almost invariably one-sided, taking as much as possible for the manufacturer and giving as little as possible to the buyer. Most significantly, many of the contracts also limit the warranty that comes with the software.

Generally, the law infers that a product must work for the tasks it's intended to be used for. A word processing program is expected to do word processing, for example. Warranty law says that a consumer is protected if the product purchased doesn't work. A limited warranty, however, is a way for the manufacturer to attempt to avoid responsibility. It may say that if the software doesn't do what you reasonably expected it to do, that's too bad. Buy another product, but leave the manufacturer alone.

As might be expected, those who have thought about software license enforcement acts from the user's perspective have been against them. Ron Beach of the North Orange County Computer Club called them "appalling." L. J. Kutten, a computer lawyer in Pennsylvania and the editor of the *Software Law Newsletter,* said they "trample on the rights of consumers."

Under these circumstances, it seems fair to assume that, at the very least, user-group members might be interested in knowing about the provisions of the legislation and in having their opinions heard by those considering such a bill.

STATE BY STATE WITH THE SOFTWARE LICENSE ENFORCEMENT ACT

Louisiana

Louisiana was the first and only state to embrace the Act. When the computer press and much of the national media were in New Orleans for the 1984 Comdex show, the Act was introduced at a joint press conference featuring Vault's Brotby and Louisiana Assistant Secretary of State J. Robert Wooley. Wooley left little doubt as to his motivation, declaring his intention to make Louisiana the "silicon bayou."

Seven months later, the bill had passed. Brotby noted that it "did not meet with any serious objections," concluding "I think that indicates it's a good, flexible law." His words are a warning to all those who think that legislatures can be adequately informed without input from their constituents. In fact, the only thing that the absence of objections in Louisiana shows is that there's little in the way of consumer protection for computer users in that state. Louisiana is the only state in which the Vault legislation was not opposed. In all other states but Illinois, the bill was defeated or postponed. In Illinois, a very limited bill was passed but never took effect.

Arizona

Grey Staples didn't find the Software License Enforcement Act introduced in Arizona to be a "good, flexible law." The Scottsdale consultant learned about the bill on a user group bulletin board and immediately began taking steps to defeat it. He learned the bill's number, obtained a copy from his legislature, and "published" the bill's text on 60 bulletin boards in the Phoenix area. He encouraged all computer users to download the bill, or make copies on their own computer systems, read it, and communicate with their legislator if the bill wasn't to their liking. Several other interested parties in Arizona appeared before the legislature or wrote in opposition to the bill. Despite the appearance of Brotby and Vault attorney Alan Grogan, the bill was tabled until the 1986 session and never passed afterwards.

Hawaii

In the course of researching an article on the topic of Software License Enforcement Acts, I learned that Hawaii's House of Representatives had passed a version of the bill. It was to be heard in about two weeks by the Hawaii Senate Committee on Consumer Protection. I called Mark Nomura, acting director of the Hawaii Office of Consumer Protection, and asked him to consider testifying against the bill. He invited me to write him expressing my opposition. I sent copies of my memorandum to him to the committee itself. One of the few people to testify, Nomura opposed the bill and contributed significantly to its defeat.

Simultaneously, attorney L. J. Kutten was engaged in a much more ambitious lobbying effort. Taking advantage of the communications capabilities of the Source, Kutten sent SourceMail letters to Source subscribers in Hawaii, urging them to communicate with their legislators and oppose the Act. He offered subscribers, free through the Source, two memoranda he had written outlining the problems with the Act. It seems that Kutten was very effective: Hawaii State Senator Steven Cobb, chairman of the committee considering the legislation, called him and told him the bill was dead.

Illinois

Kutten was joined by computer lawyer Barry Bayer in an effort to defeat the Illinois version of the Act. The bill was supposed to be a "no-nothing" bill, one that would pass easily, according to Bayer. Instead, he reported, "pure hell broke out" after Kutten sent SourceMail letters to 547 Source users in Illinois. Indefatigible, Kutten also sent letters to the user groups in Illinois listed in the *Computer Shopper*. Kutten, an outspoken writer on consumer protection, explained his motivation succinctly: "I believe in morals and ethics," he said, "and I don't believe a small cadre of hired guns should be able to ride roughshod over the rights of the people." He calls the Software License Enforcement Act the "Consumer Rip-off Act."

Meanwhile, Barry Bayer, was learning about computer politics for the first time. A member of the Chicago Bar Association Committee on Computers and the Law, Bayer was aware of the software legislation from that committee's work on it. Convinced that the bill was a poor one, he went to the state capital in Springfield to testify against it. His presence, and his behind-the-scenes contacts with legislators, user groups, and the media, kept the bill from being put on the consent calendar and approved without serious discussion. In the next week, Bayer received calls from legislators asking him if he would agree to language designed to make the bill more palatable to him and to other computer users. What Bayer finally agreed to, and what passed, was a bill "more symbolic than substantive," he said. It provided for consumer protection and affirmed that nothing in the Act should change the rights conferred on software users by the Copyright Act. Even more importantly, its effective date was after the next legislative session, giving Bayer even more time to lobby against it. Eventually, the tide of opinion, and the support of major corporate players, turned against the Illinois Software License Enforcement Act, and it has never gone into effect.

California

Attorneys played a major role in defeating the California version of the Act. Before the bill was introduced in that state, members of the Orange County Copyright and Patent Section and the State Bar Copyright and Intellectual Property Committee wrote letters to state Assemblyman Gray Davis, the bill's sponsor. Their strong opposition, raising many of the points previously addressed in this chapter, led Mercedes Azar, senior aide to Davis, to predict that the bill would never pass unless it became agreeable to consumers. It never did.

USER GROUPS AND CONSUMER PROTECTION

Given the consistent success of individuals trying to represent the interests of computer users, the natural question is what success *groups* representing those users might achieve.

Jon Seidell, head of the Independent Computer Consultants Association Committee for Social Responsibility, explains the basic rationale for such activity: "Providers of computer goods and services are organized. Information users are not."

"We're philosophically behind the idea of involvement," says Jonathan Rotenberg, president of the Boston Computer Society. "We're committed to building an expanded program of outreach and public service."

"We should form lobbying groups to keep us aware of what's going on in the legislature," says Ned Ashby, former president of the North Orange County Computer Club.

Yet the theory expressed by these individuals seems quite removed from practice. It seems that precious little is being done to protect the rights of computer users. A number of reasons, including fear of litigation, lack of interest, and lack of leadership, may explain why this is so.

CAPITAL PC USER GROUP—A LEADER FOR CHANGE

In blessed contrast to the general lack of political interest on the part of users, the Capital PC User Group, under Jerry Schneider's direction, has led the charge for greater cooperation amongst user groups and between user groups and vendors.

As previously mentioned, the Capital PC User Group was one of the parties joining to produce an *amicus curiae* brief in the case of *Vault Corporation* v. *Quaid Software*. In that case, the federal court in the Eastern District of Louisiana found that the Software License Enforcement Act passed in that state was in conflict with the federal Copyright Act, and as such was preempted. In practical terms, this ruling meant that the Software License Enforcement Act was not a valid basis for Vault Corporation's attempt to expand its rights to limit copying of its products.

The court called the license agreements that Vault attempted to enforce under this Act "adhesive contracts," meaning that they are unfair to the consumer of "shrink-wrap" software.

Schneider has since moved to an even grander scale, organizing the Association of PC User Groups, a new organization attempting to provide a unified voice for user groups throughout the United States.

TOWARD COMMUNITY

In this chapter, and in the next, I offer examples of computer users joining together to address common problems and concerns. This approach, not special interest legislation like the Software License Enforcement Act, offers the best hope for the future of computer security. As long as there are issues involving conflicting rights and expectations, some will be motivated to selfishness and lack of concern for the common good. This is not surprising or unusual. There are better ways to make changes, however, whether the issue is fighting computer piracy or other types of disrespect for rights in the computer age. Jerry Schneider's words on this topic cut to its heart: "What everyone seems to forget is that all of us—users, dealers, distributors, and vendors—are partners in the software industry. And if the industry is to continue and thrive in the future, we must all work together in a cooperative and understanding manner."

CHAPTER 18

THE CRIME-FIGHTING COMMUNITY

ROBERT MORRIS: THE SORCERER'S APPRENTICE

Talking with Jeff Schiller is guaranteed to give you hope for the future of responsible computing. Wide-eyed and smiling, Jeff appears to be that lover of knowledge and adventure that I always dreamed school would be full of. As I sat with Jeff, Ted Ts'o, Stan Zanarotti, Bill Sommerfeld, and Jon Rochlis, I wanted to enroll at MIT the next day. This was a community! Forget Robert Morris: these were the real *heroes* of the Internet, the ones who cleaned up the mess after the "sorcerer's apprentice" let his experiment get out of hand. They were among tens of thousands of students, faculty members, and researchers who communicated through a network of computer and telecommunication systems called the Internet. If there is a working solution to computer crime which has not received adequate attention thus far, it is this group. Their community joined together to fight the Internet worm.

I sat in Jeff's office at MIT, trying to pay attention as he and the others recounted the events of the past November. It was hard to concentrate. Two terminals on the floor kept changing their displays. One went from a skull to a spider; the other from a head-and-shoulder shot of an astronaut to a lavish bucolic scene.

"I got in," Jon Rochlis started, "and the secretary here said, 'We've been attacked.' I said, 'Yeah, right.' "

So had begun their part in one of the classic computer adventures, the fight against the Internet worm. Project Athena, an experiment in advanced computer communication at MIT, was one of the first Internet victims. At 9:30 P.M. on Wednesday, November 2, 1988, a workstation maintained by Mike Shanzer was infected. Within the next two hours, RAND, the University of Maryland, and the University of California at Berkeley would also be hit. Athena was a project Jeff Schiller was responsible for, so fighting the Internet worm was a natural assignment.

Pascal Chesnais of the MIT Media Lab had also spotted the problem, leaving a message for his MIT colleagues: "A virus has been detected on media-lab. We suspect that the whole internet is infected by now. The virus is spread via mail, of all things . . . So mail outside of media-lab will NOT be accepted. Mail addressed to foreign hosts will NOT be delivered. This situation will continue until someone figures out a way of killing the virus and telling everyone how to do without using e–mail . . ."

At this point, you may well wonder whether we are talking about a worm, a virus, both, or neither. In truth, the usual accuracy which characterizes conversations amongst computer professionals is absent where the Internet worm is concerned. As I discussed in Chapter 7, the word *virus* has gone from a technical definition to a more generic one. Using the generic definition now in vogue, a virus is any type of malicious software. Under this definition, the Internet worm is a virus. Most of the experts quoted in this chapter prefer to refer to it as a virus. To simplify, I will call the program in question "the Internet worm."

By 3:34 in the morning on November 3, an anonymous message sent by Robert Morris's friend, Andy Sudduth, was wending its way through the Internet. The message instructed the users of the computer communication network to take three steps to prevent further infection from the virus. Rochlis was later to write about this message, "It was ironic that this posting did almost no good. There was a 20-hour delay before the message escaped from . . . [one relay point and got to another]."

The first notice of a "fix" appeared at 5:58 Thursday morning, from Keith Bostic at UC Berkeley. Any computer user wanting to eliminate a vulnerability connected to the "sendmail" feature of the system could simply use the program Bostic had written.

At Purdue, Gene Spafford had begun putting together a mailing list of Internet users who would benefit from Bostic's fixes. Ted Ts'o received Spafford's mailing and sent it to a list of hackers internal to Project Athena. No, he warned the "watchmakers," as the hackers were also known, "it's not April 1.")

By noon Thursday, MIT Lincoln Laboratory had contacted the Network Group, which operates telecommunications for parts of the university. "We've been brought to our kneees," their message read. Boston University had cut the telecommunication links between its own computers and those of the rest of the world.

Teams of programmers around the country were trying to discover all the inner workings of the worm. They wanted to understand more than just how to stop it. They also wanted to know if it had caused any permanent damage, destroyed or altered any data, or left any "time bombs" for later execution. These time bomb programs would have been written to check the computer calendar regularly and would only become active on a certain date.

The goals of these efforts were three: isolating a specimen of the virus; decompiling the virus, or translating it into a form that could be run; and analyzing the virus's strategies and design elements to decide how to defeat it. By Friday morning the various groups had achieved the first two goals and much of the third.

Stan Zanarotti and Ted Ts'o started attacking the virus Thursday evening. They were analyzing a "core dump" which they had managed to get while the virus was infecting one of their machines. One of their first targets was ernie, an address within the computer system at UC Berkeley that the virus program seemed to be sending information to. Stan and Ted tried to figure out what the program was sending to ernie, how often, and if there was a handshake, or a communication protocol, between the two.

At about 10:15 Thursday night, the media circus began. A camera crew from the local CBS affiliate was first; later, the Internet worm was the lead story on National Public Radio's 11 o'clock news. "We were quite surprised," Jon Rochlis said, "that the real world would pay so much attention. Sound bites were heard on the 11 o'clock news, and footage shot that evening was shown on the CBS Morning News, but by that point we were too busy to watch."

Rachlis says the group "got serious" after the news. According to the congratulatory description of a faculty adviser, the group that formed around the Project Athena office undertook "a wizard-level analysis by going over the virus with a microscope and tweezers."

Efforts to "reverse engineer" the virus began around midnight Thursday night. Marc Eichin, fresh from recent experience decompiling other programs and rested from a good night's sleep, led the efforts of 8 to 10 students who were yelling back and forth amidst the partitions outside the Project Athena offices. "We would look at 10 or so instructions in assembly code and try to guess the instruction in C language which would have resulted in producing that assembly code," Ted Ts'o explained.

"It's like pattern matching," Ts'o volunteered, as I looked somewhat blankly at him. Ts'o he worked through the night experiencing both a sense of crisis and of fun. "I had a fear that it was going to do some damage to our system," he recalled, "but a suspicion that it wasn't. The fun aspect was the challenge of getting the virus first, especially with all that media hype. It was once in a lifetime."

At 5 P.M. Thursday, the MIT computers were hit again. "What makes the little beastie as nasty as it is is that it knows more than one way to enter Internet host computers and propagate itself," Jeff Schiller said. The work continued until almost noon Friday, when a press conference was held.

"It was a zoo," Schiller told me. "There were 10 camera crews present." They made an impression on the folks I was talking with. "You've been playing with computers all your life, and suddenly you're front-page news. We don't live in a world where Dan Rather reports what you're doing," said Bill Sommerfeld.

As I listened to these five men describe their efforts through those two chaotic days and nights, I realized something. The conversation almost over, it occurred to me to ask the obvious: "None of you got paid for any of this, did you?" They laughed and shook their heads. These men belonged to a community. And that's where they belonged.

Through the efforts of volunteers around the country, the virus infection that Schiller casually estimated to have affected 6,000 computers was essentially contained within 40 hours. Still, the damage to those computers is estimated as a minimum of $200,000.

THE SORCERER'S APPRENTICE

Robert Morris, the man responsible for the Internet worm, was the recipient of what seems like a rich and varied education. The son of an ecologist mother and a computer scientist father, Morris could not complain of lack of stimulation. When he was small, the family lived on a small farm in Millington, New Jersey. Sheep roamed the grounds. Robert Morris, Sr., who worked for AT&T at the time, explained that "when you're a little kid and your assignment before you go to school in the morning is to go out and feed the pigs or rabbits or pick up the eggs in the henhouse, it's a different environment. What does that kind of responsibility do for anybody? It presents a different view toward life."

Morris, Jr. vacationed in Iceland and on the English canals with his family. His parents, his brother and sister, and he all played in local orchestras. Like many bright students, he read voraciously.

Morris's brother says that Robert Morris, Sr. and Robert Morris, Jr. started to act more like colleagues than father and son as the younger Morris became more engrossed in the problems of computer security. The senior Morris had spent much of his professional career studying these issues. As early as 1961 and 1962, Morris, Sr. competed with fellow programmers at a game called Darwin. The winner would be the one whose program devoured the programs of the others. As Douglas McIlroy, one of the combatants, recalled, "Bob Morris's programs were so good we all gave up."

McIlroy later supervised Morris, Jr. and found him similarly inclined. Both father and son "are well versed in a field in which a 'game playing' mentality is essential. To make computers more secure," he said, "one must first be able to understand how to break into them."

Morris's mother said her husband and son were acutely aware of the similarities in their interests. "Their interests and careers will dovetail so that there will be a continuum of Robert Morrisses over the course of computer science," she said.

With the enormous media coverage accompanying charges that Morris was responsible for the Internet worm, partisans soon emerged to illuminate both the bright and dark sides of his past.

Mark Freidell, Morris's senior thesis adviser at Harvard, called Morris "articulate and well balanced. He isn't malicious and he isn't a nerd," Freidell said, expressing shock that Morris would be accused of responsibility for the Internet worm. Richard Draves, who roomed with Morris in high school, was not surprised. "I immediately thought of Morris when I heard about the virus," he said. "I knew he had talents in the same areas the virus exploited." Draves also recalled Morris telling him he enjoyed cracking passwords while a student at the Delbarton School in Morristown, New Jersey. "But I thought he had given up on all that."

At 14, Morris was "sleuthing from outside of the family computer," his mother said. Michael Wines of the *New York Times* wrote that "his parents acknowledged he began using his knowledge to sneak in and out of other computer files undetected."

Around this time, in August 1982, a *Smithsonian* magazine article about hacking described Morris, without naming him, as "a quiet, polite young man with soft brown hair and rosy cheeks." Author Gina Kolata reported: "he began playing games on computers when he was six years old and now spends two hours a day just fooling around *on* a computer. He has broken into password files, has read supposedly private computer mail, and has broken into computers that are linked together in networks." "I never told myself there was nothing wrong with what I was doing," Morris told Kolata. "But," she observed, "he continues anyway because he finds that probing the security of computers is exciting and challenging."

Morris had no trouble gaining employment based on his computer skills. He worked in the summers at AT&T's Bell Labs. One of his projects there involved security on Unix system computers, the area he attacked in his creation of the Internet worm.

GENESIS OF THE VIRUS

It appears that Morris's plan to release the Internet worm dates back at least to October 1988. Investigators at Cornell wrote that Morris first learned about one of the methods he put in his program during a visit to Harvard between October 20 and 22. It was around this time that he began testing one of his program's attacks.

On October 28, Morris was dancing on his desk, according to Dawson Dean, because he had discovered a secret entry path to the Unix system. He told Dean he wasn't going to do anything with the information, that he was just looking for the path for fun.

On November 2, at 5:01:59 P.M., Morris tested his program. Four minutes later it infected its first victim, another machine at Cornell. At about 9 P.M., he released the program. Morris went to dinner after releasing the program, returning to check it before he went to sleep.

By 2 A.M. Morris was worried. He called Andy Sudduth and asked him to sound an alarm about the program he'd let loose. Morris could not do it himself because the program had inactivated his computer system at Cornell.

JUDGING MORRIS

Like the German freelance aviator Mathias Rust, Robert Morris quickly became the topic of widespread conversation after his program was released. The Vancouver *Columbian* summarized the problem Morris's case presented. "Robert T. Morris is both widely admired hero and deeply despised villain in the world of computers these days."

This ambivalence was evident even in his father's public statements. As chief scientist for the National Computer Security Center, Robert Morris, Sr. was in a bind. The last thing an employee of the highly secret National Security Agency needs, particularly one so intimately tied to computer security, is a son accused of computer crime. Yet Morris, Sr. expressed pride in his son's programming talents. "I know a few dozen people in the country who could have done it," he said. "I could have done it and I'm a darn good programmer."

But Jeff Schiller was less impressed. "Real wizards don't release a code until it is polished like a gem," he said. "As we worked dissecting his code, we'd laugh about Morris's mistakes. 'Look at this,' we'd say, 'he has a wrong value here.' It was untested, unfinished code."

It was also irresponsible code, code which made little effective provision for the protection of those it might harm. "Robert Morris has a better reputation among those people who never saw his code," according to Jon Rochlis. "Each of us [who worked on reverse engineering his code] could have done much better. He could have used 'death trap' codes, for instance, instructing the program to stop running if it wasn't being run on a Cornell computer."

In addition to technical judgments, the dispute has raged over moral issues as well. Perhaps the most damning analysis of Morris's morality is found in the report produced by a group at Cornell. The report concluded:

> It appears that Morris did not pause to consider the potential consequences of his actions. He was so focused on the minutiae of tactical issues that he failed to contemplate the overall potential impact of his creation. His behavior, therefore, can only be described as constituting reckless disregard. It is the responsibility of any member of the computer science profession . . . to consider the consequences of one's acts, especially when those acts may affect thousands of individuals across the nation. Morris displayed naive conceit in assuming that he could launch an untested, unsimulated, complex worm onto a complex network and have it work correctly the first time. Even undergraduate students are taught in intro-

ductory courses that untested programs contain errors, that such errors are often subtle, and that one should never assume that one's programs function as intended without the most careful of testing.

Another of the most damning arguments I have seen is the recitation of the damage done by the worm in an article by Donn Seely:

> The worm did not destroy files, intercept private mail, reveal passwords, corrupt data bases or plant Trojan horses. It did compete for CPU time with, and eventually overwhelm, ordinary user processes. It used up limited system resources such as the open file table and the process text table, causing processes to fail for lack of same. It caused some machines to crash by operating them close to the limits of their capacity, exercising bugs that do not appear under normal loads. It forced administrators to perform one or more reboots to clear worms from the system, terminating user sessions and long-running jobs. It forced administrators to shut down network gateways, including gateways between important nationwide research networks, in an effort to isolate the worm. This led to delays of several days in the exchange of electronic mail, causing some projects to miss deadlines, others to lose valuable research time. It made systems staff across the country drop their ongoing hacks and work 24-hour days trying to corner and kill worms. It caused members of management in at least one institution to become so frightened that they scrubbed all the disks at their facility that were on-line at the time of the infection, and limited reloading of files to data that was verifiably unmodified by a foreign agent.

PUNISHMENT OR PRAISE?

The obvious next step, after judging Morris, is opining what punishment, if any, is appropriate should he be found to have violated the law. "Let him go and you make it easy for the next schmuck," says Jeff Schiller. "I wouldn't punish him because he hasn't destroyed anything," counters Richard Brandow. Brandow, who may be charged with a similar offense any day in Seattle. He let loose the World Peace virus that appeared March 2, 1988.

Since an indictment has been handed down against Morris, the question of punishment is not moot. To quote the language of his charge, should he be found guilty of "intentionally and without authorization access[ing] . . . federal interest computers . . . and prevent[ing] the authorized use of one or more of these computers," he will be subject to imprisonment for up to five years and a fine of up to $250,000.

WE ARE THE SORCERERS

Throughout this book I have tried to convey the message that computer security is a problem which affects and involves all of us. Perhaps this is nowhere clearer than in the case of Robert Morris. Here was a gifted child, an educated child, a child taught about responsibility from a very young age, creating a serious mess because he failed to contemplate the consequences of his actions.

As the society whose values Robert Morris reflects, we can profitably contemplate the consequences of actions we may have taken which contributed to his recklessness. Are we willing to take a stand for ethics as a necessary component of computer education? The alternative, I suggest, is to continue to produce sorcerer's apprentices.

Computer ethics is not an academic question. There are those who say we need all the creative freedom we can get if we are to succeed in the global competition for technological supremacy. They tend to argue against responsibility. Morris's friend Paul Graham, for instance, argues, "The fact that the United States dominates the world in software is not a matter of technology. The culture for making great software is slightly crazy people working late at night."

I believe Graham represents a position rapidly losing support. I don't think we have so lost faith in our future that only a desperate, valueless embrace of technological proficiency is seen as adequate to escape dominance by Japan and the other creditor nations of Asia.

Sitting with the real heroes at MIT, I felt quite certain that moral sensitivity goes with intellectual productivity. These kids were alive! Whether 22 or 42, their eyes twinkled when they talked about their adventure, perhaps the highlight of their professional lives. They were experiencing the joy of wizardry, wading into the unknown, slogging through on experience and instinct, solving problems quickly and with imagination.

Theirs is the attitude that leads to clear thought, creative receptivity and dynamic breakthroughs in perception. These guys work in a community that is nurturant. Contrast it with the poverty of the loneliness and terror that Robert Morris must have felt on the morning of November 3 as he wondered what the consequences of his marauding program might turn out to be. No "sorcerer's" apprentice should forget this risk as he or she contemplates undisciplined experimentation with something so powerful as a computer program.

Every "sorcerer" among us might imagine the pain and anguish Robert Morris, Sr. must feel contemplating the fate that awaits his son. Apprentices will tinker with our technologies, some far more dangerously than the younger Morris did. We cannot prevent such efforts, harmful though some may be. We can only do our best, as Robert Morris, Sr. and his wife Anna have done, to guide our children to behave responsibly when using computers. We can improve our best, however, by learning more about the impact of technology on our society, and the possible impact of crime and other computer abuse on our society as well.

Just as parents have had to educate themselves about drugs, sexual abuse, and unfamiliar religious groups to protect their children, so parents must introduce their children to computer technology with at least as much concern and care as when their offspring learn to drive a car. At the conservative estimate of $200,000, the Internet worm caused more damage than all but the biggest of auto accidents. Yet there are virtually no limits on computer use. We have learned that someone using a car has to be able to use the brake. In the same way, we must make sure our children know how to responsibly use computer technology. The next "crash" could be far more harmful than those Morris caused.

CONCLUSION

TOWARDS RESPONSIBLE COMPUTING

A writer's relationship to the audience is much more remote than that of a live performer. You cannot see my face or my posture. Yet like any entertainer, beneath the words, beneath the story, is an offering. This book is my attempt to make a gift to you.

My gift is based on a wish to share the aspects of my work which have meant the most to me and to try to articulate their meaning clearly. I wish that you could have benefits like those I've experienced in my ten years of involvement studying the social implications of computing.

The big payoff, the one that propels me when things get tough, is the awareness that I have an impact in the world of computing. I don't trust the development of technology enough to feel comfortable putting the system on automatic. I'd like to drive my car without worrying about how the gas gets to my gas station. But when something like the Exxon oil spill occurs, I conclude that not responding is a luxury I can ill afford.

After the Star Wars debate, I cannot ignore the role that I play in the use of computers for military purposes. I believe that the concerted efforts of computer scientists to communicate the technical arguments against Star Wars represent one of the most sophisticated arguments over military policy ever.

Who would have thought, during the '88 elections, that Dan Quayle would call Star Wars a fantasy and the administration would back off from it? It was like when the *New York Times* suddenly decided that it was time to get out of Vietnam. The voice of a few "radical" critics had become the majority view.

Much as I love the benefits I derive from it, technology scares me. It scares me because it amplifies the power available to people. It excites me for the same reason. When I feel more scared, I don't like to respond to technology; when I feel more excited, I do. So the secret of involvement, for me, is to feel more excited than scared. In this last chapter, I want to make your involvement easier, and more alluring as a result.

All but one story has been told. The remaining story is yours. What value have the stories of the individuals in this book to you? The answer, I hope, is that they will move you towards taking greater responsibility for the future of computing.

Responsibility is one of the trickiest words in the English language. "Who is responsible for this?" is a question often asked angrily when something has gone wrong and one wants to find someone to blame for it. Richard Nixon's term as president ended because he was forced to take responsibility for Watergate. Presidents Reagan and Bush have avoided responsibility for Contragate, so it has yet to damage either of their careers.

It is probably not surprising that few people rush to take responsibility in their lives when they see the word as equivalent to *blame*. I'd like to suggest an alternative view of *responsibility* which makes the word more inviting.

Another definition of responsibility is the "ability to respond." It is in this sense that I urge you to work for responsible computing. Anyone can respond to the growing changes in all of our lives resulting from computer use. I've told the stories of people like Bill Christison, Dennis Macleod, Grey Staples, Jerry Schneider, and Bert van den Berg to demonstrate some of the ways that individuals have responded. Their stories just scratch the surface.

You needn't watch passively as the spectacle of computer crime passes you by. There is room on the playing field for as many people and organizations as want to experience the thrill of involvement and the satisfaction of working for constructive change. (Later in this conclusion, I'll tell you how to do so.)

I cannot, of course, guarantee that your adventures will be as exciting as those I had doing the research for this book. Nor can I assure you that you will never be exposed to greater dangers, frustrations, or grief.

You will probably never visit a Solidarity safe house, now that the politics of Poland have so dramatically changed. You may never get close to Mohammed Ali or talk to a convicted computer saboteur like Katya Komisaruk. But I can guarantee that an equal amount of effort is likely to result in equally rewarding adventures, any effort at all will benefit you. I can assure you that there is no better tonic for despair about the future of our planet that getting involved in making it better.

Computer ethics must be at the heart of any serious effort to nurture the concept of "responsible computing." Without agreement about ethical standards, there is no way for those who want to be responsible to know what they should be responding to. Often those who argue that efforts to foster computer ethics are doomed assert that it is impossible to teach ethics because there is no agreement about what is ethical and what is not. I disagree. Agreement about ethical standards is a lot simpler and more common than many people seem to think. Stealing, trespassing, lying, and destroying others' property are wrong. That list covers most computer crimes.

Turning ethical precepts into ethical behavior is the key social challenge, one which computer crime shows us we have yet to overcome. For me, the hardest thing about behaving ethically is *not* knowing the difference between ethical and unethical actions. The real challenge comes at the point that I decide whether or not to consider the ethical implications of my behavior.

It's not that I sit down and ask myself, "Should I consider the implications, or should I ignore them?" I find the hardest thing is when I want to do something, and I know that if I ask if it's ethical, I'll decide it's not. The cowardly choice, the one I take from time to time, is to fail to ask the question altogether. You know the old joke: Jughead says, "I've read that eating fried food is bad for my heart, so I've decided to stop." "No more french fries?" Veronica shrieks. "No," Jughead answers, "no more reading."

Responsibility puts the emphasis where it belongs if we are to improve the safety and security of our computers. The key question is whether we can teach ourselves, and those we care about, to respond to situations of ethical danger, just as parents teach their children to react to situations of physical danger.

As we near the end of the 20th century, the major social issues of our time seem to revolve around the question of responsibility. The AIDS crisis may be the most obvious example of this phenomenon. As long as medical science is unable to provide us with a cure for the disease, our best hope for limiting its harm lies in convincing all those who might be carriers of the virus to respond to the danger that it presents to others. For all the talk and debate over drug policy in this country, most people agree argue that we will be unable to bring drug use to acceptable levels without convincing millions of individuals to stop using drugs.

Computer abuse is but one type of environmental problem. It, like all other environmental problems, will be solved only to the extent that we are able to motivate computer users and manufacturers to respond with an awareness of the many others who may be affected by their decisions concerning computers.

Before computer ethics become an integral part of the world of computing, we will need education, debate, concensus formation, and lots of serious thought and errors. Anything less will be ineffective bromides that make us feel we're making a difference without changing things very much.

The payoffs for this effort to develop computer ethics are many. The more people trust that computers are being used to make their world better, the more wholeheartedly they will buy them, use them, and secure them.

The more we ensure the security of our future computer use through the development of sane and equitable rules of behavior with computers, the better we can feel that we control our destiny, rather than allowing technological forces beyond our control to make the key decisions in our lives. The spectre of weapons relying on artificial intelligence determining whether to send out nuclear warheads and basing their decisions on computer data rather than human input was the frightening premise underlying the movie *WarGames*. I don't want to feel I have so little control over my future, and I suspect I'm not alone.

I get angry when people convince me that something needs change, but they have no information that will help me change it. I don't want to fall into the same trap, so I have collected a number of resources for responsible computing.

Depending on how you see yourself, some or all of these categories will offer information to allow you to expand your ability to respond to the challenge of making computers yours.

I have to talk a bit about despair. I think despair is the hidden curse of our times. Despair is hopelessness. It is resignation to the idea that things will never get better. It is often a generalization from one's own disappointments or those of others.

I could go on telling you how to overcome it . . . but what's the point? The point, of course, is to see why the last sentence is a joke. If you laughed at my despairing of ending my despair, you are on the road to happy living. Despair is a state of mind in which it appears that there are no solutions. It is a very depressed and depressing state—perhaps the attitude you often see reflected on the faces of people in public transportation. Hope, on the contrary, is bright-eyed, alert, curious—the kind of attitude my young daughter has. Since life is always a combination of hope and despair, to be stuck in either attitude forever without conceiving of the chance of changing to the other is laughable indeed. In today's world, it is just as bad to be a Pollyanna as a prophet of doom. More significantly, there is no real difference between the two poles. Each has abandoned contact with reality, preferring to adopt an attitude instead. The cure for despair, Joanna Macy tells us in her brilliant and important book, *Despair and Personal Power in the Nuclear Age,* starts with facing that despair. Despair and denial are two ways to avoid the pain of life. Each involves choosing a myth about reality rather than facing life's pain head-on.

I don't want to sound the slightest bit "less despairing than thou." No author can write a book without having some apprehension, at least a flash of hopelessness, and several nights of wondering if the whole project was a good idea. But I have been impressed by the logic of Macy's arguments—that despair must be, and can be, confronted if the problems of our society are ever to be overcome.

Once we face despair, Macy assures us, a "turning" can occur. As she puts it, "There comes a point . . . when we realize that our feelings of pain for the world arise from our essential interconnectedness, that they are intrinsic to the web of life itself. The very distress that had seemed to isolate us from people . . . now manifests as part of the connective tissue in which we cohere. This realization is a turning point."

To develop an awareness of your power to have an impact on the world of computing, consider the following steps (a paraphrase of Macy's advice):

1. Experience the power within you, recognizing your own power and your capacity to choose.
2. Broaden your vision of what is possible. See the possibilities clearly enough that your resolve and will to work for change are strengthened.
3. Acquire the skills for work directed toward social change.

Making these three changes will most likely not occur in a day. Deciding that they are worth your effort, however, can happen in an instant. Commitment is important, even if it comes on the installment plan. One you are committed to seeing your power, expanding your vision, and acquiring new skills, you may experience a rush of power or a sense of security. You may spend the rest of your life working towards these three goals, not only focusing on computing, but on other areas of your concern.

The most important thing is to start. The remainder of this chapter consists of an annotated list of opportunities to help you feel more in control of your future in our increasingly computerized society. Like any other list of resources, it is intended to be more extensive than exhaustive. It is certainly not intended to be exhausting! Skim through the list and see what interests you. Send out a few postcards, make a few calls, and let your intuition be your guide. It is better to begin slowly than to try to remake the world overnight.

I've broken the list into three major categories: learning, sharing, and action. Depending on your relationship with computers, some of these resources will be more applicable than others.

LEARNING

The computer revolution has yet to displace the printed word as a source of information. There are a number of books and periodicals which can serve as entry points. I list some personal favorites:

Books

Baskerville, R. *Designing Information Systems Security.* New York: John Wiley, 1988.

BloomBecker, B. *Commitment to Security.* Santa Cruz, Calif.: National Center for Computer Crime Data, 1989.

BloomBecker, B. *Introduction to Computer Crime.* 2d ed. Santa Cruz, Calif.: National Center for Computer Crime Data, 1988.

Burnham, D. *The Rise of the Computer State.* New York: Random House, 1983.

Carroll, J. *Computer Security.* 2d ed. Woburn, Mass.: Butterworths, 1987.

Gibson, W. *Neuromancer.* New York: Ace Science Fiction, 1984.

Gromyko, A. *Breakthrough.* New York: Walker, 1988.

Highland, H. *Protecting Your Microcomputer System.* New York: John Wiley, 1984.

Holsapple, C. *The Information Jungle.* Homewood, Ill.: Dow Jones-Irwin, 1989.

Johnson, D. *Computer Ethics.* Englewood Cliffs, N.J.: Prentice-Hall, 1985.

Johnson, D. *Ethical Issues in the Use of Computers.* Belmont, Calif.: Wadsworth, 1985.

Levy, S. *Hackers.* New York: Dell, 1984.

Lobel, J. *Foiling the System Breakers.* New York: McGraw-Hill, 1986.

Linowes, D. *Privacy in America.* New York: John Wiley, 1989.

Macy, J. *Despair and Personal Power in the Nuclear Age.* Santa Cruz, Calif.: New Society, 1983.

Parker, D. *Fighting Computer Crime.* New York: Charles Scribner's Sons, 1983.

Robinson, S. *Mindkiller.* New York: Berkeley, Calif.: 1983.

Roszak, T. *Bugs.* Garden City, New York: Doubleday, 1981.

Roszak, T. *The Cult of Information.* New York: Pantheon, 1986.

Ryan, T. *The Adolescence of P-1.* New York: Collier, 1977.

Schweitzer, J. *Protecting Information on Local Area Networks.* Woburn, Mass.: Butterworths, 1988.

Shelley, M. *Frankenstein.* (numerous versions available)

Sieber, U. *The International Handbook on Computer Crime.* New York: John Wiley, 1986.

Stewart, H. *Recollecting the Future.* Homewood, Ill.: Dow Jones-Irwin, 1989.

Stoll, C. *The Cuckoo's Egg.* Garden City, New York: Doubleday, 1989.

Turkle, S. *The Second Self.* New York: Simon & Schuster, 1984.

U.S. Library of Congress. *Computer Viruses: Technical Overview and Policy Considerations.* Washington, D.C.: Congressional Research Service, 1988.

U.S. Congress, Office of Technology Assessment. *Defending Secrets, Sharing Data,* Washington, D.C.: 1987.

Weizenbaum, J. *Computer Power and Human Reason.* San Francisco: W. H. Freeman, 1976.

Wood, C., et al. *Computer Security: A Comprehensive Controls Checklist.* New York: John Wiley, 1987.

Wurman, S. *Information Anxiety.* Garden City, New York: Doubleday, 1989.

Periodicals

Computer Fraud and Security Bulletin. Elsevier International Bulletins, 52 Vanderbilt Avenue, New York, N.Y. 10017. (212) 989–5800.

Computer Law and Security Report. Eclipse Publications, 18–20 Highbury Place, London, N5 1QP, England.

Computers and Security. Elsevier International Bulletins, 52 Vanderbilt Avenue, New York, N.Y. 10017. (212) 989–5800.

Computer Security Digest. 150 North Main Street, Plymouth, Mich. 48170. (313) 459–8787.

EDPACS. Warren Gorham and Lamont. 1 Penn Plaza, N.Y., N.Y., 10019 1–800–950–1216.

Privacy Journal. P.O. Box 15300, Washington, D.C. 20003. (202) 547–2865.

Processed World. 41 Sutter Street, San Francisco, Calif. 94104. (415) 495–6823.

Reset. c/o Mike McCullough, 90 East 7th Street, #3A, New York, N.Y. 10009.

Transnational Data Report. P.O. Box 2039, Springfield, Va. 22152.

2600. P.O. Box 752, Middle Island, N.Y. 11953. (516) 751–2600.

Organization Newsletters

Each of the organizations listed later in this chapter has a newsletter, a journal, or some other regular publication for members. The newsletter information is listed parenthetically after the contact information for the organization. These publications are usually quite receptive to contributions from members (or anyone else willing to write for them without pay).

Bulletin Boards

The growing number of data-maniacs will find print too slow and stodgy to satisfy them. Computer bulletin boards offer immediate opportunities to jump into conversation with some of the best minds grappling with the problems of computers in society. (The truth be told, unless the bulletin board is tightly edited, it will also present some of the shallowest and most repetitive argument you've ever seen. Such is the price of democratized access to communication media.) Some of these conceptual clearinghouses, like the Risks Forum, are well established. Others are gone before you know it. For information about the Risks Forum, call Peter Neumann at (415) 859–2375. If you belong to Compuserve, use the Arpanet, or are involved in any other computer network, you can find an abundance of bulletin boards to cover any topic of interest to you, including computer crime, computer security, computer viruses, computer ethics, and futurism.

SHARING

There is a plethora of groups eager to welcome you and value the energy you are willing to devote to their activities. If you remember back to Chapter 2, one of the reasons Stan Rifkin was welcome as an officer in the IEEE Computer Society was the shortage of people willing to fill those positions. This is not uncommon. Most of the organizations I've listed have special interest groups dealing with security, ethics, and policy issues involving computers. If they don't, the odds are great they will be receptive to your starting one.

Organizations for Computer Professionals

Association for Computing Machinery—Special Interest Group on Computers and Society (SIGCAS). 11 West 42d Street, New York, N.Y. 10036. (212) 869–7440. (*Computers and Society*)

Computer Professionals for Social Responsibility. P.O. Box 717, Palo Alto, Calif. 94301. (415) 322–3778. (Newsletter)

Data Entry Management Association, 101 Merrit, 7 Corporate Park, Norwalk, Conn. 06851. (203) 846–5070.

Data Processing Management Association, 505 Busse Highway, Park Ridge, Ill. 60068–3191. (312) 825–8124. (*Data Manager*)

IEEE Computer Society—Social Impact Group. 1730 Massachusetts Avenue, Washington, D.C. 20036–1903. (800)-CSBOOKS.

Institute for Certification of Computer Professionals (ICCP). 2200 East Devon Avenue, Suite 268, Des Plaines, Ill. 60018. (312) 299–4227

Organizations for Computer Users

Apple User Group Connection. (408) 974–6343; 800–538–9696–X500.

Association of PC User Groups (APCUG). c/o Capital PC User Group, P.O. Box 3189, Gaithersburg, Md. 20878. (408) 439–9367 (bulletin board system number).

Boston Computer Society—Social Impact Group. 1 Center Plaza, Boston, Mass. 02108. (617) 367–8080.

IBM User Group Support. (404) 988–2790 (bulletin board); (404) 988–2782.

User groups used to be the preserve of "nerds" interested in little other than technical details and occasional and restrained fellowship. With the growth of the personal computer market, user groups now offer much more varied fare. The organizations listed are large and can serve as starting points for further research. If you are particularly interested in developing a social impact group in your user group, the Boston Computer Society can give you some advice based on its experience. APCUG has a list of addresses of over 100 affiliated user groups. The Apple and IBM contacts can help you find a local user group.

Organizations for Computer Security Professionals

American Institute of Certified Public Accountants. 1211 Avenue of the Americas, New York, N.Y. 10036. (212) 575–6200. (*CPA Journal*)

American Society for Industrial Security. 1655 North Fort Myer Drive, Suite 1200, Arlington, Va. 22209. (703) 522–5800. (*Security Management*)

Association for Computing Machinery—Special Interest Group on Security, Audit, and Control (SIGSAC). c/o Steve Clemons, Norfolk Southern, 8 North Jefferson Street, Roanoke, Va. 24042–0006. (703) 981–5464. (*Security, Audit, and Control Review*)

Bank Administration Institute. 60 Gould Center, Rolling Meadows, Ill. 60008. (312) 228–6200.

Computer Security Institute. 360 Church Street, Northboro, Mass. 01532. (617) 393–2600. (*Computer Security*)

EDP Auditors Association. P.O. Box 88180, Carol Stream, Ill. 60188–0180. (312) 682–1200. (*EDP Auditor Journal*)

Information Systems Security Association, P.O. Box 9457, Newport Beach, Calif. 92658. (714) 492–3462. (*Access*)

Institute of Internal Auditors. 249 Maitland Avenue, Box 1119, Altamonte

Springs, Fla. 32701. (305) 830–7600.
National Center for Computer Crime Data. 1222 17th Ave, Santa Cruz, Calif.
95062. (408) 475–4457.

Other Professional Organizations

Ever since computer viruses spread the message that everyone
can be vulnerable to computer crime, professionals in all areas
have begun to worry more about computer security. Consequently, whatever professional organization you belong to, there
is a chance that its leaders have thought about computer
security—or wish that they had. As with the other organizations, if they do not already have a group looking into the
security implications of computing, they will probably be receptive to your starting one.

Other Organizations

Not only professional organizations worry about computer crime
these days. Your church or synagogue group, your parent-
teachers association, even the service group you meet with now
and then for lunch is likely to have more interest in computers
than ever before. They may lack only your leadership.

ACTION

If you take advantage of the opportunities to learn and to share
your learning represented by the resources I've listed, you may
find yourself as motivated to take further action as those whom
I've written about in this book. The opportunities are endless.
You can lobby for or against a piece of legislation, as L. J.
Kutten did in Hawaii and Illinois. If you are a teacher, you can
develop a computer ethics course. You can devote some of your
business's public relations or advertising funds to promoting
more responsible computing. You can meet regularly with
friends and colleagues and discuss topics of interest related to
the implications of computing.

REACTIONS

The National Center for Computer Crime Data, which I direct, has been concerned about computer crime and its implications for over the last decade. We intend to continue our efforts as long as there is a contribution we can make. To accomplish this goal as completely as possible will require your help. If you have any reactions to the ideas in this book, please contact me. Like most places in Santa Cruz, the Center is very informal. Just call, or drop a note. Your feedback will be welcomed and acknowledged. You and I are what it takes to make computers safe for the future and to make the future safe for computing.

INDEX